Business Knowledge for IT in Trading and Exchanges

A complete handbook for IT Professionals

Essvale Corporation Limited
The Forward Thinking Company

PROFESSIONAL SERIES

Essvale Corporation Limited
63 Apollo Building
1 Newton Place
London E14 3TS
www.essvale.com

This is the first edition of this publication.

Essvale Corporation Ltd is hereby identified as author
of this work in accordance with Section 77 of the
Copyright, Designs and Patents Act 1988

Requests to the authors should be addressed to:
permissions@essvale.com.

A CIP record for this book is available from the British Library

ISBN (10-digit) 9780955412486
ISBN (13-digit) 095541248X

This publication is designed to provide accurate and authoritative
information about the subject matter. The author makes no representation,
express or implied, with regard to the accuracy of the information
contained in the publication and cannot accept any responsibility or
liability for any errors or omissions that it may contain.

Cover design by Essvale Design Team
Design and typesetting by Boldface, London EC1
Printed by Lightning Source Ltd, Milton Keynes

Preface

Good customer service is the lifeblood of any business. The concept of customer service is essential to the way in which the IT function in any organisation interacts with the business. The primary role of IT is to support the business and hence the need for IT professionals working in any organisation to look upon their business counterparts as customers. The question that springs to mind is: how do you provide a service to the customer if you don't have a thorough understanding of their requirements?

To gain an insight into the customer's specific requirements, IT professionals have to understand the way in which the customer's business works. To achieve this, they need business knowledge of any industry to which they offer their support services.

The trading industry, as well as the exchange industry, is no exception. It is crucial for the IT professional to understand the business practices in both these industries to ensure the provision of a good level of service.

The trading industry is growing at a fast pace, given that trading of securities is no longer restricted to exchanges. Retail investors now trade financial products from currency to contracts for difference (CFDs) through a number of providers over the internet and this has, in part, led to the growth of the trading industry.

Traditional exchanges have to adapt to a rapidly changing business environment in the face of stiff competition from relatively new entrants into their industry. The advancement in technology has allowed electronic communication networks (ECNs) and other alternative execution venues to threaten the dominance of the traditional exchanges. In response, traditional exchanges are looking to strengthen their positions through mergers and acquisitions and also investment in technology that can enable them to offer the same levels of service as these alternative execution venues.

Acknowledgements

Essvale Corporation Limited would like to thank all authors and publishers of all materials used in compiling this publication. Also thanks to all the respondents to the research carried out to justify writing this publication.

We would like to acknowledge Nigel Woodward of Intel, Paul Miller and Dinesh Sagger of Morse, Leanne Brown of Progress Software, Sally Phillips and Rachael Harnden of OctanePR, Leslie Afflatet and Sylvain Thieullent of Hsoftware, Gilles Guyard of Ullink, Charlotte James and Jane Milner of Sungard, and Claude Courbois and Wayne Lee of NasdaqOMX.

Our thanks also go to Pat Winfield of Bookworm Editorial Services, Barney Lodge of Lodge Consulting, Boldface Typesetters, the helpful staff of City Business Library and Idea Store Canary Wharf, the editors and support staff at Nielsen Book Data, Lucy Sharp of Lightning Source, Graham Morris and Vic Daniels of Hereisthecity.com, and the staff of Amazon and other bookstores worldwide. Thanks for supporting Bizle Professional Series thus far.

Contents

ix

Introduction

The impact of trading on the state of the global economy is underscored by the events of September 2008, notably the short selling of banking stocks by traders in the wake of the financial crises that led to the collapse of Lehman Brothers, once the world's fourth largest investment bank, the rescue of Merrill Lynch by Bank of America and the bail-out of AIG, the world's largest insurer, by the US Federal Reserve to the tune of $85 billion in exchange for nearly an 80% stake in the company.

The Financial Services Authority (FSA) in the UK and the Securities and Exchange Commission (SEC), both regulators, banned the short selling of financial stocks and decreed that hedge funds, the ardent adopters of "naked" short selling, had to disclose their short positions.

When the news broke, the US markets soared, with the Dow Jones index closing up 400 points or 3.86% on the day.

Understanding the effects of the activities of traders on the workings of the financial markets is key to the self-development of the modern-day IT professional and students as well.

This book provides a springboard for the discerning IT professional or student to achieve business alignment to the business of trading and an understanding of the business models of exchanges.

It is laid out in the customary 12 chapters that make up the other titles in the series. It opens with an overview of trading and exchanges. In this chapter, topics such as the roles of traders and investors in the financial markets, trading sessions, insider trading and the business models of exchanges are discussed. The next chapter is on the trading activities in different asset classes from equities to fixed income.

Chapters 3 and 4 are about the types of orders used for trading assets and the business environment in trading and exchanges respectively. Chapter 5 contains information about the recent trends in trading and exchanges while Chapter 6 discusses the concepts of liquidity and volatility in the financial markets.

Arbitrage is the subject matter of Chapter 7 and the discussions therein include the theoretical underpinnings of arbitrage and the different types of arbitrage.

Chapter 8 is where IT meets business in trading and exchanges as it discusses the concepts of electronic and algorithmic trading.

Chapter 9 is about the common systems used in trading and exchanges and contains a discussion of the procedure of online execution that contests the conventional thinking amongst individual investors about how their trades on internet-based trading platforms are executed.

In Chapter 10, several IT projects that could be executed in investment banks, brokerages and exchanges are discussed.

The last two chapters, 11 and 12, discuss the terminology commonly used in trading and exchanges and the future of trading and exchanges from both an IT and business perspective respectively.

xi

Readers are advised to read this book in conjunction with other titles in the series such as Business Knowledge for IT in Investment Banking, Business Knowledge for IT in Investment Management and Business Knowledge for IT in Hedge Funds in order to gain a broader insight into trading as well as exchanges.

Overview of Trading and Exchanges

This chapter introduces the concept of trading and includes the history of trading and an overview of the global trading market.

Introduction

Trading is an important function in the global financial markets. It involves buyers finding sellers and sellers finding buyers. The intention of participants in a trade is to achieve the best possible price for the product that is being traded. Sellers search for buyers that can pay high prices, while buyers search for sellers that can sell at low prices. Traders – people who trade – must also find traders who are ready to trade the quantities they want. In some instances, a trader may want to trade large quantities and will have to resort to trading with a number of traders to complete his/her trade.

Arbitrage and market-making are fundamental aspects of trading as are proprietary trading by financial institutions and trading done on behalf of clients. Traders must not only have a good grasp of global economic fundamentals, but must also be knowledgeable about technical indicators and market behaviour in order to achieve success in trading in the financial markets. In addition, developing trading strategies and implementing these trading strategies are also essential ingredients for success.

Exchanges can be described as small and medium-size businesses just like any other; the difference being the intense regulation by governmental authorities to which they are subjected. They seek to fulfil economic roles in the marketplace, forge short-term and permanent alliances and are subject to competition. An exchange may be a physical location where traders meet to conduct business or an electronic platform. They are also referred to as a "share exchange" or "bourse", depending on their geographical location. Exchanges provide companies, governments and other groups with a platform for selling securities to the investing public.

Given that an exchange is the operator of a "financial market", it will be prudent at this stage to define this term. A definition by *The Economist* is as follows: "*a financial market exists to move resources across space and time, from where they are in surplus to where they are needed most. And they produce valuable information, through the prices they set, that firms, households and governments use to manage resources better.*"[1] It is safe to assume that in a well-functioning economy, a substantial number of buyers and sellers are present in this market and that their transactions stimulate a process of price discovery[2] for any individual financial product. This market may be for equities, derivatives, fixed income or other products, and can be found throughout the world in one form or another.

The financial market described above is known as the secondary market for trading, as opposed to the primary market for initial public offerings (IPOs), and attracts orders from parties such as brokers who have been pre-approved by the exchange to interact in the price-formation mechanism. It then forwards the

---

1 *The Economist*, November 13, 1999, p85.
2 A means of establishing the price for a specific commodity or security through basic supply and demand factors related to the market and what is usually used to determine spot prices.

matched order on to a clearing and settlement organisation that arranges for the payment and transfer of property. Thus it can be concluded that participants in this market are not just the buyers and sellers of financial products but the issuers as well.

The most common type of exchange is a stock exchange, which can be defined as an institution that operates a market for the orderly buying and selling of financial products, i.e. securities. The core function of a stock exchange is to ensure fair and orderly trading, as well as efficient dissemination of price information for any securities trading on that exchange. It engages in other activities such as the development of new financial products and a wide range of associated technology services. Stock markets are required to regularly produce financial reports and audited earnings reports.

Another type of exchange is the derivatives exchange, which is a central marketplace where derivatives such as futures contracts and options on futures contracts are traded. Derivatives exchanges also play an important role in the operation of the global financial system.

A commodity exchange is the type of exchange where various commodities – agricultural products, bio-fuels and precious metals – are traded. They also play an important role in the global financial system.

The Players in Trading

The major players in trading are traders and brokers. The role of the trader is to arrange his/her trades for other trades, and commission other people to arrange trades for them. The type of trader who trades for their own account is known as a proprietary trader while those that arrange trades on a commission basis on behalf of their clients are called commission traders or brokers. The type of trading that proprietary traders engage in is referred to as proprietary trading while that of brokers is known as agency trading. Proprietary trading is exemplified by the trading activities undertaken at investment banks, whereby their traders actively trade stocks, bonds, options, commodities or other items with the bank's own money as opposed to its clients' money, so as to make a profit for the bank.

Traders are said to have a long position when they trade securities they own and a short position when they have sold something that they do not own. If a trader has a long position, they expect to profit when the price of the securities they have traded rises. However, if they have a short position, they profit when the price of the securities they have borrowed falls, as they can repurchase at a lower price. Repurchasing these securities allows the traders to cover their positions.

There are two sides to the trading industry – the sell side and the buy side. The buy side refers to the traders that buy exchange services, while the sell side refers to firms that take orders from the buy side firms and then work the orders. The sell side provides the buy side with the ability to trade whenever they want to trade.

3

Sell Side

The sell side of the trading industry comprises brokers and dealers that sell securities to the buy side and also make recommendations on upgrades, downgrades, target prices and opinions based on research.

The role of dealers on the sell side is to be prepared to trade with their clients when they want to trade. The ethos of dealers is to "buy low and sell high". Brokers, on the other hand, trade at the behest of their clients. The role of the broker is to find other traders that would be interested in trading with their clients when these clients want to trade.

Firms such as investment banks fulfil the dual role of broker and dealer and have trading staff that trade as well as broker trades on behalf of their clients.

Table 1.1 provides common examples of the different types of trader on the sell side and their motivation for trading.

Table 1.1 Sell-side Traders' Motivation

Trader Type	Common Examples	Motivation for Trading
Dealers	Market makers Specialists Day traders	To generate revenue from trading profits
Brokers	Discount brokers Retail brokers	To generate revenue from commissions that can be earned by arranging trades for clients
Broker-Dealers	Investment banks	To generate revenue from trading profits and trading commissions
Inter-dealer Brokers	Specialist intermediary broking service providers	To facilitate inter-dealer trades and generate revenue from trading profits and trading commissions

Difference between a broker and a market maker

A broker is a go-between who is licensed to buy and sell securities on a client's behalf. Stockbrokers coordinate contracts between buyers and sellers, and usually charge a commission. A market maker, on the other hand, is an intermediary that is willing and ready to buy and sell securities for a profitable price.

A broker generates revenue by matching securities' buyers and sellers. Brokers have the authorisation and know-how to buy securities on an investor's behalf – not just anyone is allowed to walk into the London Stock Exchange and buy stocks; thus, investors must hire licensed brokers to do this on their behalf. A flat fee or percentage-based commission is paid to the broker for executing a trade and seeking the best price for a security. Because brokers are regulated and licensed, they have an obligation to act in the best interests of their clients. Many brokers can also offer advice on what stocks, mutual funds and other securities to buy. Owing to the availability of internet-based automated stock-brokering systems, clients often do not have any personal contact with their brokerage firms.

A market maker makes a profit by trying to sell high and buy low. Market makers establish quotes whereby the bid price is set slightly lower than listed prices, and the ask price is set slightly higher in order to earn a small margin. The role of market makers is essential because they are always ready to buy and sell as long as the investor is willing to pay a specific price. This helps to create liquidity and efficiency in the market. Market makers basically act as wholesalers by buying and selling securities to satisfy the market; the prices they set reflect market supply and demand. When the demand for a security is low and supply is high, the price of the security will be low. If the demand is high and supply is low, the price of the security will be high. Market makers are compelled to sell and buy at the price and size they have quoted.

Buy Side

The buy side of the trading industry comprises the investing institutions such as mutual funds, pension funds, governments and insurance firms that tend to buy large portions of securities for money-management purposes. These institutions also use the financial markets to solve the different kinds of problems that they encounter.

A typical situation is a temporary cashflow problem that an individual may face when their expenses exceed their income.

Table 1.2 provides common examples of the different types of traders on the buy side and their motivation for trading.

Table 1.2 Buy-side Traders' Motivation

Trader Type	Common Examples	Motivation for Trading
Investors	Individuals Endowments Charitable trusts Corporate pension funds	Generational transfer of wealth
Asset Exchangers	Global corporations Manufacturers	Acquisition of assets that they perceive to be of higher value than assets that they offer for sale
Hedgers	Shippers Agricultural organisations Mining companies	Reduction of business risk

History of Trading

The origins of trade can be traced to the beginning of communication in prehistoric times. People in this age engaged in trade by barter, exchanging goods and services with each other before the emergence of modern-day currency. Historians believe trading took place throughout much of recorded human history.

In the next chapter, trading of different asset classes will be discussed; therefore it would be beneficial to discuss the history of trading in the different classes. In this section, the history of trading in two asset classes – currency and commodities – will be briefly discussed.

History of Currency Trading

According to historians, the roots of modern currency trading can be traced back to the origins of money itself. A key principle of foreign exchange theory involves a common notion that various forms of money have value and are readily exchangeable for products, services and commodities. Currency has historically being backed by the value of various precious metals, particularly gold and silver. During the 1800s, most of the currencies in circulation around the world were backed by stores of gold bullion, an idea first conceived by the English government. However, global turmoil in the 1900s gradually led to the abrogation of the gold standard. The US dollar was, at the time, almost universally accepted worldwide as a medium for barter and trade, given the recognition of the United States as a global economic superpower.

The popularity of the US dollar continued to grow as the United States continued to contribute huge sums of money to global western stabilisation in the post-war years. Gold reserves continued to back the value of the US dollar on an international basis and, at the same time, the USA exported significant amounts of gold to back the currencies of other friendly nations. By 1970, foreign nations held $47 billion of US currency and the USA had to face the fact that it no longer had the necessary gold reserves to back the massive exposure. In 1971, the USA formally decided that its dollar would cease to be tied to the gold standard and the modern foreign exchange market was born. This became known as a "floating rate" system, under which prevailing currency exchange rates would fluctuate according to supply and demand.

History of Commodity Trading

Historians also trace the roots of commodity trading to the opening of the sea route to India (once the name given to all of Indonesia, Malaya and the rest of south-east Asia) by the mariner Dom Vasco da Gama in 1499, which established the colonial power of Portugal in the Indian Ocean.[3]

In the 100 years that followed, 200 voyages were made around the Cape of Good Hope to the east.

The spice trade was initially the main motivation, but then the discovery of 1,600 other commodities took on a more prominent role. However, only around half of all the ships sent out by the Portuguese and the Dutch ever returned. Despite the elimination of that risk, transport was still a bottleneck.

Other nations and pirates who blocked access to the eastern Mediterranean area put the expeditions at risk.

3   AME Info – Middle East Finance and Economy, A Brief History of Commodity Trading, available from www.ameinfo.com/157823.html

In 1580, the two great sea-faring nations, Spain and Portugal, combined. The resulting combination guaranteed that the sea route to Asia continued to be closed to European nations.

Trade in Asian spices, especially pepper, was subject to contracts drawn up by the crown, whereby traders (contradores) had to follow fixed prices. They then sold on the goods to retailers such as notable Dutch trading houses in Lisbon, which in turn supplied the north European market through trading agencies in Antwerp in the Netherlands.

The price volatility seen in markets in the modern day are reminiscent of those witnessed during this era. The term "tulip mania"[4] originated from a period in Dutch history when demand for tulip bulbs reached such a peak that very high prices were charged for a single bulb. During a certain period, the price paid for a single bulb exceeded that paid for a house in the centre of Amsterdam. Nowadays, the phrase is a synonym for speculation in the financial markets.

As the 16th century drew to a close, Dutch traders from across the Netherlands decided to take charge of spice imports from Asia. Companies were formed to finance the ships and equipment and these companies eventually merged. Within a few years, these companies had equipped 65 ships spread across 15 fleets, of which around 50 returned packed with goods.

These companies engaged in conflicts with the Portuguese, the English and each other. As a consequence, there was a dramatic fall in the price of spices. Therefore, economic motives compelled the Dutch merchants to co-operate and organise a merger.

The new company, VOC, was the beneficiary of a state charter that bestowed upon it sovereign rights, and this would be of great significance for its future development (the contemporary equivalent would be some of the national oil companies).

VOC was the first, and not long after became the largest, worldwide company to dominate trading. It displayed the basic features of a modern joint-stock company and initiated future economic and financial history.

In the USA in the early 1840s, Chicago, due to its infrastructure of rail and waterways, became the logical place for the mid-west farmers to meet with the dealers who were willing to ship their harvests to markets around the country. Deal making became the norm for farmers looking for a sure place to sell their crops and dealers that needed a reliable source of grain.

Initially, a "spot" market evolved as farmers, looking to find a buyer, brought their grain to the Chicago market in the hopes of selling it "on the spot" for cash. While this gave the farmer an opportunity to sell their product, the overall process was less efficient than it could have been.

The first "futures contracts" were probably handshakes between dealers and farmers – an agreement that outlined the purchase price and quantity of the grain delivered by the farmer at a future date in time. Soon, these contracts were in the form of written agreements and speculators began trading in these

---

4   A term used metaphorically to refer to any large economic bubble.

futures contracts in the hope that the laws of supply and demand would work in their favour.

By 1848, the Chicago Board of Trade (CBOT) was founded by 82 Chicago merchants, and they settled into their first premises above the Gage and Haines flour store at 101 S. Water Street where CBOT stayed until 1852. As a result, an organisation was now in place that could help farmers find buyers and provide for a more robust trading marketplace.

Traders' and Investors' Roles in the Marketplace

In the financial markets, the words "trading" and "investing " are used interchangeably, but those in the know insist that, in reality, these words represent two different activities. Experts point out that in spite of the fact that both traders and investors play a part in the same marketplace, they perform two different tasks using different strategies. The two parties are, however, invaluable to the smooth functioning of the markets.

Definition of an Investor

An investor is a market participant who commits money to investment products with the expectation of financial return. The popular perception is that investors' activities are restricted to the stock market. However, investors are also active in currency and bond markets, either directly or through investment vehicles. From a stock market perspective, investors are those who buy shares in a company, and hold on to them for a relatively long time because of their belief in the strong future prospects of the company. Investors usually take two key factors into consideration when investing in a company's shares:

■ **Value** – Investors concern themselves with the assessment of a company's shares to see if they represent value. For instance, two similar companies' shares may be trading at different P/E ratios[5] (price-to-earnings ratios), but the lower one might be the better value because it suggests that the investor will need to pay less for £1 of earnings when investing in Company ABC when compared to what would be required to gain exposure to £1 of earnings in Company XYZ.
■ **Success** – Investors typically assess the company's future success, taking a view about their financial strength and appraising their future cash flows.

Investors normally determine these factors by analysing the company's financial statements together with an assessment of industry trends that may indicate

5   This is a measure of the price paid for a share relative to the annual income or profit earned by the firm per share (Investopedia). A higher P/E ratio means that investors are paying more for each unit of income.

future growth prospects. Metrics such as the PEG (Price/Earnings to Growth) ratio are used, i.e. the ratio used to determine a stock's value while factoring in earnings growth.

The Major Investors

The types of investors that are active in the financial markets are varied. In actual fact, investors own the bulk of the money that is at work in the markets. Please note that this should not be confused with the amount of currency traded each day, which is in the hands of traders.

Below is a brief list of some types of investors:

- Institutional investors
- Retail investors
- Investment banks
- Collective investment vehicles, such as mutual funds and unit trusts

These types of investors seek to hold on to their positions in the hope that they can enjoy the continual success of the company and that they, as shareholders, can benefit from this success. There are a number of renowned investors that are firm believers in this strategy; chief among them is Warren Buffet, the Chairman of Berkshire Hathaway and, at the time of writing, the world's richest man.

Definition of a Trader

A trader is a market participant who is involved in the transfer of financial assets in the financial markets. Commodities markets are ideal for the types of activities that traders typically engage in. Since commodities are not desirable asset holdings, traders are more interested in exploiting small price movements attributable to supply and demand. Traders usually focus on:

- **Supply and demand** – traders typically monitor their trades intraday in order to identify the direction of the market and the reason behind the movements;
- **Price patterns** – traders engage in technical analysis that entails using past history with a view to predicting future price movements;
- **Market emotion** – traders exploit the fears of investors by "fading the market". This means that they sell when the prices are rising and buy when they are falling.

The Major Traders

Traders typically trade larger volumes than investors. The frequency of trading among traders varies and can be as often as every few seconds. The following is a list of the more popular types of trader:

- **Proprietary traders** – This type of trader makes money through short-term trading.

9

■ **Arbitrageurs** – This type of trader engages in arbitrage.[6]
■ **Investment banks** – Traders in investment banks trade company stock during IPO processes in the open market. They also trade shares that are not held as long-term investments.
■ **Market makers** – As stated earlier, the role of this type of trader is to supply liquidity in the marketplace.

Trading Sessions

There are two types of trading sessions – periods during which trades are arranged in the financial markets – and they are known as continuous and call markets.

Continuous Markets

Continuous markets are any markets that are generating a level of activity that is healthy enough to allow a typical trade to take place without creating a significant impact on the current market price for the security. In these markets, traders are able to trade any time the markets are open.

While the trading in continuous markets may be rapid, it remains sufficiently constant to prevent activity leading to any strong indicators that would entice traders to begin executing larger orders to buy or sell. Essentially, a continuous market is very stable, experiences a consistent level of trading, and tends to maintain a fair market price.

Continuous trading markets are very widespread. Most exchanges, from stock exchanges to futures exchanges, have continuous trading sessions.

Call Markets

In call markets, trading occurs at the same time when the market is called. In this type of market, each transaction takes place at predetermined intervals and all bid and ask orders are aggregated and transacted at once. The exchange determines the market clearing price based on the number of bid and ask orders.

Call market trades may occur simultaneously or one at a time, in a rotation. In call markets that support rotation, the rotation may occur once per trading session or as many times as possible during the trading hours.

Call markets are used as the exclusive market mechanism for a number of instruments such as government bonds and treasury bills.

Trading Hours

A market's trading hours are the period of time consisting of one day of business in a financial market, during which the market accepts orders and arranges trades. In continuous trading markets, trading takes place during normal busi-

6   Arbitrage is discussed further in Chapter 7.

ness hours. For example, the London Stock Exchange's continuous trading schedule is from 08:00 to 16:20 Greenwich Mean Time (GMT).This opening time is one hour before the start of the business day in the UK, i.e. 09:00, and the closing time is about 40 minutes before the end of the business day, which is 17:00. This is the usual practice in most continuous markets as it gives the traders the time before the open to collect and submit orders. The time after the close is used to settle trades and to report the results to clients.

As the financial markets are increasingly global in nature, some markets trade at odd hours within their time zone in order to accommodate normal trading hours in another time zone. This practice also applies nationally in the USA because of the different times zones within the country. The Chicago Stock Exchange opens trading at 08:30 Central Time to coincide with the New York Stock Exchange at 09:30 Eastern Time.

Insider Trading

An important concept in trading that needs to be discussed at this point is "insider trading". In some jurisdictions, the financial regulators have met with criticism for failing to exercise their power in the fight against high-profile insider dealing.

What is Insider Trading?
Insider trading is the trading of a corporation's shares or other securities (e.g. stock options or bonds) by individuals with potential access to non-public information about the company. In most countries, it is legal for corporate insiders such as officers, key employees, directors, and large shareholders to trade in a company's stock if they do not take advantage of non-public information. However, the term is frequently used to refer to a practice in which an insider or a related party trades based on material non-public information obtained during the performance of the insider's duties at the corporation, or is otherwise in breach of a fiduciary duty or other relationship of trust and confidence or where the non-public information was misappropriated from the company.[7]

In the USA and several other jurisdictions, there is a requirement for public disclosure or disclosure to a regulator, usually within a few business days, when trading is carried out by corporate officers, key employees, directors or significant shareholders (these are defined as holders of more than 10% of the firm's shares). Industry experts claim that a number of investors follow the summaries of these insider trades in the hope that they can imitate these and trade with a view to making a profit. Despite the fact that conducting "legal" insider trading cannot be based on material non-public information, industry experts believe that some investors are of the opinion that corporate insiders, however, may

---

7   US Securities and Exchange Commission, Insider Trading. Available from http://www.sec.gov/.

have better insights into the financial health of a corporation and that trades can also convey vital information, such as the purchase of shares indicating a greater commitment to the corporation.

In the trading industry, insider trading conducted in an illegal manner results in a decrease in overall economic growth as it is believed to raise the cost of capital for securities issuers.[8]

Illegal Insider Trading

Most jurisdictions around the world have laws prohibiting insider trading on material non-public information, though the details and enforcement procedures may vary slightly. The USA is generally viewed as having the strictest laws against illegal insider trading and making the most serious efforts to enforce them.[9]

Definition of "Insider"

An insider can be defined as a director, officer or shareholder that owns more than 10% of a class of a corporation's equity securities. This definition conforms to the requirements that are mandatory for reporting purposes. According to legal experts, trades made by these types of insiders in the corporation's own stock, based on material non-public information, are deemed to be fraudulent given that the insiders are violating the trust or the fiduciary duty that they owe to shareholders. It could be argued that the corporate insider, simply by accepting employment, has a contract with the shareholders that compels them to put the shareholders' interest before their own, in matters relating to the corporation. In a situation where the insider buys or sells based upon company-owned information, they are violating their contract with the shareholders.

In the USA and many other jurisdictions, however, "insiders" are not just restricted to corporate officials and major shareholders where illegal insider trading is concerned, but to other individuals who trade shares based on material non-public information in violation of some duty of trust. This duty may be assigned; for example, in many jurisdictions, in cases of corporate insiders giving friends tips on non-public information likely to have an effect on the company's share price; the duty the corporate insider owes the corporation is now assigned to the friend and the friend violates a duty to the corporation if they trade on the basis of this information.

A typical example was the case of Martha Stewart, the former CEO and Chairwoman of Martha Stewart Living Omnimedia, who, according to the US Securities and Exchange Commission, was told by her friend Sam Waksal that his company ImClone's cancer drug had been rejected by the Food and Drug Administration before the information was made public. This rejection was a huge

---

8   Utpal Bhattacharya and Hazem Daouk, (Feb. 2002), "The World Price of Insider Trading" Journal of Finance, Vol. LVII, No. 1.

9   Coffee, John C., (December 2007), Law and the Market: The Impact of Enforcement, University of Pennsylvania Law Review.

blow to his company and the price of the stock went down dramatically. However, Martha Stewart avoided a loss of $45,673 by selling all 3,928 shares of her ImClone stock in late 2001. The day following her sale, the stock value fell 18%.[10]

Another example is the case of Barry Switzer, then-Oklahoma football coach in the USA, who was prosecuted by the SEC in 1981 after he and his friends purchased shares in Phoenix Resources, an oil company. Switzer was at a track meeting when he overheard a conversation between executives concerning the liquidation of the business. He purchased the stock at around $42 per share, and later sold at $59, making around $98,000 in the process. The charges against him were, however, later dismissed by a federal judge on a "lack of evidence".

In Europe, the UK's Financial Services Authority (FSA) levelled allegations of insider trading in 2008 against a former partner of Casenove, a British stockbroking firm, relating to six takeover and merger deals between April 2003 and March 2005. These deals include the proposed takeover of HP Bulmer plc in 2003, the proposed management buyout of Macdonald Hotels plc also in 2003, and the proposed takeover of RAC plc in 2005.[11]

History of Exchanges

History of Stock Exchanges
The history of exchanges dates back to 11th century France when the "courtiers de change" were concerned with managing and regulating the debts of agricultural communities on behalf of the banks. Since these men also traded in debts, they could be called the first brokers.

According to some sources, the origin of the term "bourse" comes from the Latin bursa meaning a bag because, in 13th century Bruges, the sign of a purse (or probably three purses), hung on the front of the house where merchants met.

Other sources claim that it is more likely that in the late 13th century, commodity traders in Bruges convened inside the house of a man called Van der Burse, and in 1309 they institutionalised this, until then, informal meeting and it became the "Bruges Bourse". The concept spread quickly around Flanders and neighbouring counties and "Bourses" were soon commissioned in Ghent and Amsterdam.

The world's first stock exchange was located in the house of the Beurze family on Vlamingstraat, Bruges, around 1415. Historians claim that the term Bourse is believed to have derived from the family name Beurze.

Venetian bankers in Italy had begun to trade in government securities by the middle of the 13th century. Later, in the 14th century, bankers from other

---

10 Security and Exchange Commission, "SEC Charges Martha Stewart, Broker Peter Bacanovic with Illegal Insider Trading", 4 June 2003. Available from www.sec.gov/news/press/2003-69.htm.

11 Financial Services Authority. (24 July 2008). Insider Dealing: Financial Services Authority. Available from http://www.fsa.gov.uk/pages/Library/Communication/PR/2008/078.shtml.

Italian cities such as Florence, Verona, Pisa and Genoa started dealing with government securities. This came about as a result of the absence of the rule of the Duke and the council of citizens in these independent cities.

There are other differing opinions regarding the origin of the stock markets. While most historians are of the opinion that the Italians were the originators of the stock markets, others maintain that stock markets existed in a rough form in Cairo, Egypt. According to historian Fernand Braudel, the Jewish and the Muslim traders had a system of trade association and were even aware of the many ways of payment and credit – and all this way back in the 11th century. Stock market activities were observed in other countries in the 17th century. During this period, the Dutch pioneered the concept of joint stock companies, which allowed shareholders to invest in business ventures and receive a share of their profits – or losses. In 1602, the Dutch East India Company issued the first shares on the Amsterdam Stock Exchange. Some sources claim that it was the first company to issue stocks and bonds. In 1688, the trading of stocks was initiated on a stock exchange in London.

In the USA, the famous New York Stock Exchange started operating in the 18th century, 1792 to be precise, when 24 big traders convened and took the decision to deal in bonds and stocks on Wall Street on a daily basis.

History of Commodity Exchanges

As seen earlier, the Chicago Board of Trade, the world's oldest established commodity (futures) exchange, was founded in 1848 by 82 Chicago merchants. In this exchange, markets for futures trading were developed initially to help agricultural producers and consumers manage the price risks they faced harvesting, marketing and processing food crops each year. Nowadays, futures exist not only on agricultural products, but also on a wide array of financial, stock and forex markets.

The first of what were then called "to arrive" contracts on this exchange were flour, timothy seed and hay, which came into use in 1849. "Forward" contracts on corn came into use in 1851 and gained popularity among merchants and food processors.

In the meantime, what is now the USA's largest futures exchange, the Chicago Mercantile Exchange, was founded as the Chicago Butter and Egg Board in 1898 and, at that time, trading was offered in butter and eggs.

In 2007, the CME and CBOT officially merged, and are now collectively known as CME group Inc., the world's largest and most diverse derivatives exchange.

In the 21st century, online commodity trading has become increasingly popular, and commodity brokers offer front-end interfaces to trade these electronic-based markets. A commodities broker may also continue to offer access to the traditional pit-traded, or open-outcry,[12] markets that established the commodity exchanges.

---

12 This is a method of communication between professionals on a stock exchange or futures exchange, which involves shouting and the use of hand signals to transfer information primarily about buy and sell orders. The part of the trading floor where this takes place is called a pit.

The Business of Running Exchanges

Most exchanges are for-profit organisations that have a distinct, market-neutral identity within the financial services sector. They are different to insurance companies, banks, investment firms or brokerages. Their core business is to operate regulated securities and derivatives markets. These markets institute asset values via efficient price discovery, allowing the public to be informed about the worth of companies according to the latest news and economic outlook.

Exchanges offer, in addition to equities, government and corporate-listed bonds, exchange-traded funds and on-exchange financial futures and options. The diversity of instruments offered brings the know-how of public capital market operators to the service of issuers and investors by guaranteeing openness and fairness.

As financial markets are highly sensitive to the environment, operating an exchange is a proportionately complex business. While regulation helps make the market more efficient, much also depends on human talent and judgement as is the case elsewhere in the financial services industry. Governments around the world have a duty to prevail on matters of public savings as do investors and corporate issuers of securities, and operators of exchanges, in concert with these parties, typically fine-tune rules to ensure the correctness of this business model.

Exchanges are also tasked with ensuring fair and transparent price discovery.

In order to serve the needs of their clients and generate revenue that ensures business growth, exchanges need to:

- connect markets to an increasing number of players;
- invest in reserves strategically;
- upgrade their IT and telecommunication systems;
- pledge an appreciable return on capital;
- improve the quality of market data and information disclosed on companies;
- improve staff operations and competency;
- address strong national and cross-border competitive pressures;
- arrange programmes for educating users of the exchange.

Over the years, an increasing number of exchanges have introduced the shares of their companies on the markets they operate; a practice that highlights the quest for profitability and the openness to the public that characterises the industry. Exchanges are looking to increase profitability through the use of technology and an increase in operational efficiencies to reduce unit costs.

The size of the exchange industry is small when compared to the economic function of the financial markets. In addition, the corporate size of exchanges is also comparatively small in relation to banks, institutional brokerages, insurance companies and other investment firms. Each of these organisations has key financial functions to fulfil, including in the capital markets. However, due to the complex nature of the exchange business, their relatively small size hinders the ability of their managers to have an impact on public policy debates.

Three Business Models for the Stock Exchange Industry

Despite the rapid and profound change that has been witnessed in recent times in the stock exchange industry worldwide, three distinct types of exchange business models – the Global Exchange, the Regional Exchange and the Diversified Exchange – can be identified. Each of these models has its market niche and interrelates with other exchanges through various forms of collaboration and competition.

The Global Exchange

This type of exchange can be defined as an exchange that is dominant in an economically linked network of a number of financial jurisdictions. Its market capitalisation is the highest in this group and it has the greatest trading volume and liquidity of any of its direct competitors. Among the instruments it trades are highly visible international securities and derivatives that could be in the form of global shares, local currency deposits, or secondary listings of shares that have home markets elsewhere, in addition to local shares from its own well-developed domestic market. It clients range from domestic investors to global investors.

The key competences needed to create a Global Exchange are business wherewithal, market nous and a solid infrastructure; infrastructure being the pool of talented individuals in a geographic region that are available to ensure proper functioning of the market.

Typical examples are the New York Stock Exchange and the London Stock Exchange.

The Regional Exchange

This can be defined as an exchange that is dominant in its local economy. It has the highest concentration of regional listings available as it is the principal expert in these listings. Given its strong national concentration, its index is perceived as a barometer of the health of the publicly quoted section of the regional economy. This type of exchange engages in the trading of securities and derivatives and its main clients are regional investors. Other clients are international investors that seek to benefit from the available expertise and opportunities.

Like the Global Exchange, the major source of revenue of the regional exchange is the listing and trading of national securities and the focusing of knowledge on the securities on its market.

Typical examples are the Helsinki Stock Exchange and the Tel Aviv Stock Exchange.

The Diversified Exchange

This type of exchange is analogous to the Regional Exchange, but differs from it in its ability to not only list and trade securities but also the core competency it possesses in at least one related business line.

A definition of the Diversified Exchange is as follows:

An exchange that is dominant in its regional economy and that engages in economic activities outside the usual realms of where a typical exchange operates. Most regional listings occur on this type of exchange and it is the principal expert in these listings. Its clients are mainly regional investors although a relatively small number of investors may form part of the clientele. Its competitors that offer similar services are different in their economic form and function from those of the Global Exchanges and Regional Exchanges.

Industry experts opine that three types of diversified exchanges can be observed in the exchange domain: technology-focused types, one with an economic development focus and one that is a division of a broader organisation. These individual business models highlight the diversity of the success factors of a Diversified Exchange, unlike those of the Global Exchange and the Regional Exchange. The hybrid nature of these exchanges allows them to focus on particular business lines or geographical expansion though the emphasis is always on profit generation and identification of new avenues for growth.

Typical examples are the Johannesburg Stock Exchange, which is reported to have offered its proprietary trading system to neighbouring countries in Southern Africa.[13] The Paris Bourse sells its trading system to other exchanges and is another example of a Diversified Exchange.

The Global Exchange Industry

Tables 1.3 and 1.4 provide a picture of the size and recent growth of the global exchange industry in terms of domestic equity capitalisation and total value of share trading.

By the end of 2007, the NYSE Group had the highest domestic equity capitalisation, which shows a 1.5% increase on the figures for the end of 2006. It is worth noting the increasing significance of exchanges in India and China (including Hong Kong) as depicted by the position of the National Stock Exchange of India, Bombay Stock Exchange, Shanghai Stock Exchange and Hong Kong Exchanges. The respective figures for growth of market capitalisation for these exchanges show remarkable increases in 2007.

Table 1.4 shows the exchanges with the largest share trading in 2007 and 2006 in various currencies.

The figures for the Asian exchanges – Shanghai Stock Exchange, Tokyo Stock Exchange, Hong Kong Exchanges, Shenzhen Stock Exchange and Korea Exchange – in terms of share trading show their impressive individual perform-

---

13   Joshua Galper, August 1999, "Three Business Models for the Stock Exchange Industry",
     A Working Paper of MIT Sloan School of Management, p13.

Table 1.3 Growth of the global exchange industry

Exchange	USD bn end-2007	USD bn end-2006	% Change in USD	% Change in local currency
NYSE Group	15,651	15,421	1.5	1.5
Tokyo Stock Exchange Group	4,331	4,614	-6.1	-12.0
Euronext	4,223	3,708	13.9	2.7
Nasdaq Stock Market	4,014	3,865	3.8	3.8
London Stock Exchange	3,852	3,794	1.5	-0.2
Shanghai Stock Exchange	3,694	918	302.7	276.8
Hong Kong Exchanges	2,654	1,715	54.8	55.2
TSX Group	2,187	1,701	28.6	9.0
Deutsche Börse	2,105	1,638	28.6	15.9
Bombay Stock Exchange	1,819	819	122.1	97.8
BME Spanish Exchanges	1,781	1,323	34.6	21.4
National Stock Exchange of India	1,660	774	114.5	91.0

Source: World Federation of Exchanges

Table 1.4 Exchanges with largest share trading in 2007 and 2006

Exchange	USD bn 2007	USD bn 2006	% Change in USD	% Change in local currency
NYSE Group	29,909	21,789	37.3	37.3
Nasdaq Stock Market	15,320	11,807	29.7	29.7
London Stock Exchange	10,324	7,584	36.1	26.1
Tokyo Stock Exchange Group	6,476	5,825	11.2	12.2
Euronext	5,648	3,805	48.4	36.5
Deutsche Börse	4,324	2,742	57.7	45.2
Shanghai Stock Exchanges	4,070	739	450.9	426.6
BME Spanish Exchanges	2,971	1,941	53.0	41.1
Borsa Italiana	2,312	1,596	44.8	33.6
Hong Kong Exchanges	2,139	832	156.9	157.8
Shenzhen Stock Exchange	2,102	424	396.2	374.1
Korea Exchange	2,011	1,340	50.1	46.0

Source: World Federation of Exchanges

ances in 2007. According to the World Federation of Exchanges, the Philippines Stock Exchange, the Bombay Stock Exchange and the Jakarta Stock Exchange also recorded sharp rises in the value of shares traded, recording 160%, 124% and 134% respectively. It can therefore be concluded that the Asian markets are increasingly becoming a dominant force in the international economy.

Other notable exchanges in the world are listed in Tables 1.5, 1.6 and 1.7.

Table 1.5 Stock Exchanges

Name of Exchange	Country	Headquarters
American Stock Exchange	USA	New York City
Athens Exchange	Greece	Athens
Australian Stock Exchange	Australia	Sydney
Bermuda Stock Exchange	Bermuda	Hamilton
Bolsa de Comercio de Buenos Aires	Argentina	Buenos Aires
Bolsa de Comercio de Santiago	Chile	Santiago
Bolsa de Valores de Lima	Peru	Lima
Bolsa de Valores do São Paulo	Brazil	São Paulo
Bolsa Mexicana de Valores	Mexico	Mexico City
Bolsas y Mercados Españoles	Spain	Madrid
Borsa Italiana SpA	Italy	Milan
Bourse de Luxembourg	Luxembourg	Luxembourg City
Bourse de Montréal	Canada	Montréal
Budapest Stock Exchange Ltd.	Hungary	Budapest
Bursa Malaysia	Malaysia	Kuala Lumpur
Chicago Board Options Exchange	USA	Chicago
Colombo Stock Exchange	Sri Lanka	Colombo
Copenhagen Stock Exchange	Denmark	Copenhagen
Deutsche Börse AG	Germany	Frankfurt
Euronext Amsterdam	Netherlands	Amsterdam
Euronext Paris	France	Paris
Irish Stock Exchange	Republic of Ireland	Dublin
Istanbul Stock Exchange	Turkey	Istanbul
Malta Stock Exchange	Malta	Valletta
New Zealand Exchange	New Zealand	Wellington
Oslo Børs	Norway	Oslo
Singapore Exchange	Singapore	Singapore
Stock Exchange of Tehran	Iran	Tehran
Stock Exchange of Thailand	Thailand	Bangkok
SWX Swiss Exchange	Switzerland	Zürich
Taiwan Stock Exchange Corp.	Taiwan	Taipei
Tel Aviv Stock Exchange	Israel	Tel Aviv
Warsaw Stock Exchange	Poland	Warsaw

Table 1.6 Commodity Exchanges

Name of Exchange	Country	Headquarters
Australian Securities Exchange	Australia	Sydney
Brazilian Mercantile and Futures Exchange	Brazil	São Paulo
Central Japan Commodity Exchange	Japan	Nagoya
Chicago Climate Exchange	USA	Chicago
Climex	The Netherlands	Utrecht
CME Group	USA	Chicago
Dalian Commodity Exchange	China	Dalian
Dubai Mercantile Exchange	Dubai	Dubai
Dubai Gold & Commodities Exchange	Dubai	Dubai
European Climate Exchange	UK	London
Hedge Street Exchange	USA	Chicago
Intercontinental Exchange	Various	Atlanta
London Metal Exchange	UK	London
Kansas City Board of Trade	USA	Kansas City
Memphis Cotton Exchange	USA	Memphis
Mercado a Termino de Buenos Aires	Argentina	Buenos Aires
Minneapolis Grain Exchange	USA	Minneapolis
Multi Commodity Exchange	India	Mumbai
New York Mercantile Exchange	USA	New York City
National Commodity Exchange Limited	Pakistan	Karachi
Winnipeg Commodity Exchange	Canada	Winnipeg

Table 1.7 Derivative Exchanges

Name of Exchange	Country	Headquarters
Athens Derivatives Exchange	Greece	Athens
Chicago Board Options Exchange	USA	Chicago
China Financial Futures Exchange	China	Shanghai
Dubai International Financial Exchange	Dubai	Dubai
Eurex	Pan European	Various
Euronext Liffe	Pan European	Various
Italian Derivatives Equity Market	Italy	Milan
Jakarta Futures Exchange	Indonesia	Jakarta
Mexican Derivatives Exchange	Mexico	Mexico City
Montreal Exchange	Canada	Montreal
Mercado Oficial Español de Futuros y Opciones	Spain	Madrid
Moscow Interbank Currency Exchange	Russia	Moscow
New Zealand Futures & Options Exchange	New Zealand	Auckland
Porto Derivatives Exchange	Portugal	Porto
Bolsa de Comercio de Rosario (ROFEX)	Argentina	Buenos Aires
Risk Management Exchange	Germany	Hannover

South African Futures Exchange	South African	Johannesburg
Swiss Options & Financial Futures Exchange	Switzerland	Zurich
Taiwan Futures Exchange	Taiwan	Taipei
Turkish Derivatives Exchange	Turkey	Izmir

Trading in Different Asset Classes

This chapter introduces the trading activities in different asset classes from equities to fixed income.

Introduction

Financial organisations now trade many asset classes from fixed income to equities. Each asset class has its own uniqueness and the associated trading activities reflect this. While some asset classes are traded in traditional exchanges, others are traded over the counter. Demand and supply also play a part in the trading volumes of each type of asset class. For example, demand for a commodity such as crude oil around the world will increase the trading activity in this commodity as well as the derivative financial instruments such as crude oil futures contracts and options on the futures contracts. Market conditions are a major determinant in the demand for one asset class over another. For example, the collapse of Lehman Brothers and the rescue of Merrill Lynch by Bank of America in September 2008 led terrified investors to exit shares in favour of bonds, which they perceived to be a safer investment than shares in light of the market conditions. This led to an increase, in the short term, in bond trading activities.

Definition of an Asset Class

A group of securities that exhibit similar characteristics, behave similarly in the marketplace, and are subject to the same laws and regulations. (Investopedia)

Traditionally, the three main asset classes were equities (stocks), fixed income (bonds) and cash (money markets). In recent times, the categorisation has expanded to include other tradable assets such as foreign exchange and commodities.

In this chapter, trading in asset classes – equities, foreign exchange and fixed income – will be briefly discussed. Before that, an explanation of the generic trading life cycle is required.

The Trading Life Cycle

The trading life cycle can be defined as a sequence of events that pass through the front, middle and back office.

The stages of the trading life cycle are as follows:

- **Trade capture** – Trade capture for all transaction types is usually on a screen-based system, and can be through manual input or feed from another live trading system.
- **Verification and confirmations** – This is the stage at which trade details are validated and matched. It also involves an exchange of information between counterparties in the trade to confirm trade details.
- **Settlement and netting** – At this stage, exchange of payment and the asset traded takes place. If there is a netting agreement in place then netting will be performed.

- **Reconciliations** – This is where details of the trade, as recorded within the books of the organisation that executed the trade, are matched with those held by agents such as custodians and also clearing houses.
- **Accounting** – This is where details of the trade are entered into the general ledger and, if required, revaluation of the trade takes place.

The entire life cycle of a trade can also be divided into pre-trade and post-trade events. Before going into the details of the trading events, it will be prudent to explain how a trading deal is struck between two entities.

A fictional company, BizCorp, wants to use derivative contracts to hedge its risk. Suppose that the company has a floating rate liability in LIBOR (London Inter Bank Offered Rate) and it wants to convert its liability into a fixed rate. The company chooses the most feasible option by entering into an interest rate swap. BizCorp strikes a deal with a fictional bank, EssBank, and enters into a swap where it will pay a fixed rate to the bank and receive a floating rate. BizCorp and EssBank enter into a trade and the trade passes through various stages. The various trade events can be characterised into front-office, middle-office and back-office activities, which are explained as follows:

- **Front office**: This is the stage where the trade is initiated. It starts with the order being placed, and EssBank pricing the instrument and giving the quote to BizCorp. If BizCorp agrees to the details of the trade and intends to enter into the deal, the trade is then executed. The trade is then captured by the trading desk at the bank in their front-office system. Validation of the trade takes place and if this succeeds, a trade reference number is assigned. This uniquely identifies the trade, thus in the event of an amendment or cancellation of the trade, reference can still be made to the trade using the identifier. An acknowledgement is sent with the trade details to BizCorp, which confirms it back.
- **Middle office**: The middle office is responsible for limits and risk management. Captured trades are also validated and exceptions raised if there are any discrepancies. Exception management also entails trade enrichment with static data such as the standard settlement instructions (SSIs) of the counterparty, City holidays, custodian details and so on. These types of static data details are critical to the completion and settlement of the trade. The middle office is also responsible for the allocation of the trade. The trade is then passed to the back office and it becomes a live trade.
- **Back office**: The back office is the backbone of the entire life cycle of the trade. The back office is usually responsible for operational activities like record keeping, confirmation, settlement and regulatory reporting.

If the trading life cycle of an interest rate swap is broken down into pre-trade events and post-trade events, then it can be described as follows.

Pre-trade Events
- **The setting up of the master agreement**: Prior to entering into a deal, counterparties ensure that a standardised contract is in place. In the case of

a derivative contract, the master agreement is drafted in accordance with the ISDA[14] protocols.

■ **Definition of product characteristics**: It is customary for every deal to be defined by some primary characteristics, called the primary economics of the trade. For a plain vanilla interest rate swap, the economics of trade are:

■ Notional, i.e. the value of a derivative's underlying assets at the spot price;
■ Maturity;
■ Fixed rate;
■ Floating rate;
■ Trading book.

■ **Pre-trade negotiation**: In this phase, BizCorp attempts to reach an initial agreement with EssBank. This stage may include documentation, indication of the interest rate, definition of the criteria for trade execution and the bank policies with which BizCorp has to conform.

■ **Request for quote**: BizCorp will request a quote from EssBank, e.g. the fixed rate against LIBOR.

■ **Quote provision**: EssBank provides the quote by fax and email.

■ **Request for trade pricing inputs**: BizCorp requests the inputs needed to price the product. Every detail of the trade is matched and, if there are no discrepancies, the trade is priced.

Post-trade Events

Once BizCorp and EssBank are in agreement about the details of the trade, the trade is executed. Confirmation takes place by communication of the relevant categories of Swift messages. The post-trade events that follow are:

■ **Allocation of trade**: This trade is allocated to various sub entities of EssBank. This is known as allocation of trade and allows for flexibility of Profit & Loss Booking.

■ **Creation of standard identifier**: the trade is stored using a unique trade ID, which is used to identify the trade.

Post-trade Changes

■ **Amendment**: Should there be the need to amend the trade, both BizCorp and EssBank have to give their consent. The amendment can be done in terms of the economics of the trade. However, if a trade was booked incorrectly, then the amendments can be done to the booked trade with the agreed changes and it can be re-booked.

Counterparty Changes

The most common type of counterparty change is known as novation. This is the substitution of a new contract for an old one; or the substitution of

---

14 This stands for International Swaps and Derivatives Association.

one party in a contract with another party. The following is an illustration of novation.

Suppose Essbank and BizCorp have entered into a trade, and then NovaBank wants to enter and take EssBank's position, or Essbank would like to exit and let NovaBank take its position, then whoever is at an advantageous position will be paid some novation fee. What is essential is that there should be consent from BizCorp for NovaBank to come in, through a consent letter, and BizCorp is referred to as the remaining party.

Termination

- **Partial termination**: This occurs when there is a change in the notional value of the trade and it is not pre-fixed according to the agreement.
- **Full termination**: This occurs when the trade is terminated before the maturity of the trade.
- **Normal termination**: This happens when a trade is terminated at maturity.

Servicing Events

- **Rate fixing**: In a typical interest rate swap deal, the floating rate has to be fixed every period for the cash flow settlement of the floating rate leg. The fixing rule can be defined and it typically differs on a trade by trade basis. The floating rate may be fixed in advance or at the end of the period, according to the fixing rule set for the trade.
- **Payment**: This is can be described in terms of cash flow settlement. For every settlement term, there will be cash flow that BizCorp will pay and receive. The cash flow will happen in accordance with the standard settlement instructions. For interest rate swaps, it will be the Pay Flow and Receive Flow.
- **Revaluation**: This takes place at an intermediate stage, according to the market interest rates at that point of time. This means that the future cash flows are discounted to realise the present value and then the net present value (NPV) is calculated to realise the position of BizCorp on that particular trade. This is done for accounting purposes.

In conclusion, the entire trade life cycle is a maze of complex functions that entails a trade passing through a flow of different events. Manual intervention may be required in all these events, thereby increasing the time frame for processing and settlement of the various functions. The panacea to this is STP (straight-through processing), where the transactions can be conducted electronically without the need for rekeying or manual intervention.

Trading in Equities

Equities (stock) trading includes the execution of both buying and selling activities. It is not a one-sided process. Instead, it requires a buyer of a stock and a seller who is offering that particular stock.

Experts are unanimous in their opinion that without the availability of sophisticated technologies, the financial markets would not exist in their current structures. The use of sophisticated technology has enabled the trading of billions of shares around the world on a daily basis.

Types of Stock

There are two types of stock:

- **Common stock** – This type of stock is representative of the majority of stock held by the public. Holders of common stock have voting rights, as well as the right to share in dividends.
- **Preferred stock** – This type of stock entitles holders to consistent dividends. Preferred stock has first call on dividends over common stock and in the event of the liquidation or bankruptcy of the issuer, preferred stockholders will be paid out in assets before common stockholders and after debt holders.

Stock trading takes place in stock exchanges and the two basic ways these exchanges execute a trade are:

1. on the exchange floor;
2. electronically.

Exchange floor

It is safe to assume that most readers have watched movies and commentaries on television stations such as BloombergTV and CNN with a backdrop of the New York Stock Exchange (NYSE). The activities that can be observed here typify trading on the exchange floor and how the markets work. At the beginning of the trading day, the floor is filled with people (brokers) shouting over one another different numbers and words accompanied by gestures, in an atmosphere where telephones are ringing from every direction. At the same time, these people are watching monitors and studying complex graphs on terminals on their desktops.

At the end of the trading day, a vast number of transactions will have taken place and by the start of the next trading day, the rafts of activities begin from scratch.

The following is an illustration of the execution of a simple trade on a typical stock exchange such as the NYSE.

Greg Stockey is an astute investor in shares of companies whose share price he perceives to be undervalued. The following is the process by which Stockey's trade in the stock of BizHotels, a chain of boutique hotels, is executed:

1. Stockey tells his broker to buy 1,000 shares of BizHotels at market.
2. The order department of his broker, Cher Broker, sends the order to their floor clerk on the exchange.
3. The floor clerk alerts one of Cher Broker's floor traders who seeks out another floor trader willing to sell 1,000 shares of BizHotels.

4. Once there is an agreement on a price, the deal is completed. The notification process goes back up the line and Stockey's broker calls him back with the final price. The time frame for this process is dependent on the stock and the market. A few days later, Stockey will receive the confirmation notice in the mail.

Please note that this illustration is that of a basic trade; complex trades and large blocks of stocks involve considerably more detail.

Electronically

As the requirements of traders and investors have evolved, exchanges have responded by providing stock trading entirely electronically. Nasdaq is such an exchange. Compared to the NYSE, which handles a relatively small percentage of its trading volume electronically, trading in Nasdaq involves the use of computer networks to match buyers and sellers.

Large institutional investors have been observed to show a preference for electronic trading, given that it is a more efficient and faster way to trade. Individual investors also opt for electronic trading. They especially benefit from the opportunity provided for receiving instant confirmation of the trades they have executed.

It is worth noting that individual investors or traders are not allowed access to the electronic markets, hence they require the services of a broker. The process of stock trading simply involves submission of an order to a broker who has access to the exchange system, which in turn finds a buyer or seller.

Trading in Fixed Income

Fixed income securities provide a return in the form of fixed periodic payments and the eventual return of principal at maturity. The term "fixed income" is used interchangeably with bonds.

Types of Bond Markets

The Securities Industry and Financial Markets Association classify the wider bond market into five specific bond markets:

- Corporate
- Government & Agency
- Municipal
- Mortgage backed, Asset backed, and Collateralised debt obligation
- Funding

Trading of Bonds

Bonds generally can trade anywhere in the world that a buyer and seller can strike a deal. There is no central place or exchange for bond trading, as there is for publicly traded stocks. In most developed bond markets, such as the USA,

Western Europe and Japan, bonds trade in decentralised, dealer-based, over-the-counter markets, rather than in an exchange market.

The following terminology used in the bond market will be used as a starting point to illustrate bond trading:

- **Coupon** – This is the percentage interest to be paid on a bond in the course of a year. The interest is usually payable semi-annually, although it can also be payable monthly, quarterly and annually. If a bond worth $100,000 at maturity has a 6% coupon, this means $6,000 in interest is payable over the period of a year.
- **Maturity** – This is the date the bond will be redeemed or paid off. If the same $100,000 bond has a maturity date of 1 June 2008, then the investor is due to be paid off in full at that date.
- **Price** – The quoted price is usually based on the bond maturity at a price of par, or 100.00. In the case of the above-mentioned bond (6% of 1 June 2008), if the price is $105.13, this means the bond is at a 5.13% premium to its maturity price (par or 100.00). An investor who pays $105.13 for the bond will receive only $100.00 back on maturity. The market price of a bond is the present value of all future interest and principal payments of the bond, discounted at the bond's yield or rate of return. It may also include the accrued interest since the last coupon date. The price including the accrued interest is referred to as the "dirty" price while the price excluding the accrued interest is known as the "clean" price.
- **Yield** – The term "yield" usually means "yield to maturity". At a price of $105.13 for the bond, the yield to maturity is 5.31%. The yield to maturity takes into account the fact that the coupon payment is 6% per year, but that the bond is maturing at a different price than its current price. The calculation also assumes that the coupon payments each year are reinvested at the yield to maturity (5.31% in this case).

Role of Traders

Traders carry out a number of activities, including offering advice, expertise and judgement. Traders can also be described as aggregators and disseminators of

Figure 2.1 Basic Activity Chain in Fixed Income Markets

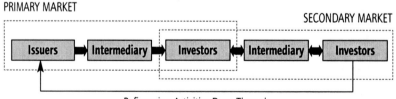

Source: Electronic Trading Systems and Fixed Income Markets, Tuck School of Business at Dartmouth

Table 2.1 Key Objectives of Key Market Participants

Issuers	Financial Intermediaries	Institutional and Retail Investors
Major issuers: 1. Governments 2. Corporations 3. Commercial banks	Intermediaries: 1. Investment banks 2. Interdealer brokers	Investors: 1. Governments 2. Pension funds 3. Large corporations 4. Individuals (high net worth and retail investors)
Key objectives: 1. To obtain a fair price for their securities with minimum transaction costs. 2. To gain access to an organised and liquid secondary market, enabling them to set a price for future issues without forgoing value to the intermediaries or investors.	Key objectives: 1. To create revenue for underwriting and distributing securities in the primary market. 2. To generate profit from turnover of inventory (bonds purchased and resold) while minimising credit or interest rate risk. 3. To sustain liquidity in the secondary markets so as to maintain a low transaction cost method of swelling their inventory in various securities. 4. To gather information relating to market value of securities to benefit trades, for their own position or those of their clients. 5. To remain anonymous so as to avoid creating panic on the market by signalling intention or information advantage.	Key objectives: 1. To purchase securities of different risk return profiles at a fair price. 2. To request information on security details and issuers' credit profiles at a low cost. 3. To seek accurate advice from experts on bonds and market conditions easily and quickly, at the lowest possible cost.

information and proprietary research. Engaging a highly experienced trader with a network of purchasers inspires confidence amongst investors or issuers as to their protection against a counterparty risk like reneging buyers or sellers. The value offered by traders is as described in Table 2.2.

Table 2.2 Value offered by Traders

Aggregate and disseminate information to issuers	Create new debt instruments	Aggregate and disseminate information to investors	Market making

Market Making				
Maintain Buyer/Seller Liquidity	Buy/Sell to Match Trading Orders	Commit Capital to Facilitate Trades	Actively locate investors for new issue bonds or trades for their own accounts	Execute and process the transaction

Source: Electronic Trading Systems and Fixed Income Markets, Tuck School of Business at Dartmouth

Role of Interdealer Brokers in Bonds Trading[15]

Interdealer brokers play different roles in each of the fixed income markets and have been key in their effectiveness and efficiency. IDBs bring together buyers and sellers so that their trades can be executed by market participants. They operate on very small spreads, but they handle extremely large transactions. Figure 2.2 is a diagrammatic representation of the role of IDBs in a fixed income deal flow.

What are Interdealer Brokers?

They can be described as firms linking the world's investment banks and any other professional traders wanting to deal in bonds, currencies and derivatives such as equity and credit derivatives.

According to industry reports, as at October 2007, one firm, ICAP, handled around £740bn of trades a day.

Interdealer brokers have always served a fundamental need in the fixed-income trading arena. They provide potential buyers and sellers with the critical market information and commentary they need to trade. This information includes the narrowness of bid and offer quotes, for instance, and conforms to a strict set of rules regarding identification of sellers. In most cases, traders with an order to buy or sell a bond (on behalf of a customer or themselves) must search for the best price available in the interdealer market. In order to achieve

15 This section draws on the Securities Industry and Financial Markets Association booklet, "The Role of Interdealer brokers in the Fixed Income Markets".

Figure 2.2 IDB Role in Trading Flows in the US Fixed Income Market

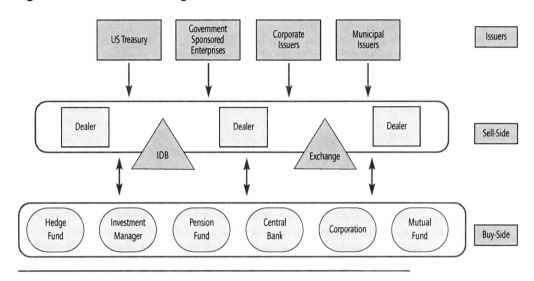

Source: The Role of Interdealer brokers in the Fixed Income Markets, SIFMA

this, they can either contact an IDB directly by telephone or obtain an aggregated quotation from an IDB's electronic screen. In some other cases, an IDB could also act as the dealer's independent intermediary so as to conceal the dealer's identity as well as their level of trading interest. The revelation of this information to the market may have a negative impact on the price at which the dealer is ready to buy or sell the security; hence the possibility of this occurring should be guarded against.

IDBs' value to the bond market
On the whole, IDBs can add value to the markets in a number of ways including:

- lowering costs;
- improving market efficiency;
- providing anonymity and confidentiality;
- facilitating information flow;
- enhancing price discovery and transparency;
- facilitating enhanced liquidity.

Types of IDB Business Model
There are essentially three types of business model that IDBs adopt in order to perform their services and they are:

1. Electronic
2. Voice

33

3. Hybrid brokerage

Electronic brokerage

This business model, which is increasingly being adopted as a result of the increased commoditisation of markets, involves the provision of real-time executable trading systems to clients. It allows for the posting of anonymous quotations on the electronic system or accessing of real-time executable quotations that are automatically executed when posted bid and offer prices are matched.

Voice brokerage

This model entails the dissemination of executable prices and indications of interest in the traditional way. IDBs and clients communicate over the phone when clients want to place orders, assess market liquidity and execute their bond trades.

Hybrid brokerage

This is a model that combines the voice process and the electronic medium. Under the hybrid model, traders can call orders into a broker or type orders into an electronic screen. This model allows anonymous execution of orders through:

- electronic negotiation and execution;
- electronic auction; or
- telephonic negotiation and electronic execution.

The Five-handed Trade

IDBs, in their role as brokers to broker-dealers and dealer banks, could essentially be dealing with intermediaries for retail or institutional customers. In other words, they could be participants in a "five-handed trade" (see Figure 2.3) described as follows:

1. An institutional investor ("1st Hand") contacts a dealer ("2nd Hand") to inform the dealer of the investor's intention to buy and sell certain bonds.
2. In the event that the bonds do not meet the dealer's trading inventory parameters, the dealer's trading desk will contact an IDB ("3rd Hand") to place a buy or sell order.

Figure 2.3 The Five-handed Trade

| 1st Hand | 2nd Hand | 3rd Hand | 4th Hand | 5th Hand |

Source: The Role of Interdealer brokers in the Fixed Income Markets, SIFMA

3. The IDB seeks out a dealer ("4th Hand") who is ready to sell or buy these bonds.
4. This dealer ("4th Hand") contacts a retail investor ("5th Hand") who is a customer and is willing to sell or buy the bonds.

As shown here, there are five parties involved in the achievement of this trade; hence the term "Five-handed Trade".

Trading in Foreign Exchange

In recent years, the structure of the global foreign exchange (forex) market has transformed significantly, reflecting a number of events such as the introduction of the common currency in Europe and the revolutionary way that market participants have chosen to manage their foreign exchange exposures.

Types of Trading Activity

A number of different types of trading activity occur in the foreign exchange market. Trades in the foreign exchange market can be categorised into the main types of:

- Spot
- Forward
- Derivatives (currency futures, FX swaps, currency options)

All of these types of trade involve exchanging one currency for another (at least in principle), even though in many respects the nature of the different types of trade are quite different.

Components of a Typical Spot Forex Trade

A forex trade is a contract agreed upon between two entities – the trader and the market maker. The components that make up the contract are:

- the principal amount, i.e. the amount involved in the trade;
- the currency pairs, i.e. the currency to buy and the one to sell.
- the exchange rate between the two currencies.

In the spot market, the exchange rate is agreed on the trade date (or "done" date) with the date of exchange as soon as possible thereafter.

The standard time for "immediate" settlement is two business days after the trade date (T + 2). This is called the spot value date. (The only exception to this convention is USD/CAD which has a spot value date of T + 1).

Forex trading is always done in currency pairs. Suppose that on a certain day the spot rate for GBP/USD (i.e. pounds sterling to US dollars) is 1.8034. If a trader had bought £1,000 on this date, they would have paid $1,803.40. If about two business days later the spot rate is 1.8242 and the trader now sells

Figure 2.4 Spot Trade Timeline

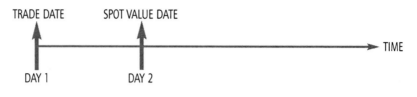

the £1,000 in order to receive $1,824.20, the trader would have a made a profit of $20.80.

A currency pair is essentially a quotation of two different currencies. The first currency in the pair is the base currency or transaction currency. The second currency in the pair is quote currency, payment currency or counter currency. Such quotations show how many units of the counter currency are required to buy one unit of the base currency.

The majority of currencies are traded against the US dollar (USD), which is traded more than any other currency. The most widely traded currency pairs in the world are known as "the Majors". They are the most liquid and the trades involving the majors are estimated to make up about 90% of total forex trading.

The currency pairs that constitute the Majors are: EUR/USD, GBP/USD, USD/JPY, USD/CHF, AUD/USD and USD/CAD.

Motivation for Buying and Selling

Buying ("going long") – The currency pair implies buying the base currency and selling an equivalent amount of the counter currency (to pay for the base currency). It is not necessary to own the counter currency prior to selling, as it is sold short. A trader buys a currency pair if they believe the base currency will go up relative to the counter currency, or equivalently that the corresponding exchange rate will go up.

Selling ("going short") – The currency pair implies selling the first, base currency, and buying the second, counter currency. A trader sells a currency pair if they believe the base currency will go down relative to the counter currency, or equivalently, that the counter currency will go up relative to the base currency.

An open trade or position is one in which a trader has either bought or sold one currency pair and has not sold or bought back an adequate amount of that currency pair to effectively close the trade. When a trader has an open trade or position, they stand to profit or lose from fluctuations in the price of that currency pair.

Spreads, Prices, Quotes and Indications

■ **Spread** – This is the difference between the bid and offer prices. This means the difference between the market maker's selling price to its clients and the price at which the market maker buys currency from its clients.

▦ **Pips** – This is the smallest price change that a given exchange rate can make. Given that most major currency pairs are priced to four decimal places, the smallest change is that of the last decimal place – for most pairs this is the equivalent of 1/100 of one per cent, or one basis point.

▦ **Quotes** – This is the price of a currency (in terms of counter currency). There are two types of quotes in the forex market:

  ■ **Direct quote** – This is the price of 1 USD in terms of another currency, e.g. euro, Japanese yen, etc.

  ■ **Indirect quote** – This is the price of 1 unit of a currency, say 1 GBP, in terms of US dollars.

▦ **Indication** – This is price information provided by a market maker to a trader about market price level.

▦ **Cross rates** – These are rates that are established between two currencies using their exchange rate against a common currency, usually the US dollar. This can be illustrated as follows.

Sally Cross, a UK-based fund manager, intends to move funds to the Japanese market to exploit the rising equity prices. Her intention is to buy Japanese yen (JPY) and sell sterling (GBP) and so she contacts EssBank, whose spot rates against the US dollar are as follows:

GBP/USD = 1.7656
USD/JPY = 112.6

Therefore: GBP/JPY = 112.6 x 1.7656 = 198.81 is the cross rate that Essbank will quote to Sally Cross.

Outright Forward Transactions

Sometimes market participants do not want to exchange currencies in two business days' time. For example, suppose that a chocolate bar exporter is expecting to receive payments for their new range of bars in one month's time. Those receipts will be in US dollars, but the exporter wishes to receive pounds sterling. Additionally, this exporter wishes to fix today the amount of pounds sterling they will receive. The requirements of this exporter cannot be satisfied with a spot transaction (a spot transaction would be settled in two days but the exporter isn't going to receive their US dollars for another month), but they can be satisfied via an outright forward transaction. An outright forward transaction is identical to a spot transaction, except that the settlement date (and the exchange of currencies) is more than two business days ahead. Hence spot and forward transactions are usually analysed as one type of instrument since the only difference is the date on which the exchange of funds occurs.

Illustration of an outright forward transaction

BizLink, an import/export company, has ordered goods from a supplier in Canada. There are two payments of CAD 1,000,000; the first is due immediately, which is covered by a spot rate transaction, and the other is due in three months' time. BizLink intends to lock in the USD/CAD exchange rate for the future payment and needs to buy CAD 1,000,000 in three months. The current spot rate for USD/CAD is 1.500. This spot rate needs to be adjusted by the "forward points".

The calculation of forward points is achieved by using the 3-month interest rates specific to each currency. These points can either be at a "discount" or "premium" to the spot rate. The current spot rate is adjusted by either the discount or premium points in order to arrive at the outright rate.

In this instance, the spot points are +0.0025, hence the outright forward rate is USD/CAD 1.5025. When the forward matures in three months' time, BizLink will send the bank USD 665,557.40 and the bank will remit CAD 1,000,000 according to BizLink's specifications.

Types of Order

This chapter discusses the various types of order that traders use in the financial markets. It also contains a brief discussion of order presentation systems.

Introduction

We place orders in our everyday lives for items such as cars, electronics, CDs, books and so on. Thus, the concept of an order is one almost everyone is familiar with. In the trading industry, however, orders are trade instructions that specify what traders want to trade, whether to buy or sell, the quantities, the timing, the method and most importantly, the terms of the trade.

Orders can be described as the basic building blocks of trading strategies. Traders use orders to specify exactly what they want to trade. Successful traders are aware of the importance of order submission strategies to the success of their trading activities. Orders that are well specified as well as well timed can determine the quality of the trade, the cost of the trade and even whether the trade will happen or not.

Traders submit orders according to a set of rules for matching buy and sell orders used by many markets to arrange their trades.

The concept of orders in the trading industry can be compared to the concept of taking out a mortgage loan on a property. An applicant that shops around and arranges a mortgage directly with the lender that offers the best deal can be compared to a trader who monitors the market for the best price for the security they want to buy or sell. The applicant that chooses to go through a mortgage broker to search for the best deals on mortgage loans is similar to the trader that executes orders through a broker.

A Typical Example of an Order
Ms Betty Deale wants to sell 10,000 shares of Apple Inc (AAPL) at no less than $169.55 per share, but on the proviso that she can trade during the current trading session and also trade the whole quantity in one go. To achieve this, Ms Deale issues an all-or-nothing day order to sell 10,000 shares of AAPL, limit $169.55.

Benefits of Using Orders

At this point, the question that needs to be answered is: what are the benefits of using orders in the trading industry?

Orders are essential, given that most traders do not personally arrange their trades. Traders who arrange their own trades – usually dealers – do not use orders. In practice, they decide immediately what they want and how to do it.

Most small traders find that it is uneconomical to continuously monitor the market. It is this type of trader who usually uses orders to signify their interests when they are not paying attention to the market.

There are obvious advantages for traders who arrange their own trades over those who use orders to express their intentions including the following:

- The former are able to respond to market conditions as they change while the latter must foresee such changes and append contingencies to orders that effectively represent traders' interests even when conditions change.

▧ When orders do not adequately represent traders' interests under these circumstances, traders need to cancel and resubmit their orders. This can take up time that a trader would normally use to exploit changing conditions. Thus, traders need to carefully specify their intentions when they use orders to trade.

▧ Traders that arrange their own orders can use computer software to monitor and manage their orders in line with changes in market conditions.

Some Essential Terms

The following are terms that are essential to the understanding of the execution of orders:

▧ **Bid** – This is an indication from a trader that they are willing to buy a security.

▧ **Offer** – This is an indication from a trader that they are willing to sell a security.

▧ **Sizes** – These are quantities that traders are willing to buy or sell.

▧ **Firm prices** – These are prices that traders can demand to trade at.

▧ **Soft prices** – These are prices that traders can revise even after they offer them.

▧ **Best bid** – This is the highest bid price in the market.

▧ **Best offer** – The lowest offer price is the best offer.

▧ **Market quotation** – This is a report of the best bid and best offer prices available in the market.

▧ **Bid/Ask spread** – This is the difference between the best bid and best offer prices.

▧ **Standing offers** – These are open offers to trade.

▧ **Liquidity** – This is a measure of the ability to trade assets or securities in the market without affecting the asset's price. An order is said to offer liquidity if it allows other traders to trade. Traders who want to trade quickly are demanding liquidity, while traders who accept offers that other traders have made take liquidity.

▧ **Uptick** – This is when the last (non-zero) price change is positive.

▧ **Downtick** – The opposite of uptick. This is when the last (non-zero) price change is negative.

▧ **Trades prices** – These are prices at which orders are filled.

▧ **Order status** – An order is pending after a trader submits the order to a broker, but before the broker agrees to accept it. The order is working when the broker accepts it, but before it is filled or cancelled.

Market Orders

The simplest and most common type of order, a market order, is an instruction to trade at the best price that is available in the market at the present time. As long as there are willing sellers and buyers, a market order will be filled. This type of order is also known as "at the market" or an "unrestricted order". A market order guarantees execution, and it often has low commissions due to the minimal work brokers need to do.

One disadvantage of a market order is that the price is paid when the order is executed. The price may not always be the same as that presented by a real-time quote service. This often happens when the market is volatile. Placing an order "at the market", especially when it involves a large number of shares, offers a trader a greater chance of getting different prices for different parts of the whole order.

Small market orders, however, usually fill straight away with little or no effect on prices. A small market buy order will usually trade at the best (lowest) asking price, and a small market sell order will usually trade at the best (highest) bid price.

Example of a market order

Honeywell International Inc (HON) trades on the NYSE. Dealers are bidding $51.16 for HON and offer it at $51.36.These quotes are good for 1,000 shares on the bid side and 800 shares on the ask side. Ms Deale submits a market order to buy 400 shares of HON. She buys all 400 shares at $51.36.

Limit Orders

A limit order is an instruction to trade at the best price available, but only if it is better than the limit price specified by the trader. In other words, it is an instruction to buy a security at no more (or sell at no less) than a specific price. This gives the trader some control over the price at which the trade is executed, but may prevent the order from being executed.

This is the main difference between a market order and a limit order in that the broker cannot guarantee that the latter will be executed.

A buy limit order can only be executed by the broker at the limit price or lower while a limit order to buy may never be executed if the market price exceeds the limit before the order can be filled. Because of the additional complexity, some brokerages will charge more for executing a limit order than they would for a market order.

There are other ways in which both buy and sell orders can be constrained. Two of the most common additional constraints are Fill or Kill (FOK) and All or None (AON). FOK orders are either filled (partially or completely) on the first attempt or cancelled outright, while AON orders stipulate that the order must be completely filled or not filled at all (but still held on the order book for later execution).

An important aspect of limit order execution is the recording of unexecuted limit orders. In continuously trading markets; the usual practice is for a broker or exchange to attempt to trade a newly submitted limit order as soon as it arrives. If it happens that no trader is willing to take the opposite side straight away at an acceptable price, the order will not trade. Instead, it will remain an offer to trade until someone is willing to trade at its limit price, or until the trader who submitted it cancels it.

Standing limit orders are recorded in a file called a limit order book. This is maintained by either a broker or an exchange. In some markets, however, even a dealer might be responsible for maintaining the limit order book.

Limit orders are especially useful on a low-volume or highly volatile stock.

Example of a limit order
The following is an example of a limit order:

Ms Deale wants to buy the stock of a "hot" IPO that was initially offered at $15, but she doesn't want to end up paying more than $30 for the stock; therefore she places a limit order to buy the stock at any price up to $30. Since she entered a limit order rather than a market order, she would not be buying the stock at, say, $100 which could lead to immediate losses should the price of the stock drop later in the day or the weeks ahead.

Stop Orders

A stop order, also referred to as a "stop" and/or "stop-loss order", automatically converts into a market order when a predetermined price is reached (this is referred to as the "stop price"). This means that a stop order is essentially an instruction that stops an order from executing until the price reaches the stop price specified by the trader.

At that point, the ordinary rules of market orders apply; the order is guaranteed to be executed, but the trader simply doesn't know the price – it may be higher or lower than the current price reported on the ticker symbol.

A trader typically uses a buy stop order when buying stock to limit a loss or protect a profit on short sales. The order is entered at a stop price that is always above the current market price. Similarly, a sell stop order helps investors to avoid further losses, or to protect a profit that exists, if a stock price continues to drop. A stop order to sell is always placed below the current market price.

The advantage of a stop order is that the trader does not have to monitor how a stock is performing on a daily basis. The disadvantage is that the stop price could be activated by a short-term fluctuation in a stock's price.

The use of stop orders is much more frequent for stocks that trade on an exchange rather than in the over-the-counter (OTC) market.

Stop-Limit Orders

Those that are new to trading with orders regularly confuse stop orders with limit orders, given that both specify price conditions. The more experienced traders are aware that the difference lies in the purpose of the specified price. While a limit order can only be executed at a price that is equal to or better than a stipulated limit price, a stop order is an instruction to trade when the market attains or exceeds a stipulated stop price. To illustrate this difference, take a limit sell order for a limit price of £10. A trader will usually submit a limit sell order when the price is below £10. This order can be filled only if the price is equal to or rises above £10. In contrast, in the case of a stop sell order for a stop price of £10, the order the trader submits when the price is above £10 will only activate when the price drops to the specified stop price.

A stop-limit order is therefore an order to buy or sell a stock that combines the features of a stop order and a limit order. Once the stop price is reached, the stop-limit order becomes a limit order to buy or to sell at a specified price.

The advantage of a stop-limit order is that the trader can control the price at which the trade will be executed. But, as with all limit orders, a stop-limit order may never get filled if the stock's price never attains the specified limit price. This may be the case in fast-moving markets where prices fluctuate uncontrollably.

The use of stop-limit orders is much more common for stocks that trade on an exchange than in the OTC market. In addition, a broker might not allow a trader to place a stop-limit order on some securities or accept a stop-limit order for OTC stocks.

Stop-Limit Order Example

Gary O'Deal is interested in purchasing AstraZeneca stock only if its price goes up to $33, and then only if he can buy it for less than $33.40. He submits a limit buy order with a limit price of $33.40 and a stop price of $33.

Trailing Stop Orders

These are orders that traders use to protect gains and limit losses automatically. With a trailing stop order, a trader can set a stop price as either a spread in points or a percentage of current market value. For example, a trader purchased 1,000 shares of Wal Mart Stores Inc. at $40 per share; the current price is $47. He wants to lock in at least $5 of the per share profit he has made but wishes to continue holding the stock, hoping to benefit from any further increases. To meet his objective, he could place a trailing stop order with a stop value of $2 per share.

The following is what happens in practice: his order will sit on his broker's books and automatically adjust upwards as the price of Wal Mart's common stock increases. At the time his trailing stop order was submitted, his broker knew to sell WMT if the price fell below $45 ($47 current market price − $2 trailing stop loss = $45 sale price). Suppose WMT increases steadily to $52 per share; now, his trailing stop order has automatically kept pace and will guarantee at least a $50 sale price ($52 current stock price − $2 trailing stop value = $50 per share sale price). In other words, the trailing stop order will increase in his favour and lock in any gains he has made in the interim. If WMT were to fall to $50, the trailing stop order would convert to a market order for execution; his shares would be sold, and should result in a capital gain of $10 per share.

Tick-Sensitive Orders

In order to understand a tick-sensitive order, it would be useful to understand the concept of an uptick as well as a downtick. The following is an illustration.

Gary O'Deal observes that the last trade price for General Electric (GE) stock on the NYSE is $29.31. The previous trade price was $29.33. This stock is on downtick given that $29.31 is less than $29.33. GE stock is now traded four times, each time at a price of $29.31. GE is on a zero downtick at this stage. Gary O'Deal now attempts to sell GE for $29.32, and if this happens, he will sell on an uptick.

This way of classifying prices by their relation to previous prices, as shown in the illustration above, allows traders to submit orders conditional upon the last price change. This type of order is called a tick-sensitive order. Tick-sensitive orders can be either a sell uptick order or a buy downtick order. The fulfilment of a sell uptick is conditional upon an uptick or zero uptick and a trade price that is higher than the last different price. Similarly, fulfilment of a buy downtick is conditional upon a downtick or zero downtick and a trade price that is lower than the last different price.

In practice, on receipt of tick-sensitive orders, brokers check straight away to see whether these orders can be matched with other orders without breaching the tick conditions. These orders are held in the event that the brokers cannot match them and filed as soon as an opportunity arises.

Tick-Sensitive Order Example

Peter Van Teak wants to buy Time Warner (TWX) at less than the offer price, but he is not available to cancel and resubmit orders in the event of a price rise. The solution to this conundrum is to submit a buy downtick order to his broker, Bill Brock.

When Mr Brock receives the order, TWX is on a zero uptick at $2.06. Mr Brock is unable to buy TWX for Mr Van Teak when the price drops to or below $2.05. Unfortunately, the price rises to $2.07. Brock knows that all he can pay is $2.06, hence he continues to monitor the market. When a market sell order is received, Van Teak buys for $2.06.

Market-If-Touched Orders

A market-if-touched order, also referred to as a "board order", is a conditional order that becomes a market order when a security reaches a preset (touch or trigger) price. Traders submit market-if-touched orders to buy when prices fall to their touch prices or to sell when prices rise to their touch prices, in contrast to stop orders. The definitions of a buy market-if-touched order and a sell market-if-touched order are as follows:

- A buy market-if-touched order is an order to buy at the best available price, if the market price goes down to the "if touched" level. As soon as this trigger price is touched, the order becomes a market buy order.

45

◼ A sell market-if-touched order is an order to sell at the best available price, if the market price goes up to the "if touched" level. As soon as this trigger price is touched, the order becomes a market sell order.

A trader submitting a not-held order exhibits great faith that the broker will be able to attain a better price than the current one. Although the broker has price and time discretion, they cannot be responsible for any losses that the trader may suffer as a result of this type of order. Often this type of order is applied to international equities due to the fact that the trader trusts the broker's judgement more than they trust their own.

Market-If-Touched Example

Google Inc. (GOOG) shows an asking price of $504.72 on the NYSE. Glen Iffy decides to buy 1,000 shares, but doesn't want to enter the market until the price drops to $504.62. He clicks the Ask price button on the screen of his front-office system to create a Buy order, and then selects MIT in the system to specify a Market-If-Touched order. He then enters the trigger price of $504.62, and submits the order. This order will remain in the system until the trigger price is touched, and will then be submitted as a market order.

Market-Not-Held Orders

This is essentially a market order but with the crucial difference that the broker has discretion to execute the order when they feel it is best. If the broker feels that the market will decline, they may hold the order to try to get a better fill. Market-not-held orders are practised widely in international equities trading and commodity trading.

The rationale behind traders' use of market-not-held orders is that they feel that brokers are better at trading and often more experienced. Brokers generally have more awareness of current market conditions.

In practice, traders use this type of order when:

◼ they are very confident about their brokers;
◼ they lack adequate market and price evaluating tools;
◼ prices are expected to rise;
◼ they place large-sized orders.

Although the basic idea is to get the best possible execution utilising the broker's knowledge, market-not-held orders do not guarantee any profits.

However, it is worth noting that traders cannot hold brokers accountable should the brokers fail to trade at the best possible price. There are common scenarios where brokers feel they can get better prices than current prices and therefore hold out. This strategy could lead to them trading at even worse prices as prices could move away from them. There is an understanding between traders who submit market-not-held orders that indicates that there is no accountability on the part of brokers if they fail to trade.

Most brokers and floor traders execute market-not-held orders manually rather than electronically to get the best desired price, so the process can be time-consuming. Most brokers usually hold the orders unexecuted when the price is falling. Market-not-held orders favour novice traders who face a dilemma in taking good decisions and who lack the knowledge of evaluating results and doing technical analysis. They are not so attractive to experienced traders having access to market data and technical analysis tools and who quickly respond to market changes.

In recent times, some traders have been submitting market-not-held orders to brokers who operate electronic order desks that use complex econometric models to formulate optimal order submission strategies.

Other Order Instructions

Traders use other order instructions with specifications that indicate the validity and expiration of their orders as well as arrangements of multiple trades with their brokers to fill their large orders. Some of these order instructions are briefly discussed here:

- **Day orders** – These are orders to buy or sell a security that automatically expire if not executed on the day the order is placed. A day order will not be executed if the limit or stop order prices were not met during the day.
- **Good-till-cancelled (GTC)** – This is an order to buy or sell a security at a set price that is active until the trader decides to cancel it or the trade is executed. If an order does not have a good-till-cancelled instruction, then the order will expire at the end of the trading day the order was placed. In most cases, GTC orders are cancelled by brokerage firms after 30–90 days. This type of order is traditionally placed at price points away from the price of the stock at the time the order is placed. For example, if a trader, Gary O'Deal, holds a stock whose current price is $30 but is of the opinion that the price will go to $35, at which point he intends to sell, he can use a GTC order. Once he submits a GTC order to sell and the price of the stock reaches $35 at any point over the next few months, his shares will be sold.
- **Open orders** – These are orders to buy or sell that remain in effect until they are either cancelled or executed.
- **Good-until orders** – These are buy or sell orders that are good until a date specified by a trader. Good-this-week (GTW), an order only valid in the week of its placement and cancelled if the order is not filled during the week of issue, is a special case of a good-until order.
- **Immediate-or-cancel orders (IOC)** – These are orders requiring that all or part of the order is executed immediately after they have been brought to the market. Any portions not executed immediately are automatically cancelled. This is applicable to large orders where there is difficulty in filling quickly. Also known in some markets as Fill-or-Kill (FOK).

47

- **Good-after orders** – These are also known as good-after-time (GAT) orders and are good after some specified date. For example, a trader in Beijing wants to buy 1,000 shares of Microsoft stock on the NYSE. It's 2:00 pm Thursday, 8 January in China, but only 1:00 am Thursday morning in New York. The trader creates a limit order to buy 1,000 Microsoft shares, and then sets the "Good After Time" field in his front-office system to 20080108 09:30:00 EST (8 January, 2008, 9:30 am Eastern Standard Time). He submits the order, which is held in the system until the market opens in New York.
- **Market-on-open orders (MOO)** – This a market order executed on the market's open at the market price. This means that a broker can fill the order only at the beginning of the trading session. For example, Gary O'Deal wants to sell 100 shares of Pfizer Inc., and decides that the opening price for this stock has historically proved to be the best price of the day. He submits a market order to sell the 100 shares and specifies that the order is to be submitted at the next day's opening.
- **Market-on-close orders (MOC)** – This is a market order that is submitted to execute as close to the closing price as possible. This means that a broker can fill the order only at the close of the trading session. For example, Gary O'Deal wants to sell 1,000 shares of Lucent Technologies at the best market price, and decides that the closing price for this stock has historically proved to be the best price of the day. He submits a market order to sell the 1,000 shares and specifies that the order is to be fulfilled at the closing price.

Order Presentation Systems

In financial markets, traders obtain quotes and access information about orders from order presentation systems. Some of these order information systems are briefly described in this section:

- **Screen-based trading systems** – These are systems that present orders on computer screens. They are favoured by traders because they are easy to update and can be used anywhere.
- **Messaging systems** – These systems are used by traders to transmit private messages to other traders when negotiating their trades.
- **Board-based trading systems** – In some markets, traders still use this type of system. They are not electronic, but involve manual displays of orders written by traders or exchange clerks on big boards.
- **Bulletin boards** – These systems are used for posting indications of interest (IOIs).[16] Some vendors tailor IOIs to traders by building features that pop up on their workstations in anticipation of trades that will interest the traders' clients.

16 These are orders for a new securities offering which are placed prior to final registration and represent only a tentative interest rather than a firm commitment to buy. This content can be found on http://www.investorwords.com/2434/indication_of_interest.html. An indication of interest is not a commitment to buy, an important point because selling a security while it is in registration is illegal.

The Business Environment

This chapter discusses the business environment in trading as well as the exchange sector.

Introduction

Exchanges around the world operate public capital markets, which are critical components of the global economy. The distinct roles played by exchanges in the capital markets establish a formal environment for the trading, clearing and settlement of securities and other investment products. For this reason, the activities of exchanges in their macroeconomic role are impacted by traditional environmental factors such as political, economic, socio-cultural and technological factors.

In most economies, exchanges are key private sector players in the regulation of the trading value chain, i.e. they oversee the activities of other players whose activities are in turn critical to the value chain. These other players include government authorities, clearing agents, settlement agents, depositories and custodians, broker–dealers and IT service providers.

Environmental Factors affecting the Trading Industry

Regulatory

Exchanges around the world are regulated by rules approved by governments in their respective jurisdictions. These rules govern operational aspects of the exchange business such as trading, clearing, trade surveillance, admission of members to the exchanges, Initial Public Offerings (IPOs), and reporting among others. For example, the Markets in Financial Instruments Directive (MiFID) is a regulation in Europe which requires that financial services firms take all reasonable steps to provide best execution for their clients under Article 21.

Impact

Regulation shapes the competitive landscape of exchanges as well as the trading industry. Overly restrictive regulation can stifle innovation in an exchange and limit trading opportunities.

Regulation also impacts on the revenue-generating capabilities of exchanges. For instance, if an exchange's policies on IPOs are favourable, then it can attract more listings. A typical example is the recent rise to prominence of the Tadawul, the Saudi Stock Exchange. It is reported to have surpassed the London bourse to become the world's second busiest market for IPOs in the first five months of 2008. According to Reuters, the total of Tadawul IPOs rose 322% from a year earlier to $8.50 billion. This notable increase was on the back of high-profile IPOs such as Al Inma Bank, which raised $2.80 billion, the $1.87 billion listing of mobile telecom company Zain, and the $1.20 billion IPO of petrochemical company Petro Rabigh. These high-profile IPOs are partly responsible for the increased profitability of this exchange.

Economic

Interest rates, inflation rates and exchange rates are some of the economic factors that affect trading and exchanges. The interrelation between these economic factors is a major determinant in the demand for traditional assets such as equities, fixed income, foreign exchange and commodities.

For instance, the direction of interest rate movement is of primary importance to the stock market. Stock investors watch for signs from the economy and regulators that may suggest which way interest rates will move in the future. These give an indication as to where interest rates are headed in the short run.

Interest rates control the flow of money through the economy. When rates are low, consumer spending increases and corporate entities can borrow money for expansion and other needs at more affordable rates. The availability of cheaper money in an economy boosts consumer confidence and the tendency is for the consumer to spend more. In broad terms, an economy with an inexpensive flow of money creates new jobs.

However, in a fast-growing economy there is the risk of a rise in the inflation rate. When a government in a country sees signs that inflation is on the rise or there is a chance it could rise, it can control this by raising interest rates. Higher interest rates slow the flow of money, making it more expensive for both consumers and businesses to borrow. This slowing effect reduces the chance of inflation, but it also reduces corporate profits, which in turn adversely affects stocks prices.

When stock markets are volatile, investors opt for bonds as they provide an element of stability that offsets some of the volatility of stocks. The irony is that bond prices move inversely to interest rates. When interest rates go up, bond prices go down and when interest rates go down, bond prices go up. This is applicable to previously issued bonds trading on the open market.

Impact

Movements in interest rates, inflation rates and exchange rates will have an impact on the volume of equities traded on stock exchanges, which also impacts on their revenue streams. Similarly, these economic factors will also impact on the prices of commodities such as oil, wheat and sugar and the volumes traded on commodities exchanges.

Currency trading is also affected by these factors as movements in exchange rates favour day currency traders who are active in the foreign exchange market.

Socio-cultural

These environmental factors are centred on the needs of investors. A typical example is the demand for Islamic finance products, which is fuelled by the need for Muslim investors to adhere to the rules of Sharia in their investment objectives. Under Sharia Islamic law, making money from money, such as charging interest, is usury and therefore not permitted.

One of the more popularly traded Islamic financial instruments is the Islamic bond, also known as Sukuk. These are designed to get around the Islamic prohibition of charging interest. For example, they treat the bond holder as the owner of some of the company's assets. The bond holder then receives rent, not interest, for the use of these assets.

Impact

Exchanges are looking to list financial instruments that meet the changing demands of investors. For example, in 2007, Dubai Islamic Bank listed a $750 million Sukuk on the Dubai International Financial Exchange (DIFX), after selling the Islamic securities to investors in Europe, Asia and the Middle East. This Sukuk was the first one ever issued by the bank, which specialises exclusively in Islamic instruments.

Technological

The advancement of technology has been instrumental in the way trading has been conducted and how exchanges have operated in recent times. The rapid development of the internet has been a boon to retail traders (investors) trading stocks and currency on a daily basis around the globe.

Technology has also led to the proliferation of alternative execution venues for traders. A typical example is the so-called dark liquidity pools, which are mostly crossing networks of one form or another that match buyers and sellers anonymously, reducing information leakage and market impact, often with lower direct trading costs.

Impact

Technology providers are offering new technologies to the trading industry to help them trade efficiently and manage risk effectively. Technology is also a source of competitive advantage to exchanges. The London Stock Exchange, for example, is using a service-oriented network architecture framework to deploy what is regarded as the world's fastest real-time trading information system, which is reported to have increased competitive advantage for the Exchange and helped to promote more trading in the London market.

Competitive Landscape

As investors worldwide, especially institutions, are embracing the trend as well as perfecting the act of trading on several exchanges at once, the competition for stock exchanges has intensified lately. Capital may flow into, say, Intel shares trading on the London Stock Exchange, but may leave if liquidity shifts to Germany. It was reported not so long ago that brokers trading several blue-chip Brazilian securities saw liquidity shift from the Bolsa de Valores de São Paulo (Bovespa) to the New York Stock Exchange due to a government-imposed banking fee, which caused higher overall trading costs in Brazil than in New York.[17]

17   Barham, p51 and Rich, p17.

Many exchanges today are working to redefine their current business models to optimise their competitive advantage in a highly globalised world.[18]

It has been noticeable that in some jurisdictions, competition for stock exchanges is not limited to other stock exchanges. There are two main types of alternative trading systems (ATSs) that function outside the regulatory structure of stock exchanges yet offer investors the same service of matching trades. These are:

1. **Electronic communications networks (ECNs)** – The unique feature of these systems is that they publish their prices on publicly accessible display systems. In the United States, for instance, these ECNs are registered as broker–dealers with the national Securities and Exchange Commission and have received a no-action letter from that organisation.[19]
2. **Non-ECN alternative trading systems** – These carry out the same function as ECNs, but do not publicly post their prices. In many instances, given that they are call markets where prices are taken from a major market or are determined on the spot for large block trades at certain prearranged times, these non-ECN ATSs do not post prices.

Trades can also be matched in-house, if possible, by the use of a totally different type of system called broker–dealer internalisation of order flow. This negates the need to send trades to a public trading facility.

Competition between trading platforms raises the possibility of price fragmentation in addition to loss of trading business. Duplication of functions among stock exchanges, ATSs and broker–dealer systems may not only result in fragmentation, but also leaves investors with no central source of liquidity in financial markets. Price fragmentation threatens the central franchise of a stock exchange: management of a market where true price discovery occurs and investors and issuers receive the best possible prices for their transactions.[20]

In the global financial markets, fragmentation and competition are becoming bedfellows. In the US capital markets, the stock exchanges, ATSs, and broker–dealer internalisation systems all compete for order flow; while in Europe and Asia, there is intense competition among long-established electronic order-driven trading systems as well as competition between the traditional national exchanges and their newer rivals.

---

18 Galper, Joshua, "Three Business Models for the Stock Exchange Industry", Working Paper, International Federation of Stock Exchanges, August 1999. Boland, Vincent, "Stock exchange chief sees merger by 2003", *Financial Times*, 17 January 2000.
19 A no-action letter for ECNs is a statement made by the US SEC that no action will be taken against the operation of an ECN's business as defined by the Alternative Trading System policy guidelines.
20 Michaels, Adrian, "Brokers face up to realities of the Internet revolution", *Financial Times*, 8 November 1999, p5.

All these developments may lead to an increase in price fragmentation in these markets.

Profile of Major Exchanges around the World

London Stock Exchange (LSE)

The London Stock Exchange is hailed as Europe's largest stock exchange (and one of the oldest), and it lists more than 3,200 depository receipts, Eurobonds, and company shares (some 650 based outside the UK).

In 1997, after 200 years as a regulated exchange, the LSE launched the Stock Exchange Electronic Trading Services (SETS). SETS is the platform for trading the constituents of the FTSE All Share Index, exchange-traded funds and exchange-traded commodities, along with over 180 of the most-traded AIM and Irish securities.[21]

The LSE includes the main market, the Professional Securities Market (or PSM, listed debt securities), and the Alternative Investment Market (or AIM, which lists new and growing companies).

Key figures for the fiscal year ending March, 2008 are:[22]

Revenue: £546.4M
One year growth: 15.6%
Net income (profit after taxation): £178.2M
Net income growth: 16.1%

Deutsche Börse

One of the major hallmarks of the Deutsche Börse is the securities exchange platform it offers through the Frankfurt Exchange, the derivatives trading on the Eurex market (the world's largest), the market information with the DAX index and the STOXX index (33%-owned), and clearing services with subsidiary Clearstream.

It is also the co-owner of the Eurex futures market with the Swiss Exchange and developed the electronic trading platform Xetra, which it licenses to other exchanges, including the Vienna Exchange.

Key figures for the fiscal year ending December, 2007 are:[23]

Sales: €2,185.2M
One year growth: 18%
Net income: €911.7M
One year income growth: 13.6%

21 Source: www.londonstockexchange.com/en-gb/about/cooverview/history.htm.
22 2008 Annual Report and Accounts of London Stock Exchange plc.
23 Annual Report 2007 – Deutsche Börse.

NYSE Euronext Inc.

NYSE Euronext operates the New York Stock Exchange (NYSE), one of the oldest and largest stock markets in the world. There are some 2,800 companies listed on this exchange and these include most of the largest US corporations. Some foreign companies in search of the greater liquidity that is accessible in the US markets also list on the NYSE.

A major milestone in its history was the purchase of Euronext for around $10 billion to create the first transatlantic exchange and the largest global stock market, with exchanges in Paris, Brussels, Amsterdam and Lisbon, plus automated trading desks, in addition to the NYSE. This structure allows NYSE Euronext to own six derivatives and futures markets, including London-based LIFFE.

Key figures for the fiscal year ending December, 2007 are:[24]

Sales: $4,158.0M
One year growth: 75.0%
Net income: $643.0M
Income growth: 213.7%

NASDAQ OMX Group Inc.

The Nasdaq OMX Group is billed as the leader in floorless exchanges and is believed to have surpassed NYSE Euronext as the world's largest stock exchange. The merger between the Nasdaq Stock Exchange and OMX, the owner of Nordic Marketplace (and its Nordic Exchange, Northern Europe's largest integrated securities exchange), and other European markets in 2008 resulted in the creation of the group.

Nasdaq OMX trades in more than 3,900 companies, including exchange-traded funds (ETFs), equities, derivatives, commodities, and structured products. The company's market services segment (quotations, order execution, reporting services, and more) represents about 85% of its sales.

Key figures for the fiscal year ending December, 2007 are:[25]

Sales: $2,436.6M
One year growth: 47.0%
Net income: $518.4M
Net income growth: 305.3%

Tokyo Stock Exchange

The Tokyo Stock Exchange is the most well-known stock exchange of Japan. The stocks that are listed under the Tokyo Stock Exchange are classified into the following:

24 Source: MarketWatch, Inc.
25 Ibid.

1. First Section, aimed at large companies;
2. Second Section, for mid-sized companies;
3. Other sections for the high-growth start-up companies.

There are 89 domestic and 19 foreign securities companies that participate in Tokyo Stock Exchange trading.

The Tokyo Stock Exchange was a physical stock exchange where trading took place using the open outcry system until 30 April 1999, when the Tokyo Stock Exchange closed and switched over to an electronic method for transactions.

The following are the main indices that are used to track the performance of the Tokyo Stock Exchange:

- Nikkei 225 of companies, which is used by Japan's largest business newspaper – the Nihon Keizai Shimbun;
- J30 Index, which caters for the large industrial companies that are serviced by Japan's major broadsheet newspapers.
- Topix Index, which is based on the share prices of the First Section companies.

Key figures for the 2007 fiscal year are:[26]

Sales (operating revenue): Y75,505M
One year growth: 1%
Net income: Y17,701M
Net income growth: -12%

Profile of Major Players in Trading

The players profiled in this section are firms that are non-banking institutions, which are active in the trading space.

BGC Partners Inc.
BGC Partners Inc. is an inter-dealer broker that provides integrated voice and electronic services to wholesale market participants worldwide. The firm's service offerings include price discovery, trade execution, straight-through processing, and clearing and settlement. These services are offered to participants in the global fixed income, interest rates, foreign exchange, equity derivatives, credit derivatives, futures and structured product markets.

BGC separated from Cantor Fitzgerald in 2004 and merged with eSpeed in April 2008. The merger resulted in the creation of BGC Partners Inc.

The financial data of the company for 2007 will not be listed as a result of the merger.

26 Source: www.tse.or.jp/english/about/ir/financials/highlights/index.html.

GFI Group

GFI Group is a provider of inter-dealer brokerage services in global over-the-counter (OTC) cash and derivatives markets, including credit derivatives and fixed income, financial derivatives, cash equities and equity derivatives, energy and commodities.

Founded in 1987, the group is headquartered in New York, USA and employs more than 1,700 people. GFI provides services and products to over 2,400 institutional clients, including investment banks and hedge funds.

Financial data for the year ended 31 December 2007:[27]

Revenues	$970.5M
Net income after tax	$ 94.9M

ICAP

ICAP is a voice and electronic inter-dealer broker that provides specialist inter-mediary broking services to trading professionals in the wholesale financial markets. The group offers services in commodities, foreign exchange, interest rates, credit and equity markets, as well as data, commentary and indices.

Investment banks use the firm's specialist service that matches up buyers and sellers in the wholesale financial markets and pay a commission to use the firm to complete trading transactions.

Financial data for the year ended 31 March 2007:[28]

Revenues	$2,090.9M[29]
Net income after tax	$ 404.1M[30]

Tullett Prebon

Tullett Prebon is an inter-dealer broker that acts as an intermediary in the wholesale financial markets. The business covers major product groups including equities, energy, fixed income and derivatives.

The business adopts a business model whereby it brokers financial market products on either a "name give-up" basis (where the counterparties to a transaction settle directly with each other) or a "matched principal" basis (where Tullett Prebon is the counterparty to each leg of a transaction).

Financial data showing overall results for 2007:[31]

Revenue	£753.8M
Operating profit	£131.8M

27 Source: GFI – Annual Report 2007.
28 Source: ICAP Annual Report for the year ended 31 March 2007.
29 Dollar numbers converted at the average exchange rate for the year of US$1.89 (year ended 31 March 2006 – US$1.79).
30 Ibid.
31 Source: Tullett Prebon Annual Report 2007.

There are a number of providers that allow retail investors to trade currencies and contracts for difference (CFD). These include Interbank FX, GFX Group SA for foreign exchange and City Index and IG Markets for CFDs.

Table 4.1 Head-to-head comparison of some notable FX Platforms

	Number of Currency Pairs Offered	Minimum Spread (in pips*)	Minimum Margin Requirement (%)	Minimum Account
dbFX	34	2	1	$5,000
FX Solutions	20	3	0.25	$250
BARX	300	1/10	1	£3,000
Saxobank	300	2	1	£2,000
Spreadbet Forex (CMC)	84	2	1	£200

* 1 pip is 0.0001 of the exchange rate
Source: City A.M.

Clearing and Settlement Firms

Clearing and settlement firms fall into the category of firms that assist traders to settle the trades they have made. They also fulfil the role of preventing issues that may arise as a result of trading activities by uncreditworthy or untrustworthy traders.

Clearing Firms

The principal role of clearing firms, also referred to as clearing agents in some markets, is to provide a common facility to match the records of counterparties in a trade and also confirm that both traders (buyers and sellers) agreed to the same terms.

In practice, traders are expected to record details of their trades when they arrange trades on the floor of any exchange or over the telephone. Items recorded include the identities of the traders with whom they trade and the terms of the trade.

Once trades clear, traders can then commence the settlement of these trades.

In the USA, for instance, once a trade has been executed, records will be sent to the National Securities Clearing Corporation (NSCC®), the largest securities clearing agency in the country, for clearance and settlement. All trading activity is transmitted to NSCC via computer as "locked in" transactions, meaning a computer has already matched the details of the trades from buyer and seller. Trades executed will be routed to NSCC for settlement via the Regional Interface Organisation (RIO).

In general, once trades clear, traders can then commence the settlement of these trades. However, trades will not clear if there is a mismatch in the records. The clearing agent is required to report the discrepancies to the traders, who then go about resolving them. The expression used when there is such a discrepancy in the details of a trade in a securities market is DK (which stands for Don't Know). Thus, such trades are known as DKs. In the futures market, these kinds of trade are known as out-trades.

Clearing may also involve netting down trades to minimise the number of securities that must be received or delivered at settlement.

Cleared trades are settled within a specific time after the trade date, based on the type of security being traded.

Settlement Agents

The principal role of the settlement agent is to facilitate the settlement of trades. The settlement process entails the receipt of cash from buyers and securities from sellers. If each party fulfils their obligations in this respect, the settlement agent forwards the cash to the seller and the securities to the buyer.

One of the major benefits that traders derive from using settlement agents is the efficiency they offer for the settlement of trades. The method of net settlement offers the required efficiency in the settlement process. In practice, net settlement entails the netting of the buy and sell trades for each security to a single net security position by the settlement agent. This method is also applied to all money credits and debits, netting them into a single net money position for individual clients. Settlement is then done on the basis of net positions.

Some settlement agents use a system known as continuous net settlement (CNS). This is an automated book-entry accounting system used for centralising the settlement of compared security transactions and maintaining an orderly flow of security and money balances.

The CNS processing cycles output reports that provide participants with a complete record of security and money movements, and related information.

In most securities markets, the normal convention for settlement cycles, denoted as T+3, is three business days after the arrangement of a trade. There are other settlement cycles, T+1 and T+2, which signify that the settlement occurs on a transaction date plus one day and plus two days respectively.

To illustrate these conventions, suppose Bob Setts, a trader, buys 500 shares of Hutchison Whampoa Limited stock on 25 August 2008, which is the transaction date. If the settlement cycle for this trade is T+3, then the date on which ownership of the security is actually transferred and money is exchanged, i.e. the settlement date, will be 28 August 2008.

The reason for this time-lag in the settlement process is that in the past, security transactions were done manually as opposed to electronically. Investors (traders) would have to wait for the delivery of a particular security, which was in actual certificate form, and delay payment until reception. Given that delivery times could vary and prices could fluctuate, market regulators set a period of time in which securities and cash must be delivered. Not so long ago, before June 1995, the settlement date for stocks was T+5, or five business days after the transaction date.

If Bob Setts were to buy UK government debt, i.e. gilts, on 25 August 2008, the settlement date for this transaction would be 26 August 2008, as the settlement cycle for this type of securities is T+1.

There are also situations where traders can arrange special settlement instructions on the transaction date and this is known in the industry as cash settlement.

Clearing Houses

Clearing corporations, or clearing houses, provide operational support for securities and commodities exchanges. They also help ensure the integrity of listed securities and derivatives transactions in open markets.

For example, when an order to buy or sell a futures or options contract is executed, the clearing house compares the details of the trade. Then it delivers the product to the buyer and ensures that payment is made to settle the transaction. In other words, it guarantees that the buyer and the seller fulfil the terms of their contract. This is accomplished by acting as a buyer for every seller and as a seller to every buyer, i.e. as a central counterparty.[32] Thus, they are the issuers and guarantors of the buyers' and sellers' contracts.

Clearing houses are usually owned by clearing members, who are collectively responsible for settling all trades. Each futures exchange has its own clearing house. All members of an exchange are required to clear their trades through the clearing house at the end of each trading session and post collateral, called margins, to secure their obligations. For example, if a member broker reports to the clearing house at the end of the day a total purchase of 224,000 pounds of sugar and total sales of 112,000 pounds of sugar, they would be net long 112,000 pounds of sugar. Assuming that this is the broker's only position in futures and that the clearing house margin is six cents per pound, this means the broker would be required to have $6,720 on deposit with the clearing house, i.e. its margin payment. Given that all members are required to clear their trades through the clearing house and must maintain sufficient funds to cover their debit balances, the clearing house is responsible to all members for the fulfilment of the contracts.

Traders that are not members of a clearing house need a clearing member to guarantee the settlement of their trades. In the event that the trader fails to settle a trade, the onus is on their clearing member to ensure that the trade is settled. If the clearing member is unable to settle a trade, for whatever reason, the clearing house would levy its other members to settle the trade.

The creditworthiness of members of clearing houses is an important factor in the minimisation of settlement risk – the risk that one party will fail to deliver the terms of a contract with another party at the time of settlement – that can arise in the course of trading with other traders. In addition to the monetary deposit that clearing houses demand from their members, they also control

32 A central counterparty is a market operator who steps in as a legal counterparty between buyer and seller in a trade.

this type of risk by requesting accurate information regarding members' financial situations and trading activities, and evidence that they have not exceeded the position limits stipulated for them.

Depositories and Custodians

Depositories and custodians are institutions that have the legal responsibility of holding cash and securities on behalf of their clients. They fulfil the role of helping to settle trades by ensuring the quick delivery of cash and security certificates to settlement agents. They are also responsible for the safekeeping of clients' assets.

There are number of depositories, referred to as the Central Securities Depository, around the world. The largest of them is the Depository Trust Corporation (DTC), which holds over $20 trillion in assets for both US and non-US clients. This categorises the firm as one of the International Central Securities Depositories (ICSDs), which are central securities depositories that settle trades in international securities and in various domestic securities, usually through direct or indirect (through local agents) links to local CSDs.

Another major depository is the ECSDA, which stands for European Central Securities Depositories Association. It is composed of 42 CSDs situated in the geographical area of Europe.

Mechanics of T+3 Settlement Cycle

In this section, the mechanics of the T+3 settlement cycle, depicting the roles of the settlement agent, clearing house and the depository, are illustrated. The fictitious firm BizOp will assume the role of clearing and settlement agent while the fictitious firm EssTrust will assume the role of central security depository.

On 25 August 2008, a transaction for 1,000 shares of General Motors stock takes place between two fictitious brokers, BizNova and Vale Global Investors (VGI), on behalf of their clients.

Trade Date (T) – 25 August 2008

The clearance and settlement cycle commences on 25 August 2008. On this date, trade details are electronically transmitted in real time to BizOp for processing. BizOp sends automated reports to BizNova and VGI, which are legally binding documents that show trade details. These reports are essentially confirmation that this transaction has entered the clearance and settlement streams.

T+1 – 26 August 2008

BizOp guarantees settlement and this commences at midnight between T+1 and T+2. At this juncture, BizOp assumes the role of the central counterparty in this transaction, i.e. it takes on the buyer's credit risk[33] and the seller's delivery risk.[34]

T+2 – 27 August 2008
BizOp issues broker summaries of all compared trades (including the trade in question). Information on the net positions of each security due or owed for settlement is also contained in these summaries.

T+3 – 28 August 2008
This is the settlement date for the delivery of the shares to the buyer (BizNova) and payment of money to the seller (VGI). Both brokers instruct their selling banks to send or receive funds to/from EssTrust as BizOp's agent. The General Motors shares do not change hands physically. The transfer of ownership is done electronically by EssTrust between the brokers' accounts by book-entry movements.

Credit Rating Agencies

Credit rating agencies (CRAs) are companies that are responsible for assigning credit ratings for issuers of certain types of debt obligation as well as the debt instruments themselves. Credit ratings are used by investors, issuers, investment banks, broker–dealers, and governments. Credit rating agencies are particularly beneficial to investors as they increase the range of investment alternatives and provide independent, easy-to-use measurements of relative credit risk; this generally increases the efficiency of the market.

The most recognised rating agencies are Standard & Poor's, Moody's Investors Service, and Fitch Ratings.

Standard and Poor's (S&P)
This agency was founded in 1860 by Henry Varnum Poor. Major milestones in the history of S&P include the 1941 merger between Poor's Publishing and Standard Statistics to form the Standard & Poor's Corporation and its acquisition by The McGraw-Hill Companies, Inc. in 1966.

According to industry reports, as of August 2008 the total amount of outstanding debt rated by S&P globally is approximately US$32 trillion, in 100 countries. In 2007 alone, Standard & Poor's Ratings Services published more than 510,000 ratings, including 208,000 new and 302,000 revised ratings.

S&P is headquartered in New York City, USA, and employs approximately 8,500 employees located in 23 countries and markets.

33 This is the risk due to uncertainty in a counterparty's ability to meet its obligations.
34 This is the risk that a counterparty in a trade will not deliver the securities that were traded.

Moody's Investors Service

Moody's Investors Service was established in New York, USA, by John Moody in 1900. That year, the company, known then as John Moody & Company, published Moody's Manual of Industrial and Miscellaneous Securities. The manual contained information and statistics on stocks and bonds of financial institutions and government agencies, and manufacturing, mining, utilities, and food companies.

According to industry reports, Moody's ratings and analyses track debt covering more than:

- 100 sovereign nations;
- 12,000 corporate issuers;
- 29,000 public finance issuers;
- 96,000 structured finance obligations.

Fitch Ratings

Fitch Ratings was established as the Fitch Publishing Company on 24 December 1913 by John Knowles Fitch. Initially, it was a publisher of financial statistics whose consumers included the New York Stock Exchange. Major milestones in the company's history include the introduction in 1924 of the "AAA" to "D" ratings scale and the establishment of Derivative Fitch, a rating agency, in 2006 that is dedicated to providing ratings and a suite of comprehensive services for the credit default obligation (CDO) and credit derivatives markets.

Fitch Ratings has two headquarters: one in New York City, USA, and the other in London, UK. It also has joint ventures in more than 49 locations and covering entities in more than 90 countries.

Indices

Indices track the performance of a specific "basket" of stocks considered to represent a particular market or sector of the regional stock market or economy. There are essentially two classes of stock market indexes: the broad-base index which represents the performance of a whole stock market and more specialised indices that track the performance of specific sectors of the market. Typical broad-base indices are the S&P 500 Composite Stock Price Index, which is an index of 500 stocks from major industries of the US economy; the FTSE 100, which is a share index of the 100 most highly capitalised companies listed on the London Stock Exchange; and the Nikkei 225, the stock market index for the Tokyo Stock Exchange; while a typical specialised index is, for example, the NASDAQ Health Care Index, which contains securities of NASDAQ-listed companies classified according to the Industry Classification Benchmark as Health Care. They include health care providers, and medical equipment, medical supplies, biotechnology, and pharmaceuticals suppliers.

Table 4.2 Other Stock Market Indices

Index	Symbol	Country
MerVal	MERV	Argentina
All Ordinaries	AORD	Australia
Bel 20	BFX	Belgium
Bovespa	BVSP	Brazil
S&P/Toronto Composite	GSPTSE	Canada
Shanghai SEComposite	SSEC	China
CAC-40	FCHI	France
DAX Composite	GDAXI	Germany
Hang Seng	HSI	Hong Kong
Bombay BSE Sensex	BSESN	India
Jakarta Composite	JKSE	Indonesia
Tel Aviv 100	TA-100	Israel
Kuala Lumpur SEComposite	KLSE	Malaysia
Amsterdam Exchange	AEX	Netherlands
Trading System	RTSI	Russia
Straits Times	STI	Singapore
KOSPI(Seoul Composite)	KS11	South Korea
Taiwan TSEC Weighted	TWII	Taiwan

Security Identifier Types

Security identifier types are symbols used to identify a security product or issue. The management and distribution of these identifiers are handled by different organisations. Common types of security identifier are Committee on Uniform Security Identification Procedures (CUSIP), International Securities Identifying Number (ISIN), and Stock Exchange Daily Official List (SEDOL).

CUSIP

CUSIP numbers are 9-character alphanumeric security identifiers distributed by the American Bankers' Association and operated by Standard and Poor's. The CUSIP Services Bureau is North America's National Numbering Association (NNA) and the CUSIP identifiers are the national securities identification number for products issued from both the United States and Canada.

CUSIP identifiers enable the accurate and efficient clearance and settlement of securities. In addition, they facilitate the easy processing of income payments made during the life cycle of an issue. They allow:

- holders, analysts and brokers to quickly identify and access data that is specific to certain security issues;
- custodians and sub-custodians to effortlessly communicate with each other on securities trades;

- depositories to accurately manage transactions and examine historical data;
- accurate management of transactions and the examination of historical data often carried out by custodians.

Structure of a CUSIP

Figure 4.1 depicts the structure of the CUSIP identifier for General Electric stock.

Figure 4.1 General Electric CUSIP identifier structure

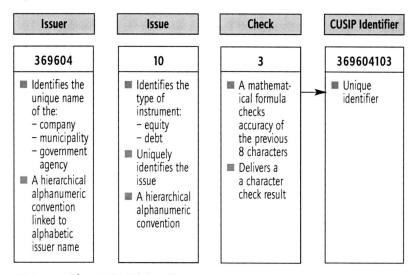

Data sourced from CUSIP Global Services

Instrument coverage

There are more that 8.4 million unique financial instruments issued by corporations, municipalities and government agencies throughout the world that are covered by the CUSIP numbering system. Table 4.3 shows some of these instruments categorised as debt, equities and other types of instruments.

Table 4.3 CUSIP Financial Instruments

Debt	Equity	Other
Certificates of deposits (CDs)	Common shares	Equity-linked notes (hybrids)
Corporate bonds	Exchange-traded funds	Derivatives
Commercial paper	Indices	Credit derivatives (CLIPS)
Asset-backed securities	Preferred shares	Capital securities (hybrids)
Structured products	Warrants	
Mortgage-backed securities		
Collateralised debt obligations (CDOs)		

Source: CUSIP Global Services

CINS

CINS, which stands for CUSIP International Numbering System (CINS), is a 9-character alphanumeric identifier that uses the same numbering system as CUSIP. It, however, also contains a letter of the alphabet in the first position representing the issuer's country or geographic region. CINS is an extension to CUSIP in response to US demand for global coverage, and is the local identifier of over 30 non-North American markets and was developed in 1989.

Structure of a CINS

Figure 4.2 depicts the structure of the CINS identifier for Daimler stock.

Figure 4.2 Daimler CINS identifier D1668R123

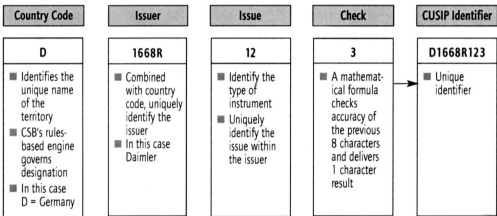

Country Code	Issuer	Issue	Check	CUSIP Identifier
D	1668R	12	3	D1668R123
■ Identifies the unique name of the territory ■ CSB's rules-based engine governs designation ■ In this case D = Germany	■ Combined with country code, uniquely identify the issuer ■ In this case Daimler	■ Identify the type of instrument ■ Uniquely identify the issue within the issuer	■ A mathematical formula checks accuracy of the previous 8 characters and delivers 1 character result	■ Unique identifier

Data sourced from CUSIP Global Services

ISIN

ISIN, which stands for International Securities Identifying Number, is another unique identifier for securities. It is a global code used to indentify instruments in different countries to facilitate cross-border trading. The ISIN code is a 12-character alphanumeric code that consist of three parts: a two-letter country code, a nine-character alphanumeric national security identifier (CUSIP number), and a single check digit. Securities with which ISINs can be used include debt securities, shares, options, derivatives and futures.

Structure of an ISIN

Figure 4.3 depicts the structure of the ISIN identifier for Siemens stock.

Figure 4.3 Siemens ISIN: DE0007236101

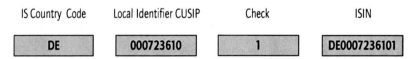

IS Country Code	Local Identifier CUSIP	Check	ISIN
DE	000723610	1	DE0007236101

RIC

Reuters Identification Code is a ticker-like code used within the Reuters system to identify instruments worldwide. For equities, for instance, the RIC code is denoted as: Ticker.Exchange.

Thus, the RIC code for Microsoft stock on the Nasdaq exchange is: MSFT.OQ, MSFT being the ticker and OQ used to denote the Nasdaq exchange.

The RIC code for Hewlett Packard stock on the New York Stock Exchange is: HPQ.N, HPQ being the ticker for Hewlett Packard and N used to denote the NYSE.

Similarly, the RIC code for Unilever stock on the London Stock Exchange is: ULVR.L, ULVR being the ticker for Unilever and L used to denote the LSE.

RIC codes use tickers for common indices and money-market instruments. For instance, the US 5-year money market bond is assigned the ticker US5YT, the "T" at the end referring to "Treasury". Commodities as well as contracts for difference (CFDs) are similarly assigned tickers; crude oil for instance is CL. The RIC code for gold CFD, for example, is 0#YGG. Indices have a leading period; for instance, .GSPC identifies the S&P 500 and .FCHI identifies the CAC40.

Other Security Identifier Types

Table 4.4 Other Security Identifier Types

Name	Description
SEDOL	This is a seven-digit number used to identify UK-listed securities. A security's SEDOL is the basis of its ISIN. The ISIN is the SEDOL plus the prefix "GB00" with a single check digit suffixed.
SICOVAM (Société Interprofessionelle pour la Compensation des Valeurs Mobilières)	An identifier used to identify French securities listed on French stock exchanges. SICOVAMs are no longer issued, ISINs being used instead.
Valoren	Telekurs Financial, the Swiss numbering agency, assigns Valoren numbers to identify financial instruments.
EPIC	Commonly used on the UK stock market.

Trends in Trading and Exchanges

This chapter discusses some of the recent trends in trading and exchanges including CFD trading, the emergence of liquidity pools and the popularity of day trading.

Introduction

There have been great transformations in the structures of trading and exchanges over the years. The advancement of technology has been one of the key drivers for these transformations as electronic methods have become integral to the way trading is conducted on exchanges and over the counter.

The growth of the hedge fund industry and also the retail sector in trading (i.e. day traders, swing traders and so on) has also impacted on the trading industry and exchanges. The trading requirements of these groups are markedly different to the traditional requirements of the brokers and dealers of yesteryear. The hedge funds, in particular, pursue very complex and unique trading strategies and these drive the way they go about trading. They require far more sophisticated technology to achieve their investment and trading objectives, which usually involve identifying even the smallest movements in the prices of securities.

Retail investors (traders) have benefited from the growth of the internet over the years and this has allowed them to trade anything from stocks to indices and currency. Non-banking institutions have also proliferated due to the range of possibilities that can be achieved on the internet. Technology has allowed these players to compete on an even keel with traditional banking institutions in their service offerings with regard to stock and currency trading. In addition, technology has enabled these players to improve on their service levels in a bid to differentiate their offerings.

That said, the recent trends shaping the trading and exchanges industry are discussed below.

The Growth of Electronic Communication Networks

An electronic communication network (ECN) in the financial markets is a type of computer system that expedites trading of financial products such as stocks and currencies outside traditional stock exchanges. A succinct definition of ECNs is offered by the US Securities and Exchange Commission as follows:

Electronic trading systems that automatically match buy and sell orders at specified prices.

Another interesting definition offered by Investopedia is:

An electronic system that attempts to eliminate the role of a third party in the execution of orders entered by an exchange market maker or an over-the-counter market maker, and permits such orders to be entirely or partly executed.

An ECN connects major brokerages and individual traders and facilitates direct trading between these entities without having to go through a middleman. The SEC describes ECNs as integral to the modern securities market.

Benefits of the ECN Structure

▦ **Lower trading costs** – The communication and matching systems that ECNs use allow their clients to trade at lower costs. ECNs sidestep human intermediaries such as dealers by matching buyers and sellers directly. In the USA, for instance, industry figures show that dealers on the New York Stock Exchange have operating margins of approximately 50% and 25% respectively.

▦ **Faster trade execution** – The use of cutting-edge technologies by ECNS allows for significantly faster order execution than established exchanges' trading systems. For instance, industry figures show that an average execution time for an ECN is 2–3 seconds in comparison with more than 20 seconds for an order through an exchange.

▦ **Provision of complete price information** – ECNs usually provide investors with more complete price information than traditional exchanges by giving them access to their limit order books. Investors use this information to better assess market conditions and optimise their trading strategies.

▦ **Provision of trader anonymity** – Anonymity is potentially important for informed institutional investors as it protects against copying of their trading strategies by less informed traders. Furthermore, in the event of other market participants gaining prior or simultaneous knowledge of transactions, there might be attempts on their part to trade before the institutional investors are able to complete their trades.[35] This sort of practice or any leakage of information is a serious matter in the financial markets. ECNs provide trader anonymity by displaying only the price and the size of an order.

▦ **Access to limit order book** – The access provided to customers and brokers is a major feature of ECNs. In general, ECNs initially attempt to match customer limit orders within the ECN. When an internal match is found, the trade executes immediately. ECNs offer subscribers several options in the event that internal matches are not feasible. The subscriber can choose the option of leaving the limit order on the ECN's book, cancel the order, or route the order to another ECN or market.

Competition amongst ECNs

The competitive state of the ECN landscape is exemplified by the manner in which they compete with each other by targeting different clientele and following various strategies. Some ECNs use only limit orders and they are "desti-

---

35 This practice is known as front running and refers to taking a position in a security based on non-public information such as an impending transaction by another person in the same or related security. Also known as trading ahead.

nation-only" ECNs, which implies orders do not leave the ECNs until they are cancelled, regardless of whether or not they could execute somewhere else. If a match is not found, the ECN posts the order on a traditional exchange once it becomes the ECN's best quote, and waits for an incoming order to trade at its price. Other ECNs take market orders, i.e. orders to buy or sell a stock immediately at whatever is currently the best available price, and limit orders, and if internal orders are not matched, route them to a traditional exchange to seek the optimal price. These outbound-routing ECNs are in search of external liquidity. If the regional bets bid or offer, the bet price available across all markets, is from another market, an outbound-routing ECN sends its orders there. It is worth noting that outbound-routing ECNs are some of the best customers of destination-only ECNs.

ECNs adopt various differentiation strategies including:

- employing proprietary methods/algorithms, as in the case of outbound-routing ECNs, to select exchanges that could possibly provide the best combination of price, quality and speed as well as certainty of execution for their customers;
- batching orders for short periods and conducting regular "call markets" to establish a stock price;
- posting all or part of their limit-order books on internet sites;
- providing limited access to price information.

Fee Structure

The ECN fee structure is such that they charge fees for their services to subscribers who pay directly and non-subscribers who pay indirectly. Subscribers are charged fees which include a fixed component, the cost of purchasing the ECN terminal and line feed, and a per-share fee for execution of stock trades. Subscribers usually submit limit orders without paying a fee. However, they may pay a nominal access fee per share for orders that are executed against a standard limit order.

The Growth of Algorithmic Trading

The era of algorithmic trading has begun. Algorithmic trading promises to cut costs, eliminate human error, and boost trading efficiency and productivity. The use of algorithms to make complex decisions and place thousands of orders in milliseconds has grown in popularity, particularly among equity and currency traders in recent times. Algorithmic trading, also known as algo trading, is defined as the placement of a buy or sell order of a defined quantity into a quantitative model that can automatically generate the timing of orders and the size of the orders on the basis of the parameters and constraints of the algorithm specified to achieve a certain trading objective.

The following is a definition of an algorithmic trading system by Investopedia:

A trading system that utilises very advanced mathematical models for making transaction decisions in the financial markets. The strict rules built into the model attempt to determine the optimal time for an order to be placed that will cause the least amount of impact on a stock's price.

Within the equities markets, large blocks of shares are typically purchased by dividing a large share block into smaller lots and the decision as to timing of the purchase of the smaller blocks is taken by the complex algorithm. Large institutional investors are some of the major users of algorithmic trading, given the large amount of shares they purchase on a daily basis. These investors are able to achieve the best possible price without significantly affecting the stock's price and escalating purchasing costs owing to these complex algorithms.

Brief History of Algorithmic Trading

In the financial markets, the computerisation of order flow was first witnessed in the early 1970s with significant milestones such as the introduction of the New York Stock Exchange's "designated order turnaround" system (DOT, and later SuperDOT), which routed orders electronically to the proper trading post to be executed manually, and the "opening automated reporting system" (OARS), which aided the specialist in determining the market clearing opening price.

Financial markets with fully electronic execution and similar electronic communication networks grew in the late 1980s and 1990s. In the USA, the advent of decimalisation, which resulted in the change of the minimum tick size from 1/16th of a dollar ($0.0625) to $0.01 per share, could have been partly responsible for the rise of algorithmic trading as it changed the market microstructure by allowing smaller differences between the bid and offer prices, decreasing the market-makers' trading advantage, therefore decreasing market liquidity. In addition, regulations such as Reg-ATS changed the way in which the sell side and the buy side thought about trading.

This reduction in market liquidity prompted institutional traders to split up orders in accordance with computer algorithms so as to execute their orders at a better average price. These average price benchmarks are calibrated and calculated by computers by applying the time weighted (i.e. unweighted) average price (TWAP) or more usually the volume weighted average price (VWAP).[36]

The opening of more electronic markets has made the creation of other algorithmic trading strategies possible. These strategies are more easily implemented by computer systems because the systems can react more rapidly to temporary mispricing and examine prices from several markets simultaneously.

In the early 2000s, algorithmic trading really started to take off as the execution product for the sell side. It soon became a product that was mass delivered to the buy side as the buy side became interested in taking on the trading of some of its order flow on its own instead of sending all its orders to the broker–dealers.

---

36 VWAP and TWAP are discussed further in the latter chapters of this book.

In recent years, the biggest growth area in the algorithmic trading universe is in customisation of algorithms. As the buy side has become more sophisticated in understanding trading and how it wants to trade in today's marketplace, the more it desires customised strategies tuned to exactly the way it wants the strategies to work.

Algorithmic trading has spread across multiple asset classes – from equities to futures and options to foreign exchange – as people look for cross-asset trading to hedge their positions.

Market Growth

It is an understatement that the market for algorithmic trading systems has grown in recent times. Estimates from Boston-based consulting firm Aite Group LLC show a 15% increase in the percentage of equities trading volume driven by algorithmic trading between 2004 and 2008 (see Figure 5.1). Therefore it is unsurprising that IT spending is expected to have exceeded $300 million by the end of 2008.

A third of all EU and US stock trades in 2006 were also driven by algorithms, according to Aite Group. This figure is expected to reach 50% by 2010, according to Aite.[37]

Figure 5.1 Percentages of Equities Trading Volume Driven by Algorithmic Trading

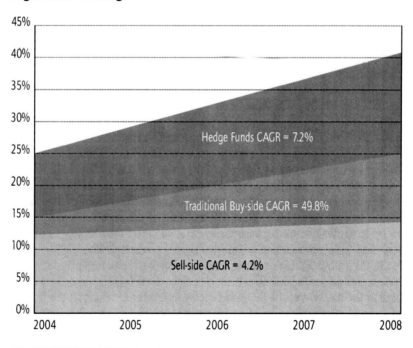

37 Iran Daily, "The Ultimate Money Machine", Economic Focus, 7 May 2007.

In 2006, at the London Stock Exchange, over 40% of all orders were entered by algo traders. American markets and equity markets generally have a higher proportion of algo trades than other markets, and estimates for 2008 range as high as an 80% proportion in some markets. Foreign exchange markets also have active algo trading (about 25% of orders in 2006).[38] Futures and options markets are considered to be fairly easily integrated into algorithmic trading,[39] with about 20% of the options volume expected to be computer generated by 2010.[40] Bond markets are moving towards more access to algorithmic traders.[41]

Trading in CFDs

Trading in contracts for difference, frequently referred to as CFDs, is becoming increasingly popular among both institutional and private traders because of the flexibility they offer. CFD trading is a speculative instrument for trading shares, indices, futures and commodities. It is a retail-level market derivative utilised by traders for its leverage advantages. CFDs are also known as equity swaps in the institutional marketplace.

What is a CFD?

A CFD is an arrangement made in a futures contract whereby differences in set-tlement are made through cash payments, rather than the delivery of physical goods or securities. (Investopedia)

Another interesting definition is:

A CFD is an agreement between the investor and the dealer or broker who pro-vides contracts for difference to reconcile the difference between the opening and the closing price of a CFD trade position of an investor. The overall agree-ment is done on a cash basis.

Trading in CFDs is akin to trading in ordinary shares. A trader can trade any quantity of CFDs they desire, in much the same way as conventional share trad-ing, at the price quoted by CFD providers, which is the same as the underlying market price. These providers charge a commission on trades and the total value of any transaction is basically the number of CFDs bought or sold multiplied by the market price.

---

38 Heather Timmons. "A London Hedge Fund That Opts for Engineers, Not MBAs", New York Times, 18 August 2006.

39 The Economist, (April 2007), "It's all Derivative", Market View. Available from www.economist.com/finance/displaystory.cfm?story_id=E1_JDNPSDQ.

40 The Economist, (June 2007), "The best newsreaders may soon be computers". Available from http://www.economist.com/finance/displaystory.cfm?story_id=9370718.

41 Paul Temperton, "Trading with the Help of 'Guerrillas' and 'Snipers'", Financial Times, 19 March 2007.

However, there are some distinct differences from trading ordinary shares that have made them increasingly popular as an alternative instrument to speculate on the movements of shares or indices.

Advantages of CFDs
- Traders can maximise trading capital as CFDs are traded on margin.
- Traders can trade CFDs long or short to profit from rising and falling markets.
- Risks can be managed by using "Stop Losses" and "Limit" orders.

CFD Trading Strategies
- **Going long** – Using the long strategy with CFDs would benefit the trader with any positive move of the underlying stock. If the trader rolled a long position into the next trading day, they would need to pay the amount borrowed at the going interest rate plus a fee (usually an additional percentage) to the CFD provider.
- **Going short** – Traders can also benefit from the fall of the underlying share price without too many complications by using a CFD short strategy which entails selling shares to enter the trade hoping the shares will fall in price. Short positions usually pay out interest daily on rolling positions. If there are dividend payments, the holder of the stock pays the amount to the CFD provider.
- **Hedging** – This allows the trader to change the risk profile of any holdings they may have. By use of the hedging strategy, the trader essentially offsets an existing stock position to reduce the market risk. This course of action will temporarily reduce the trader's exposure to a stock price movement without the full sale of the underlying stock.
- **Index constituent changes** – Traders use this CFD trading strategy by either shorting or going long on the underlying index. This is a very favourable strategy, especially when the companies included in an index are shifting and being reweighted.

Typical CFD Long Trade
Stephanie Ordar, a trader at BizGroup, believes the price of Vodafone shares will rise and so decides to pursue a long strategy using CFDs. At 10.00 (GMT) on 10 Dec 2007, she receives a quote of a bid price of 140.35p and an offer price of 140.9p for these CFDs. She buys 7,000 VOD.L CFDs at the offer price of 140.9p.

Total face value of the CFDs is £9,863.00.
Initial margin (10%) is £986.30
Commission on the trade (0.2%) is £19.73

A week later Stephanie Ordar's prediction was proved right and Vodafone rose to 145 – 145.5 so she decided to close their position by selling 7,000 Vodafone CFDs at 145p (bid price). The commission on the trade at 0.2% was £20.30.
Stephanie Ordar's profit from the trading strategy is as follows:

Level on 10th December	140.9p
Level on 17th December	145.0p
Difference	4.1p
CFD market (4.1 x7,000)	£287.00

Overall Profit

In order to calculate the overall profit, the commission and financing charges on the deal should be factored in.

Profit on trade	£287.00
Commission	-£40.03
Financing charge*	-£12.50
Overall profit on the trade	£234.47

*Incurred because of the long position

Trading of Structured Products

Structured products are popular with investors when there are high levels of volatility in the stock markets. Anxious investors tend to cash in their equity investments and seek to minimise their exposure to risk by taking refuge in lower-risk asset classes. Innovative financial products such as structured products seem to be the logical choice in these circumstances. For this reason, trading of structured products has become increasingly popular among broker–dealers such as major investment banks.

What are Structured Products?

Structured products are financial products designed to facilitate highly customised risk-return objectives. They are typically a fixed-term investment that offers investors a predefined return based on an index – such as the FTSE or S&P 500 – or a basket of indices over a three- or five-year period. There is usually a guarantee that the original capital will be repaid at maturity.

The implications are that should the index rise at the end of the period, the investment will mirror a fraction of the rise in the particular index. Similarly, in the event of a fall in the value of the underlying investment, the investors still get most of the capital back at the end of the term.

Investors are keen on structured products because they can provide access to markets with a degree of capital protection in the event that they go down and, in addition, they are able to provide upside gearing – or extra growth – for investors who are of the opinion that the markets are going up.

Features of Structured Products

- Investors do not receive dividends from structured investments linked to equities.
- Given that investment terms are usually three to five years and that most

77

structured products do not have any sort of secondary market, investors are committed for the duration.
▓ Structured products are less popular with investors when equities markets are doing well, given the high price for the guarantees that structured investments give.
▓ Structured products are slightly similar to insurance. This is because the cost of the capital protection they offer usually sacrifices dividend income, and perhaps even some of the potential upside.
▓ The majority of structured products on the market are from high investment-grade issuers such as global financial institutions. Therefore, the credit quality of an issuer is a risk that is associated with structured products.

Structured products, having enjoyed a degree of popularity in Europe, are now gaining traction in the USA. They are accessible to retail investors just as stocks and bonds are. According to industry experts, the ability of structured products to provide customised exposure, including to otherwise hard-to-reach asset classes and subclasses and areas such as emerging regions, makes structured products a beneficial complement to the conventional components of diversified portfolios.

The figures from Blue Sky Asset Management in 2008 show that total sales of structured investments in the first six months of 2008 in the USA were $27.6 billion, in Asia excluding Japan $84.2 billion, and in Europe €127 billion.[42]

Emergence of Retail FX Trading

The popularity of global currency trading has soared in recent times as investors have sought to profit from exchange rate fluctuations. The extent of the popularity of trading in FX from a retail perspective is exemplified by recent reports of housewives in Japan casually gambling the Japanese yen in exchange for much higher interest rates from a multitude of currencies ranging from the Turkish lira to the Bahraini dinar.

In financial markets, the retail FX market is a subset of the larger foreign exchange market. Industry estimates show that as of June 2008, around $3.2 trillion was traded on the foreign exchange each day, making it the world's most liquid financial market. This market is estimated to be growing 30% a year, attracting investors who are looking to exploit the fast pace of the markets and the opportunity to make substantial returns in a short space of time.

Definition of Retail FX and Retail Investor
Retail FX can be defined as the sale of foreign exchange products and services directly to the private customer. (Deutsche Bank)

42 Esther Shaw, "In Volatile Times there are Still Investments that Offer a Safe Haven", City A.M., 1 August 2008.

A retail investor is an individual who buys and sells securities on their own behalf – not for an organisation. Retail investors (non-professional investors) typically trade in much smaller quantities than institutional investors. Retail customers define the end of the distribution chain. (Deutsche Bank)

Retail FX Market

According to the Aite Group, the retail FX market grew quickly between 2001 and 2007 (see Figure 5.2) despite a slow start in the mid- to late-1990s. In 2001, the estimated average daily trade volume in the retail market stood at US$10 billion, representing 0.8% of the overall FX market. By the end of 2006, the average daily trade volume reached over US$60 billion, representing over 2% of the entire market, signalling plenty of room for future growth.[43]

The success of the retail FX firms mainly responsible for this stellar growth depends on their ability to develop and support reliable and comprehensive front-to-back office operations. Another reason cited for this growth is the advancement in internet technology, which has allowed for 24-hour trading.

Banks are now increasingly attracted to the growth in this space, which is seen as a good sign for existing players as banks can help enhance the profile of retail FX in the minds of investors and provide the necessary legitimacy for the industry. According to industry reports, major banks such as Citi, Goldman Sachs, UBS, Deutsche Bank, and ABN Amro have entered the market with online FX trading platforms.

The growth of the retail FX market shows no sign of abating as a number of leading global retail FX firms are introducing market products and offerings that will further enhance access and acceptance of the retail FX space.

Figure 5.2 Estimated Average Daily Trade Volume in Retail FX

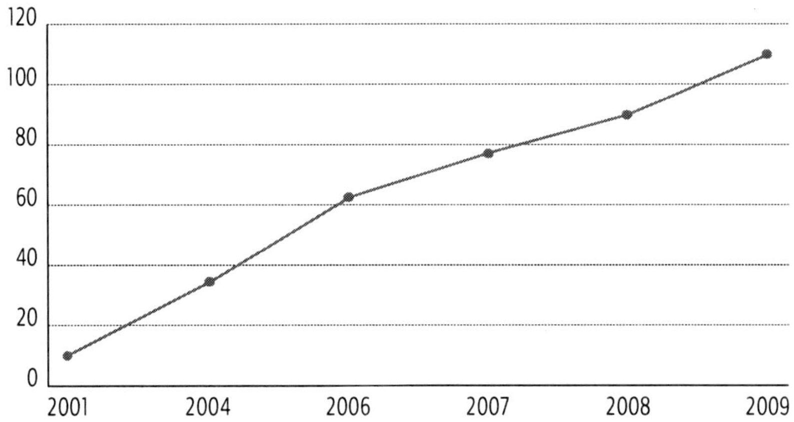

Source: Aite Group

---

43   Aite Group, (2007), "Retail FX Market: The Next Frontier", Report 200707161.

Trading Strategies

Currency traders adopt three main strategies described as follows:

1. **The Carry** – Traders who use this strategy sell currencies with low interest rates and buy those with high rates.
2. **The Momentum** – This strategy is used to track the direction of currency markets.
3. **The Value Trade** – This is a value-based strategy whereby the trader takes a view on the currency's value.

There are literarily hundreds of currency pairs that can be traded in the foreign exchange markets, each of which have their own characteristics and considerations that traders understand and analyse. Analysis of a currency pair considers its liquidity, transaction costs (the spread) and its volatility.

As a general rule, major currencies typically have better liquidity, tighter spread and lower volatility; whereas that same general rule holds that emerging market currencies have poor liquidity and more volatile movements.[44]

Impact of Technology

As technology has become an enabler for competitive pricing as well as a sophisticated margin/credit facility, it has also become a major catalyst to broaden the appeal of FX. At the same time, technology also plays a key role in helping retail FX providers differentiate their service levels. Some providers also use technology to tie into bigger financial institutions, such as banks, to enhance liquidity that can enable them to increase the amount they can offer per trade to their retail customers.

The Arrival of Mobile Trading

The use of wireless technology for trading in the industry will be a revolution. Combined with automated trading, it would allow retail FX traders to make the most of the round-the-clock nature of FX trading.

Popularity of Spread Betting

Once a niche sector of the trading industry, spread betting – which is essentially gambling on the direction of shares, commodities or stock market indices – is becoming increasingly popular, especially among ordinary investors.

The spread-betting industry thrives on downward market movements, providing opportunities for traders to make large gains over very short periods. Unlike traditional equity trades, spread betting allows traders to profit when markets fall. If they manage to bet on the correct direction a stock or index is heading, they can reap instant benefits. In recent times, spread betters have used short positions to hedge other equity investments in order to reduce the effects of any market falls on their overall portfolios.

44 Katie Hope, "Why Japanese Housewives go Crazy for Forex", *City A.M.*, 25 June 2008.

A typical example is how spread betters profited on events surrounding the movement of the Dow Jones Index on Friday, 29 February 2008. On the night of 28 February, the index closed at just under 12,600 points following a slight correction and days of strong gains. Many investors were of the opinion that it was therefore due to fall.

Given that by the close of Friday the index had fallen by 315 points, traders that took a short position could have made over £600 if they had bet a minimum of £2 a point.

How does Spread Betting work?

A spread-betting company quotes a bid (selling) and offer (selling) price for an index, say the FTSE 100:

- Bid price – 5012
- Offer price – 5014
- Spread 2 points (difference between the bid and offer price)

A trader takes the view that the index will rise and "buys" at £20 a point at 5014. Their strategy is to allow their bet to run until the market closes in the hope that the FTSE will rise. If the FTSE should indeed rise to, say, 5,059, the trader will make a profit from the difference between the closing price of 5,059 and the opening price that they were quoted (5,014) times £10, giving a total of £450. If the trader were to bet that the market would fall, they could sell at 5012 in the hope that it would drop below this level.

One of the major differences between trading the stock market and spread betting is that with spread betting, the trader doesn't actually own the shares, they just bet on the performance of the share price. For this reason, capital gains tax does not apply to gains from spread betting.

Rise of Fixed-Odds Betting

Fixed-odds betting, also referred to as binary betting, is another form of financial betting that is becoming increasing popular in the financial markets. As a trading opportunity, it is newer than spread betting. Industry experts have likened the difference between the two to the difference between limit and no-limit poker: limit and fixed odds provide the trader with a lot more control over their potential risk while still having the opportunity to make substantial profits.

With fixed-odds financial betting, a trader can bet on movements in an ever-widening range of assets. These include individual shares, equity indices, commodities and exchange rates.

How does Fixed-Odds Betting Work?

The mechanics of fixed-odds betting are akin to those of basic sports betting. They entail risking an amount of money on a particular outcome of a particular event, such as an index price or the exchange rate of a currency pair going

81

above or below a particular level. If the outcome is as predicted, the trader receives a payout from the book-keeper (provider) according to the odds quoted when they placed the bet.

The above description highlights the difference between fixed-odds betting and spread betting. With spread betting, the amounts that can be won are unlimited. In the same vein, the amounts that can be lost are limitless. However, with fixed-odds financial betting, the losses cannot exceed the initial stake.

The following is a typical dataset that could be used for fixed-odds betting on a currency pair, such as GBP/JPY, on a certain date, such as 9 August 2008.

Data	Typical value
I wish to win	GBP 1,000
If in	10 days time (19-Aug-08)
The (currency pair)	GBP/JPY
Is (higher/lower)	Higher
Than	211.90

How are Fixed-Odds Bets Quoted?

Fixed-odds financial bets work on the same principles as wagers on sporting events. A trader can bet on the price of a certain stock, such as IBM, attaining whatever price by a certain date at the same odds as, say, a bet on Manchester United Football club to defeat Real Madrid at 7/1. However, despite the odds being 7/1, the trader will not see them quoted in this format. Instead, the trader is informed that they stand to win that multiple of their stake. Therefore, for a £50 bet, they will be told they will make a profit of £200 or a net return of 400%.

Popular Fixed-Odds Bets

- **One Touch bet** – The concept of this type of bet is based on a price hitting a certain level once within a certain period. A typical example for a one touch bet would be if a trader, Mr James Bett, expects the price of a commodity such as gold to reach $1,200 within a certain time frame on the basis of his chart analysis, factoring in a weakening dollar and strong demand and also the rising cost of oil. The current price on the date, 8 July 2008, that the trader decides on his bet is $1,190.00. The trader states that he wants to win £100 if at some time before close of trading on 22 July 2008, the price of gold reaches $1,200 an ounce.

    High-powered software using mathematical formulae works out the cost of this bet to be £91.95. In other words, this is the amount Mr Bett needs to put down to get back the £100 in the event that his bet is successful. The winnings on the bet are therefore £8.05, which is equivalent to about 9% return.

    If the price of gold drops to, say, $1,000 on, say, the 10th of July, the likelihood that the trader will win decreases. The options are either to close the bet or salvage the "remnants" of the stake or pin his hopes on the possibility that the price will bounce up to $1,200 by the end of the bet.

■ **No Touch bet** – This is based on the concept that a price will not hit a certain level by a certain date. This is the opposite of the One Touch bet.

■ **Double Touch bet** – The concept underpinning the double touch type of fixed-odds betting is that of the expectation that a price will hit two particular levels by a certain date. It is popular with traders when markets are volatile. As the name implies, it is basically two One Touch bets rolled together. The bet is on a price hitting two levels – one above and one below – as opposed one level.

■ **Bull and Bear bet** – The concept underpinning this type of bet is that a price, "Bull", will be above a certain price at expiry and the "Bear" price will be below a certain level at expiry.

One of the obvious benefits of fixed-odds betting is the opportunity it affords traders to trade assets they do not own and hence not have to pay any capital gains tax on profits from the bets.

Increasing Popularity of Direct Market Access

Direct market access tools allow traders and investors to trade directly on stock exchanges' electronic order books. Direct market access can be defined as the option for clients to send orders electronically by means of order routing to a marketplace without manual intervention from a trading desk. DMA allows the individual to decide on an investment strategy as well as match buyers and sellers via specific destinations on not only exchanges but also on electronic communication networks.

There are, however, two distinct types of DMA models observed in the trading industry, described as follows:

■ **The "traditional" model**: This requires the client to transmit their order first to a clearing firm's centralised order routing system which then delivers it to the appropriate exchange. This was the initial step in removing the need for a telephone call to place the order. The process has been further enhanced by various innovations for the smooth routing of the order through the clearer's own infrastructure.

■ **"Pure" DMA model**: This model is becoming increasingly significant and is driven by the dominant hedge funds and proprietary trading groups. It involves the elimination of the intermediary's "plumbing" and goes direct to the exchange's trading platform, thus reducing latency.[45] This is particularly essential for sophisticated "black-box" trading strategies, which are dependent on speedy execution for their success.

45 The responsiveness or "turnaround time" for an order on a trade execution venue.

Key Benefits of DMA

The key benefits of DMA from an exchange perspective are:

- **equality of orders placed** – each and every order is of equal status and prioritisation is only on the basis of price and time;
- **visibility** – all market participants make a full contribution to central market liquidity as orders are visible to the entire market;
- **the depth of order book** – DMA allows visibility of the number of buyers versus the number of sellers and prices at which they are willing to trade;
- **price setting** – limit orders can be entered at the price of the trader's choosing and be available to the entire market;
- **tighter spreads** – given the public display of limit orders as opposed to these being held privately, market spreads become narrower, providing the order placer with a higher chance of getting their trades executed at the price, and the market possesses a tighter public price which traders can use as a reference;
- **auction participation** – DMA allows participation in the pre-market and post-market auctions where the highest or lowest price regularly arises;
- **regulation and market supervision** – participants have peace of mind as the exchanges regulate and supervise the marketplace;
- **availability of order book** – availability of the order book is guaranteed during trading hours.

Impact of DMA on the Trading Industry

In the USA, there has been a rapid adoption of DMA by institutional investors in recent times. It is routinely used as a panacea to the fragmentation of liquidity across execution venues in this region. It is also increasingly popular with the buy side of the trading industry that is seeking best execution and wants greater control over its strategies as a result of regulatory pressures. The overriding advantage of DMA is the opportunity it affords the trader to rent a broker's infrastructure and use the broker's clearing facilities, and still be able to control the order. The cheaper commission associated with DMA trading – 1 cent a share compared with 2 cents a share for program trading[46] and 4 cents per share for block trading[47] – makes DMA trading an attractive option for the buy side.[48]

Some industry experts estimate that by 2008, 38% of buy-side shares will be executed via DMA, up from 34% in 2004. Others predict DMA flow in the US market will increase to 20% of equities share volume by 2010, gradually replacing manual executions. In Europe, DMA flow for equities is expected to grow from 8% of traded value as of 2008 to 15% in 2011.

Among the earliest and still the major adopters of DMA are hedge funds, with industry observers describing their use of this technology as "aggressive".

---

46 The use of computers by institutional investors to trade large volumes of securities.
47 Trading of a block of shares in quantities of 10,000 or more.
48 Schmerken, I., "Direct Market Access Trading". Wall Street and Technology, 4 Feb. 2005.

Figure 5.3 Growth of US DMA vs Overall Equities Share Volume (2002–2010)

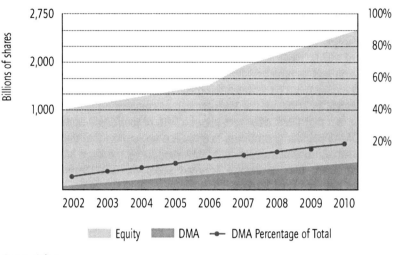

Source: Celent

In its earlier form, DMA was mostly associated with a small but prominent sector of the hedge fund industry that conducted statistical arbitrage.[49] This subsector aggressively exploits even the slightest movement in prices away from market efficiency,[50] resulting in profits attributable to the speed of execution as well as the amount of the securities traded. The use of sophisticated systems have made it possible to take advantage of these small yet transitory movements. It also removes the need for human intervention and allows the funds to rapidly strike on predictable correlation between instruments.

It is safe to conclude that without DMA the development of statistical arbitrage funds would have been impossible as a statistical arbitrage trading strategy is highly specialised and dependent on intensive statistical analysis, proprietary mathematical trading models and, naturally, sophisticated trading systems.

DMA has, nowadays, gone mainstream owing to the increasing demand for execution services and the growth of thriving statistical arbitrage funds that are getting the best out of the technology. The hedge fund universe as a whole has adopted DMA, hence it is no longer the exclusive preserve of these overly accurate clandestine trades.

49 Statistical arbitrage is a type of hedge fund strategy.
50 Market efficiency refers to the notion that prices on traded assets, e.g. stocks, bonds, or property, already reflect all known information.

Hedge funds' demand for DMA stems from their requirement for high-speed, low-cost access and the ability to run their own technical models. Regional brokers in different countries who, under MiFiD, are required to give their clients access not just to one local market but also to others quoting the same stock are also fuelling the demand for DMA.

In Europe, the spotlight is increasingly on the cost of execution with the advent of MiFiD. Experts opine that the regulatory requirement to unbundle commission and to report to the client the amount of money spent on execution and money spent on research has given more focus to the cost of execution and research. In addition, the transparency of commission spend has emphasised the fact that DMA only costs about a fifth of traditional trading methods.

As DMA's popularity continues to grow, it is no surprise that there have been notable acquisitions of independent DMA vendors by the large broker–dealers. In recent times, BNY Brokerage acquired Sonic Financial Technologies and CitiGroup acquired Lava Trading.

Popularity of Day Trading

Day trading involves trading securities during the trading day but closing all positions by the end of the day with a view to making a profit from the difference between the buying price and the selling price. The trader, a more accurate description than investor, will not have any holdings or short positions to carry forward to the next day.

Day trading can be further subdivided into a number of styles, including the following:

- **Scalpers**: A style of day trading that involves the rapid and repeated buying and selling of a relatively large volume of stocks within seconds or minutes. The aim is to earn a small per share profit on each transaction and at the same time minimise the risk.
- **Momentum traders**: This style of day trading entails seeking out and trading stocks that are in a moving pattern during the day, in an attempt to buy such stocks at bottom prices and sell at top prices.

Day trading is most commonly associated with individual investors, although the proprietary trading operations of investment banks do often day trade as well. However, compared to traders at investment banks, individual investors have much less access to information, much less sophisticated systems and much less support in terms of research and trading systems. These are all crucial elements that ensure the success of short-term trading. In addition, these banks can trade far more cheaply than private investors.

The cost of trading is a major stumbling block for day traders. This is because the returns that are needed to cover trading costs are huge if one considers that the profit has to be made in a short period of time, i.e. in a matter of hours.

Day trading is a very high-risk strategy that requires the expenditure of considerable time. While some investors make spectacular returns from day trading, just as many make spectacular losses. The two are often the same people, as it is common knowledge that investors may be lucky for a while and then, confident in their ability to make money by day trading, keep putting their money back in, and eventually make large losses.

Contrary to the popular perception, there are many different markets available for day trading including futures, options, currencies and stock markets. Most people are aware of the stock markets, but few non-traders are aware of the many other markets that are available to day traders, many of which are much more popular than the stock markets.

All of the day-trading markets are provided via exchanges such as the following:

- CME (Chicago Mercantile Exchange) in the USA
- CBOT (Chicago Board of Trade) in the USA
- DTB (Deutsche Bourse) in Europe
- MONEP (Euronext Paris) in Europe

The exchanges set the contract specifications for the markets, and process all of the trades on their markets. The exchanges can be accessed directly, but day traders usually use direct access brokerages, which allow the day trader to access all of the different exchanges directly but via the same trading interface.

Day trading has been gaining popularity in leaps and bounds in recent years with the advent of improved communication technology, affordable computers, the lure of large, intraday price swings and competitive commission.

In Japan, for instance, not so long ago there were reports of a 40% rise in the leading stock index, the Nikkei 225, over a six-month period, attributed to the surging popularity of day trading by investors. The Japanese dealers association claimed that despite the absence of internet trading before 1999, 29% of all equity trades in Japan between March and September 2005 were traded on the internet. By September 2005, the association also reported that there were 7.9 million accounts at Japan's electronic brokerage firms, up from 296,941 in 1999, when the first type of firm opened.[51]

Day trading was also popular in the USA in the late 1990s, but the popularity waned when the telecom and dot-com bubble burst and traders suffered substantial losses. The erstwhile bull market in these types of stock turned, and overleveraged speculators offloaded their holdings, hastening and exaggerating the decline in prices.

Nevertheless, day trading has its benefits. These benefits of stock trading, for instance, include the following:

51 Fackler, M., "In Japan, Day Trading like its 1999", *New York Times*, 19 February 2006.

■ Traders do not have to be concerned with overnight news as they are completing trading within the span of a single day. They are aware of their profits and losses at the end of the day.

■ There are no risks of riding losses since traders finish off their trading activities within a day and avoid losing more the next day as they don't hold on to their stocks. Therefore, if any of the stock that the traders had held suffers significant losses over a few days, they are not affected to a great extent.

■ Traders are able to capture large price swings as they are focused on the anticipation of news or events that result in this large price swing on a particular stock.

■ There is instant feedback on the state of the trader's trading revenue as they are buying and selling the same shares in a single day. Traders are aware of how much they have on a given day.

Popularity of Swing Trading

Swing trading is, quite simply, a style of trading that attempts to capture gains in a stock within one to four days. Swing traders typically employ technical analysis to seek stocks with short-term price momentum. The emphasis is on the price pattern of the stocks as opposed to fundamental or intrinsic value.

Difference between Swing Trading and Day Trading

The main difference between day trading and swing trading is that swing traders will normally have a slightly longer time horizon than day traders for holding a position in a stock. Like day traders, swing traders also attempt to predict the short-term fluctuation in a stock's price. However, swing traders choose the option of holding stocks for more than one day, if necessary, to give the stock price some time to move or to capture additional momentum in the stock's price. Swing traders, in practice, hold on to their stock positions anywhere from 1 to 15 days.

It is well known in the industry that swing trading has the capability of providing higher returns than day trading. However, unlike day traders who liquidate their positions at the end of each day, swing traders assume overnight risk. There are some significant risks in carrying positions overnight. For example, news events and earnings warnings announced after the closing bell can result in large, unexpected and possibly adverse changes to a stock's price.

The following are simple rules that underpin swing trading:

■ choice of trading style;
■ matching of trading style to objective;
■ matching of broker to trading style;
■ use of a low-risk, high-reward trading method;
■ ensuring that trading method works in all markets;
■ trading of the best stocks.

A swing trader generally aims for a 10–15% return on all trades.

The Emergence of Liquidity Pools

The emergence of dark liquidity pools has been a threat to traditional exchanges in recent times. The advent of best execution regulations such as Regulation NMS in the USA and MiFID in Europe is partly responsible for dark liquidity sources emerging in increasing numbers to provide the required anonymity and liquidity for block trade execution.

The following is a definition of dark liquidity pools by the *Financial Times*:

Dark liquidity pools are private interbank or intrabank platforms that are widely used to trade stocks away from exchanges. They are widely used by clients such as hedge funds to buy and sell large blocks of shares in anonymity, avoiding the risk of moving the public price of a stock on an exchange as a result of copycatting by other traders.[52]

Sources of dark liquidity include alternative trading systems (ATS), crossing networks and other dark pools. The main difference between these systems and conventional liquidity sources such as stock exchanges is that trades on these systems draw their prices from the market. Differentiation among dark pools is on the basis of type of liquidity, timing and level of transparency. It is worthwhile to note that while such decentralised pools of liquidity provide anonymity, they also create fragmentation and the associated price transparency is minimal.

Dark liquidity provides funding for trading in most asset classes including equities and fixed income and is an essential source of liquidity for trading activities.

As stated earlier, the popularity of dark liquidity sources is partly due to the best execution regulations. In the USA, for example, prior to the introduction of Regulation NMS, the Securities and Exchange Commission (SEC) introduced rules that were intended to modernise and strengthen the regulatory structure of the equity markets in the country and allowed exchanges to provide a centralised marketplace with the requisite liquidity for buyers and sellers to fulfil block trades. With the introduction of Regulation NMS, there is a requirement for trades to be executed at the national best bid or offer (NBBO) for any given security, which requires publishing quotes.

However, Regulation NMS does not require dark pools to publish quotes, hence traders use them to maintain anonymity and to make sure that there is minimal leakage of information. For instance, ATSs are not required to print quotes unless they accrue more that 5% of US equity volume.

In Europe, dark liquidity pools are expected to increase in number as trades can now be executed on other trading venues apart from traditional stock exchanges. The best execution regulation, i.e. MiFID, requires traders to search for the best bid or offer price of any given security and also supports the exploration of all liquidity sources in the bid to achieve best execution.

52 Gangahar, A, and Grant, J. "Responding to Liquidity Pools", the *Financial Times*, 23 June 2008.

The following figures depict the relevance of dark pools in the financial markets:[53]

■ In 2006, dark pools and crossing networks captured nearly 10% of the total equity market, with an average of 420 million shares executed per day.
■ The figure above is expected to increase to 512 million shares by the end of 2007.
■ Growing at 42% compound annual rate, the volume of dark liquidity trades could triple to 1.5 billion a day by 2010, a level equalling more than 15% of total equity share.

An interesting development in the marketplace is the response of traditional exchanges to the threat of liquidity pools. As exchanges are under persistent pressure to seek out the best ways to accommodate new types of traders beyond the simple flow of trading activities from brokers on behalf of large institutional clients, they are nowadays offering – or planning to offer – their own platforms that are similar to dark pools.

This development may result in consolidation of dark pools or even the acquisition a number of dark pools by some of the larger exchanges. Some industry observers believe that consolidation in the dark pool space could lead to the creation of structures that may apply for exchange status, posing a further threat to the exchanges.

The Emergence of E-minis

The trading of e-minis involves the buying and selling of stock index futures within a single day, or intraday using a computerised system. It involves the use of real-time market data, via the internet, to determine buy and sell signals, and orders that can be placed electronically via the internet with no middleman or broker intervention in the process of order execution.

The "e" in the name stands for electronic, which implies trading does not take place in a trading pit, but rather trade is strictly electronic. The term "mini" refers to the contracts being smaller than the original pit-traded contracts.

E-minis are popular with active traders who want to trade electronically, and seek maximum control in addition to best profit potential. Trading the e-mini index futures has become a way of life for many traders. These futures are advantageous due to no Pattern Day Trading Rule, plenty of volatility, tight spreads between the bid/ask, the fact that they can be sold just as easily as bought, plus low margin requirements that allow almost any trader to participate.

53 Jerome Johnson and Larry Tabb, (January 2007), "Navigating Crossing Networks and Other Dark Pools of Liquidity".

The e-minis market is traded by many people including amateur and professional traders as well as pivot traders,[54] gap traders[55] and pit traders.[56]

Definition of E-mini

An e-mini is a futures contract that can be traded electronically on the Chicago Mercantile Exchange (CME) and is based on the S&P 500 index,[57] as opposed to normal S&P futures contracts.

Some Benefits of Trading E-minis

- E-minis offer a fast and efficient opportunity to trade the benchmark S&P 500 Index (and the underlying 500 large-cap US issues) with a single contract.
- The smaller contract size of e-minis makes them suitable for a broad range of individual and institutional customer needs.
- They accommodate a variety of strategies, such as hedging, to defend against adverse price movements, spreading with other stock-index futures and gaining broad market exposure. This can aid in the minimising of losses for small investors.
- The costs associated with trading e-minis are lower than those of trading a basket of equities or exchange-traded funds (ETFs).
- E-minis offer substantial liquidity and tight bid/ask spreads.
- The e-mini S&P is traded on the Chicago Mercantile Exchange (CME) GLOBEX platform. This ensures speed, reliability, anonymity and global trading around the clock.

Comparison of Margins for Full-sized Futures Contracts and Mini Futures Contracts (E-minis)

Just like full-sized futures contracts, e-minis have margin requirements. For readers that are not aware, margin is collateral that the holder of a position in futures contracts has to deposit to cover the credit risk of their counterparty (most often their broker). The collateral can be in the form of cash or securities, and it is deposited in a margin account. On US futures exchanges, "margin" was formerly called performance bond.

Tables 5.1 and 5.2 show a comparison between the margin requirements for full-size futures contracts and e-minis.

54 Pivot traders are traders who use pivot points in their trading strategies. Pivot points are support and resistance levels derived from the previous period's high, low and closing values. There are a variety of pivot values with which to trade, including monthly, weekly and daily values.
55 Traders that adopt the gap trading strategy, i.e. exploiting the change in price levels of a security between the close and open of two consecutive days.
56 Traders that trade in person using the open outcry method at the trading floor, in the designated area for this particular market, called a pit.
57 The S&P 500 is a stock market index containing the stocks of 500 Large-Cap corporations, most of which are of US origin.

Table 5.1 Margins for Full-sized Futures Contracts

Contract	Exchange	Symbol	Margin
Corn	CBOT	C	$1,350
Dow Jones	CBOT	DJ	$7,005
Gold (Pit)	COMEX	GC	$4,725
Silver (Pit)	COMEX	SI	$4,725
Soybeans	CBOT	S	$2,970
Wheat	CBOT	W	$6,075

Source: Investopedia

Table 5.2 Margins for Mini Futures Contracts

Contract	Exchange	Symbol	Margin
Mini Corn	CBOT	YC	$270
Mini Dow Jones	CBOT	YM	$3,503
Mini Gold (Pit)	CBOT	YG	$1,121
Mini Silver (Pit)	CBOT	YI	$810
Mini Soybeans	CBOT	YK	$594
Mini Wheat	CBOT	YW	$1,215

Source: Investopedia

Case Study

The following case study illustrates how a day trader, Mr Bob Deale, traded e-minis for profit.

Mr Deale's hunch that the markets would rally following a sell-off[58] in the markets for four consecutive days prompted him to trade in e-minis. He chose the option of trading the index futures as opposed to buying the cash index (i.e. through funds). This allowed Mr Deale to trade the index futures, where he had far more margin power and where nearly round-the-clock trading enabled him to make a purchase before the cash market opened. The early morning price was 1341.50, which was 10 points below the S&P 500's opening price.

Mr Deale purchased the e-mini S&P contract as opposed to the regular S&P index contract. The e-mini is a fifth of the contract size, therefore the margin requirements are far less. The margin payment for a single regular S&P contract that is valued at $200 per point, which equates to about $268,000 on a 1341.50 price, is about $20,000. However, an e-mini contract, valued at $40 per point, requires about $4,000 or less if the contract is held overnight. Mr Deale opted to day-trade and purchased 10 specific-date e-mini S&P contracts, and to minimise his losses in the event of his analysis and entry proving ill-timed or faulty, he entered into an intraday protective stop on his e-mini position.

Before the end of the day, Mr Deale disposed of the contracts at more than 20 points as the

58 The quick selling of securities, such as stocks, bonds and commodities. The resultant increase in supply leads to a decline in the value of the security.

e-mini had risen to 1361.85, which was over 20 points above the cash index's closing price for that given day. His profits were thus 20x40x10 which is equal to $8,000.

E-minis are bought and sold at least 500,000 times on a typical trading day. Industry observers believe that e-mini futures trading is one of the fastest selling products available.

The Rise of Exchange-Traded Funds

Industry experts hail exchange-traded funds (ETFs) as a valuable component for any investor's portfolio, from the most experienced institutional fund managers to a novice investor. Other experts opine that ETFs are the hottest investment products of the century. Billions of dollars are reported to be flowing into these funds, and firms are falling over themselves to bring novel ETFs to market. ETFs are also referred to as Spiders, OPALs, iShares, VIPERs, Diamonds, Qubes, StreetTracks and HOLDRs.

What is an ETF?
An ETF is an index investment crossed with an exchange-listed corporate security and open-ended mutual fund. They enable investors to trade "the market" with a single investment as easily as if they were buying an individual stock. ETFs represent ownership of a portfolio of common stocks that closely track the performance of a specific index, either broad market, sector or international. In an active secondary market, individual investors can buy and sell as little as a single ETF share during trading hours.[59]

Most ETFs are unit investments trusts, which are essentially investment companies with a finite life that raise capital from investors and use the proceeds to buy a fixed portfolio of securities. Trading of ETFs occurs throughout the day over an exchange, and investors are able to buy and sell shares via a broker or in a brokerage account just as they would shares of any publicly traded company. ETFs have relatively low expense ratios[60] when compared with index mutual funds and open-ended mutual funds.

Fund Category	Average Expense Ratio
Open-ended mutual funds	1.34%
Index mutual funds	0.65%
Exchange-traded funds	0.52%

Source: Morningstar Database

59 Phyllis J. Bernstein, (Jan 2002), "A Primer on Exchange-Traded Funds". Available from www.aicpa.lorg/PUBS/JOFA/jan2002/bern.htm.
60 The measurement of the cost of operating a mutual fund. An expense ratio is calculated annually by dividing a fund's operating expenses by the average dollar value of its assets under management.

Background

ETFs are new when compared to the relatively established mutual funds. The first US ETFs were created by State Street Global Advisors, with the launch in 1993 of Standard and Poor's Depository Receipt Trust, called SPDR 500 ("Spiders"). In 1994, Morgan Stanley created OPALs, which stands for Optimised Portfolio of Listed Securities and is listed on the Luxembourg Stock Exchange. The mid-cap SPDR was created in 1995 and tracks the S&P Mid-CAP 400 Index, while in 1998, Diamonds, which tracks the Dow Jones Industrial Average, was added to the number of ETFs on the market. Other ETFs followed, including Qubes, introduced by NASDAQ to track the NASDAQ 100 Index, and WEBS, which stands for World Equity Benchmark Shares but is now known as iShares.

Creation

The trigger for creating ETFs is the anticipated demand for a fund to track a particular market index such as the NASDAQ 100. When this occurs, an institutional investor or large intermediary such as State Street Global Advisors – referred to as the Authorised Participant (AP) or market maker or specialist – transfers a portfolio of stock that closely approximates the specified index to a fund manager. These APs are middlemen who assemble the appropriate basket of stocks, usually enough to purchase 10,000 to 50,000 shares of the ETF. The fund manager then places the stock in a trust and issues ETF shares to the AP. It is at liberty to hold the new securities or sell them to other investors.

In general, only the major fund management firms, with experience in indexing, can create and manage ETFs. These firms are in constant contact with major investors, pension funds and other fund managers around the world that have the pools of stocks need to create an ETF. The firms also line up customers to buy a newly introduced ETF.

ETF shares are freely traded between investors on traditional exchanges such as the American Stock Exchange, Tokyo Stock Exchange and London Stock Exchange.

Figure 5.4 shows the creation and redemption process for ETFs.

1. The market maker buys a basket of shares (in the stock), as specified by the ETF custodian, and pays cash.
2. This basket of securities is then exchanged with the ETF custodian for a set number of ETF units or shares (creation).
3. The market maker then has an inventory of ETF shares than can be used to satisfy market demand for buy/sell orders.

The minimum size of a basket of shares is called a creation unit.

Redemption is simply this process in reverse. The market maker buys a defined number of ETF shares, forwards them to the custodian and receives an underlying basket of shares which can be sold in two ways:

1. by redeeming the ETF: this involves submission of shares to the ETF fund in exchange for the underlying shares;
2. by selling the ETF for cash in the secondary market.

Figure 5.4 Creation and Redemption Process for ETFs

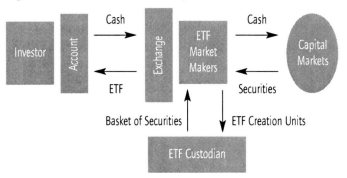

Source: London Stock Exchange

Comparison between ETFs and Mutual Funds

	ETFs	Mutual Funds
Trading	Buy or sell on exchange during trading hours.	Buy or sell at net asset value at the end of the trading day.
Purchase/sale options	Trade only through brokers. Sponsors do not sell shares directly to the public.	Generally available directly from the fund sponsor. Mutual funds are available through brokers.
Expenses	Operating expenses are generally low. Costs to buy or sell are based on brokerage commission rates plus a spread between bid and ask prices.	Mutual funds may be subject to one or more of the following: – a sales load paid to the broker who sold the fund; – exit fees when shares are sold, and referred sales charge intended to discourage frequent trading.
Redemptions	Broker–dealers buy creation blocks, exchanging them for a basket of securities and some cash. This protects other shareholders from a taxable event.	Sponsor sells shares from its portfolio to make cash payments to redeeming shareholders. These transactions typically result in a taxable event to other shareholders.
Dividend distributions	Rarely made.	Typically made quarterly depending on what stock the fund holds.
Commissions/ sales load	Standard brokerage commissions to buy and sell.	Some funds carry a sales load as an adjustment to the purchase price.

Tax consequences	Same as for traditional stocks based on long- or short-term trading period.	Sales taxed like traditional stocks based on investor cost basis and holding period. Mutual fund shareholders also receive dividend and capital gains distributions based on fund holding.

Source: Phyllis J. Bernstein. (Jan 2002). "A Primer on Exchange Traded Funds".

The ETF Market

According to Morgan Stanley, by the end of 2007 there were 1,171 ETFs trading worldwide, with assets approaching $800 billion. In the USA alone, the combined assets of the nation's exchange-traded funds (ETFs) were $578.07 billion as of June 2008, according to the Investment Company Institute. The net value of shares issued and redeemed by all ETFs in the USA was $10.3 billion, while the number of exchange-traded funds by type was 697, also as of June 2008. The breakdown of assets of exchange-traded funds by type and number of exchange-traded funds by type are shown in Figures 5.5 and 5.6 respectively.

Figure 5.5 Breakdown of Assets of Exchange-Traded Funds by Type

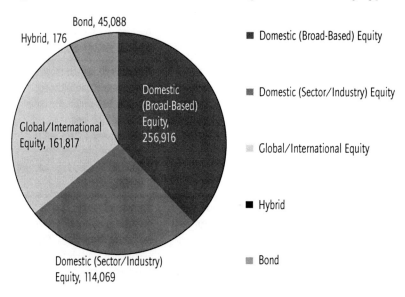

Source: Investment Company Institute

5. Trends in Trading and Exchanges

Figure 5.6 Breakdown of Number of Exchange-Traded Funds by type

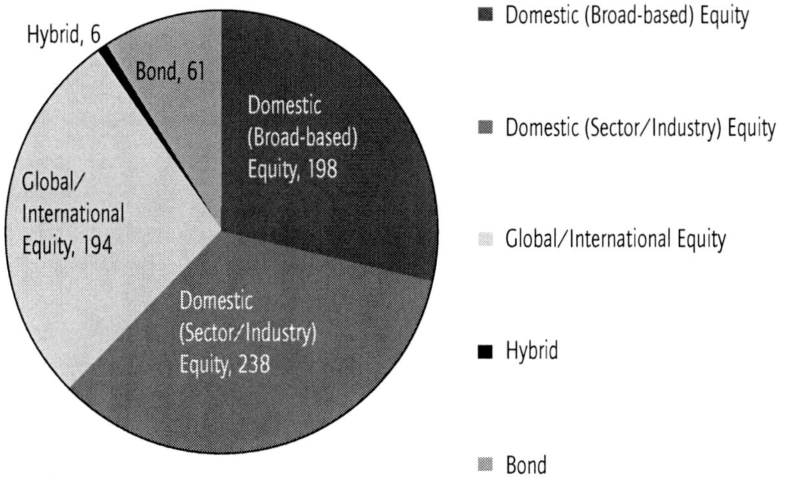

Hybrid, 6
Bond, 61
Domestic (Broad-based) Equity, 198
Global/ International Equity, 194
Domestic (Sector/Industry) Equity, 238

- Domestic (Broad-based) Equity
- Domestic (Sector/Industry) Equity
- Global/International Equity
- Hybrid
- Bond

Source: Investment Company Institute

97

Liquidity and Volatility

This chapter discusses the concepts of liquidity and volatility in trading. Also included is a description of the volatility index.

Introduction

Liquidity plays a vital role in the functioning of financial markets. Markets are liquid when those who have asset holdings can sell them at prices that do not involve considerable losses, so as to gain access to the finance they need to fulfil other commitments. In the light of this, measuring liquidity is almost an impossibility. However, it is well known that a market is more liquid when there are more investors active in that market. Thus, the volume of transactions occurring in a market is an indicator of the extent of liquidity in the system.

Liquidity has various meanings. However, there are three concepts of liquidity that are relevant to the financial markets:

1. Macroeconomic liquidity;
2. Market liquidity;
3. Balance sheet liquidity.

Macroeconomic liquidity has to do with "overall monetary conditions", including interest rates, credit conditions and the growth of monetary and credit aggregates.

Liquidity is essential for the real economy and financial markets to function well; the more liquid the market, the better.[61] Liquidity is important to players in trading for various reasons. Traders are in favour of more liquidity in the markets as it allows them to implement their trading strategies at a cheaper cost. Liquidity is also important to exchanges as it draws traders to their markets. As for regulators, they prefer liquid markets as they are usually less volatile than illiquid ones.

Definition of Liquidity

Market liquidity refers to the extent to which one is able to quickly and easily buy and sell financial assets in the market, without moving the price.[62]

Features of Liquid Markets
A liquid market is one that is:

- **tight** – which implies that the costs of trading small amounts are themselves small, i.e. bid-ask spreads are small;
- **deep** – costs of trading large amounts are small, i.e. big trades do not cause price movements;
- **resilient** – discrepancies between prices and true values for the asset in question are small and corrected quickly;

61 David Longworth, "Liquidity, Liquidity, Liquidity", Thursday, 18 October, 2007. Available from http://liquidityblog.blogspot.com/2007/10/bank-of-canada-liquidity-liquidity.html.
62 Ibid.

■ **desirable** – a highly liquid market is a desirable trading venue as trading costs are low, resulting in an increase in the number of trades being executed on the market. The eventual outcome is increased liquidity, i.e. liquidity leads to liquidity.

On the other hand, an illiquid market is one where market participants will be able to trade securities at prices different from the last traded price. The larger the size of the trade, the further the price will be from the observed price. Large volumes of the security can be traded only with a long time lag.

The Search for Liquidity

Trades occur in financial markets as the successful outcome of a bilateral search for trading partners. The main objective of a trader involved in bilateral searches is to find liquidity. In the event that a buyer finds a seller who is willing to trade at mutually acceptable terms, the buyer has found liquidity. Similarly, should a seller find a buyer who is willing to trade at mutually acceptable terms, the seller has found liquidity.

Bilateral search for liquidity is fundamental to the way trades are conducted. Two factors are essential to the success of bilateral searches:

1. the cost of searching;
2. the availability of trades that match the trader's orders.

Experts identify two types of traders that are in the bilateral search for liquidity: the active trader, who actively searches for liquidity, and the passive trader, who takes a more passive approach and hopes that active traders can find them to match their orders.

Active Traders
Active traders are often impatient traders who think that by entering a trade early they will receive a better price, and therefore make a larger profit. In terms of liquidity, they request liquidity by initiating trades. In terms of cost, however, they have to factor the cost of the potential loss of previous best matches to their orders into the cost of persisting with their search.

Experienced active traders are aware that the cost of additional searches could potentially outweigh the benefits and tend to stop searching before this occurs.

Active traders demand immediacy and push prices in the direction of their trading. In practice, this type of trader typically submits market orders and thus pays a premium for instant execution.

Passive Traders
This type of trader typically displays their interest with a view to attracting active traders. Passive traders normally employ limit orders and supply immedi-

101

acy and stabilise prices. The odds of locating a trading partner typically increase if the passive trader widely and credibly disseminates their interest in trading. The dissemination is normally via quotes and postings of indication on bulletin boards, and in some cases by directly informing their brokers.

In some markets, passive traders tend to commit to trades at the price they post. As a result, their chance of attracting an active trader is greatly enhanced.

Active traders' confidence that they are able to arrange trades with passive traders leads to a reduction in their overall costs.

Dimensions of Liquidity

Despite growing evidence that liquidity matters economically, exactly what liquidity is and how it should be measured remain theoretical questions that are open to debate. There is a notion that is being touted by experts as an answer to these questions, and that is perfect liquidity. An asset is perfectly liquid if one can trade immediately, at a price not worse than the uninformed expected value, the quantity one desires. By the same token, a perfectly liquid market is one where participants would get the same price for a security irrespective of the quantity they traded, irrespective of the time at which they traded and irrespective of whether they bought or sold. All three dimensions of liquidity – time, price and quantity – matter to traders.[63]

One other interesting dimension of liquidity is the availability of credit or the ease with which institutions can lend or borrow money. This is referred to in the industry as funding liquidity. This type of liquidity is also essential in the marketplace as it provides traders with the resources with which to finance trading positions to alleviate the consequences of price shocks and increased liquidity.

Market liquidity captures the aspects of immediacy, breadth or tightness, depth, and resiliency in markets. These aspects are referred to as the dimensions of liquidity. They are briefly described as:

- **tightness** – often measured by the bid/ask spread, and refers to the costs of providing liquidity;
- **depth** – which refers to the maximum size of a trade for any given bid/ask spread;
- **resiliency** – which refers to how quickly prices revert to fundamental values after a large transaction;[64]
- **immediacy** – which refers to the speed with which a trade of a given size and cost can be completed. According to Brady (1989), this seems to have been a problem on the New York Stock Exchange during the stock market crash of October 1987, when orders had to wait up to 75 minutes for execution, apparently due to long printing queues.

63 Laurie Simon Hodrick and Pamela C. Moulton, "Liquidity".
64 Ibid.

The dimensions of market liquidity are illustrated in Figure 6.1.

Figure 6.1 Dimensions of Market Liquidity

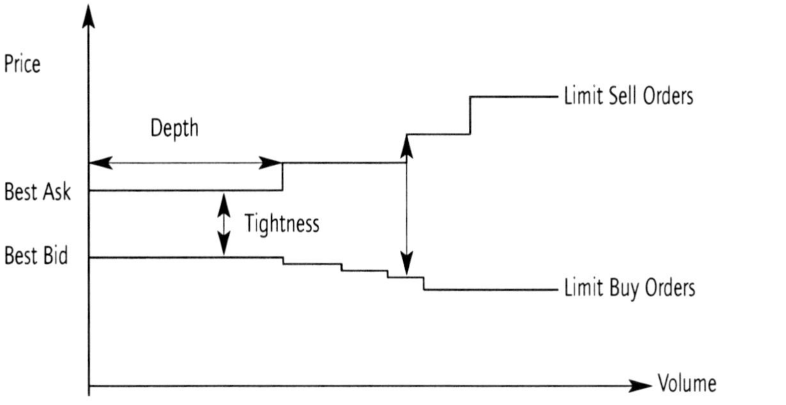

Source: Economic Research Group of Deutsche Bundesbank

In Figure 6.1, tightness is represented by the vertical distance between the lowest ask and the highest bid prices. Market depth is measured on the horizontal axis in order size, and the corresponding spread for the amount is quantified on the vertical axis. Resiliency denotes the speed with which the bid and ask schedules revert to their initial positions following the execution of an order.

Liquidity Demanders and Suppliers

It is often beneficial to describe economic agents or market participants as suppliers or demanders of liquidity. Liquidity supply has traditionally been associated with the "sell side" of the market. Liquidity demanders in this view are therefore the buy side. From a narrower perspective, liquidity supply and demand differentiate participants who are available to trade or offer the option to trade, and those who spontaneously decide to trade. Thus, liquidity suppliers are passive and demanders are active. In any given trade, the active side is the party who seals the deal by accepting the terms offered by the passive side. In other words, the passive side "makes" the market and the active side "takes".

In modern-day financial markets, the role of liquidity demander or supplier is a strategic choice that can be quickly reversed, given the rise of markets that are widely, directly and electronically accessible. Hence, the alignment of liquidity demand and supply with particular institutions is of less significance.

In this section, the contributions of market makers, block traders and arbitrageurs to market liquidity will be discussed.

Market Makers

As seen in Chapter 1, market makers are dealers who quote both a buy and a sell price in the hope of making a profit on the turn or the bid/offer spread. As a result, they usually trade very frequently and often try to buy after they sell, and vice versa. Market makers add to the liquidity and depth of the market by taking a short or long position for a time, thus assuming some risk, in the hope of fulfilling their objective, i.e. making a small profit.

The principle of market making entails taking relatively small inventory positions, given that market makers do not generally know the fundamental values of the instruments that they trade very well. This is crucial, as their exposure to losses in the event that the market moves against them is higher if they take large inventory positions. Market makers attempt to use price discovery in such a way that their order flows are two-sided and balanced.

In terms of liquidity supply, market makers achieve this in the form of immediacy. They usually quote a firm bid and offer for at least a minimum quantity of each security in which they are a market maker. If they are asked to trade larger quantities that would make them uncomfortable with their inventory positions, they demand liquidity from other traders.

Block Traders

Block traders are dealers who take a position in block trades to accommodate customer buyers and sellers of blocks of a large amount of the same security, contract or portfolio of many instruments. Hence, they are suppliers of liquidity to these clients.

In practice, block traders avoid well-informed traders, given that they take large positions and these well-informed traders could be parasitic. Parasitic traders are traders who profit only by exploiting other traders. They use exposed information to create trading strategies that profit at the expense of the exposing traders. They generally do not add value to the market. In particular, parasitic traders neither provide liquidity nor make prices more efficient. Since parasitic traders take from the markets without giving, they tend to degrade them.[65] In order to mitigate this risk, block traders give carefully consideration to the types of trader they deal with. This exercise in caution means that there is no urgency in their trading. They normally do not want to supply liquidity in the form of immediacy, given that impatient traders are usually well informed.

The aspect of liquidity that block traders offer their clients is depth. These traders can offer much larger sizes than market makers can offer, since they know their clients well.

Arbitrageurs

Arbitrageurs are traders who seek to profit from price inefficiencies in the market by making simultaneous trades that offset each other. An arbitrageur would, for

65 Lawrence E. Harris, "Order Exposure and Parasitic Traders", a paper prepared for Deutsche Börse AG Symposium "Equity Market Structure for Large- and Mid-Cap Stocks," Frankfurt, 12 December 1997, p 2.

instance, search for price discrepancies between stocks listed on more than one exchange, then buy the undervalued shares on one exchange while short-selling the same number of overvalued shares on another exchange, therefore make risk-free profits as the difference in the prices on the two exchanges narrow.

The resultant effect of the trading activities of arbitrageurs is the creation of a link between demand for liquidity in one market with the supply of liquidity in another market. Therefore, arbitrageurs are regarded as "porters" of liquidity as opposed to suppliers of liquidity, given that they buy in one market and sell in a closely related market. In liquidity terms, they in effect demand liquidity in the market that has the requisite availability and supply this liquidity in the market where there is trader demand for it.

Arbitrageurs can be described as market markers that simultaneously connect buyers in one market with sellers in another market.

The concept of arbitrage will be discussed in more detail in Chapter 7.

Volatility

Volatility can be described simply as the relative rate at which the price of a security moves up and down. Thus, if the price of a stock moves up and down rapidly over short time periods, it has high volatility. If the price almost never changes, then it has low volatility.

Traders and investors have realised over the years that market volatility is unavoidable. Financial markets by their very nature tend to move up and down over the short term.

Volatility is characterised by large price fluctuations and heavy trading in the markets. This is often as a result of an imbalance of trade orders in one direction (for example, all buys and no sells). Some experts opine that volatility is caused by things like news about listed companies, a recommendation from a renowned financial analyst, a popular initial public offering (IPO) or an announcement of unexpected earnings results. Others believe that day traders, short sellers and institutional investors are responsible for volatility.

There is a close link between volatility, risk and profit. Traders always pay attention to volatility as it can significantly impact on their trading revenues. Traders with long positions make profits when there is an increase in prices and losses when there is a decrease. Similarly, those with short positions make losses when there is an increase in prices and profits when there is a decrease.

Definition of Volatility
Volatility is a statistical measure of the dispersion of returns for a given security or market index. Volatility can be measured by using either the standard deviation[66] or the variance[67] between returns from that same security or market index. Commonly, the higher the volatility, the riskier the security. (Investopedia)

Trading in Volatile Market Conditions

Volatility provides an array of trading opportunities for those traders who are able to react quickly and get on the right side of the market. It can be unsettling for some traders and investors, and when markets are volatile a number of them may prefer to sit tight rather than trade.

There are, however, some strategies that traders adopt for trading profitably in volatile markets. In this section, a number of the trading strategies will be briefly discussed.

Installation of Stop-losses

Traders that take bets in volatile markets usually install stop-losses which are stop bets if the losses reach a certain level. They carefully decide on how wide the stop-losses should be. Unexpected market movements can be sources of frustration for traders using stop-losses.

Traders give due consideration to wide daily ranges[68] when markets are volatile. For example, 10% daily movements in prices for blue chip stocks were witnessed in June 2008. A 200-point swing in a single session on the Dow Jones is also not uncommon.

This presents opportunities for day traders that do not hold assets overnight.

Trends Trading

Another common strategy is trends trading. Trend traders take a risk when they purchase a stock since they are relying on the stock's trend to remain strong over the long term. Any slowing of the trend can result in lost opportunity costs, while any reversal can turn a profit into a loss. A simple approach to trends trading is to identify a recent high or low and trade the breakout through that level. A typical example was in May 2008 when the price of crude oil peaked at $135 per barrel and then moved back towards $120 per barrel in June. The ensuing rally[69] then broke through $135 and observers witnessed the market at $139 per barrel in very short order.

Similarly, trend trading can work for traders that are short on certain stocks when the markets are down. For most of 2008 the banking sector suffered and the trend was clearly identifiable. In March, the price of Royal Bank of Scotland stock, for instance, dropped to 300 pence, but started to rally in April.

However, during the following month the price of the stock dropped below 300 pence to 250 pence in little over a week, providing an opportunity for traders that were short on the stock to trade the breakout at this level.

---

66 In financial markets, standard deviation is applied to the annual rate of return of an investment to measure the investment's volatility. Standard deviation is used by investors as a gauge for the amount of expected volatility.

67 Variance measures the variability (volatility) from an average. Volatility is a measure of risk, so this statistic can help determine the risk an investor might take on when purchasing a specific security (Investopedia).

68 A trading range is the spread between the high and low prices traded during a period of time.

69 A rally is a period of continuous increases in the prices of stocks, bonds or indexes.

It is worth noting that the scenarios depicted above can also be considered to be a type of breakout trading. Breakout trading is defined as follows:

A type of trading that involves the use of technical analysis to seek out potential trading opportunities, identifying situations where the price of an asset is likely to experience a substantial movement over a short period of time. Breakout traders normally seek key levels of support and resistance and will engage in transactions when the asset's price passes through these levels. Short positions are taken when the price breaks below a level of support while long positions are taken when the price of an asset breaks through a level of resistance.

Trading against the Short-term Trend

Trading against the short-term trend is another trading strategy that traders adopt in the face of considerable volatility with no real overall short-term direction.

One approach taken by some traders is to "sell the market" should it move back to the previous trading day's highs, and to "buy the market" should it drop towards the previous day's low.

The rationale behind this approach is that traders believe that these changes are as a result of sentiments during the previous trading day and speculate on the premise that the same thing will occur again.

There are, however, risks inherent in this strategy as the previous level could end up getting breached. Traders normally mitigate these types of risk by carefully placing stops so that they can exit trades should the market persist in that direction.

Betting on Options

Traders usually consider spread betting on options as opposed to the individual market itself in times of increased market volatility. A trader that buys a call, or put, derives the benefit of knowing the absolute downside right from the beginning of the trade.

The maximum the trade can lose is the price of the option, but still has the infinite profit potential of a trade on the underlying market. There is, however, a price to be paid in the sense that the prices of options increase in times of increased market volatility.

Traders that favour this option find that it can be an attractive way to take advantage of what, in their opinion, is an extended move in a particular market, and have an awareness of their maximum risk from the start.

To illustrate this concept, suppose a trader, George Betts, feels in August 2008 that the FTSE 100 index is going to be lower on 1 September 2008 than the level at the time (6200 points). He buys a 6100 August put option at £3 per point.

The option is trading at 102 to buy. Thus, his maximum risk is £306 (102 x 3). Even if he is completely wrong about the direction and the markets were to rally 500 points, his maximum risk will still be the same value.

Use of Binaries and Bungees

Traders are increasingly adopting binaries and Bungee bets to achieve their trading objectives in times of increased volatility.

Bungee bets entail using stop-losses for particular trades to limit the downside in case the market moves past a predefined level. A Bungee bet allows a trader to capture favourable price movements in volatile daily markets and at the same time strictly check on their maximum possible loss.

Bungees have a built-in "floor" or "ceiling" level akin to a stop level, which ensures that the trader cannot lose more than a given amount on their position. In contrast to a normal stop, however, should the underlying market pass through their floor or ceiling, their position remains open. Hence, if the market bounces back in their favour later in the day, a profit can still be made.

Figure 6.2 A Typical Bungee Buy Price Movement

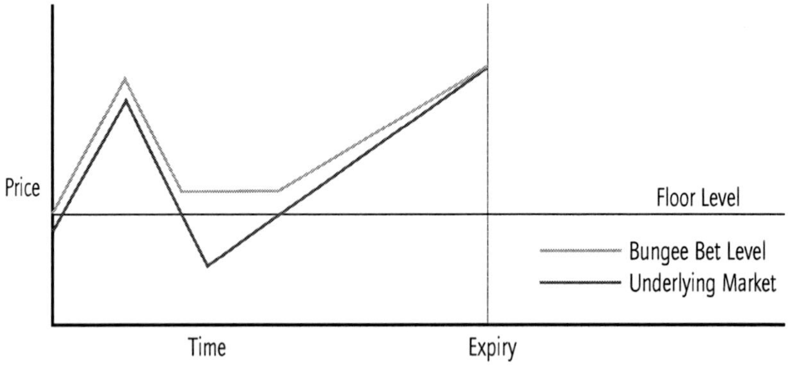

Source: IG Index

Illustration of a Bungee bet

George Betts buys a FTSE 100 Daily Bungee with a Floor at 5040 at £5/point, in the hope that the FTSE will rise. Assuming that the offer price (there is no bid price for a Bungee buy) is 5080, this implies that if the FTSE 100 closes the day above 5080, Betts will make a profit, but he knows he cannot lose more than 40 points (£5/point x 40 = £200) as the Floor level is fixed at 5040.

The FTSE now falls to 5039, meaning his Floor level has been breached. The Floor holds his risk at 5040, but his position is kept open. His strategy is to wait until the end of the day in the hope that the FTSE will bounce back. Should this happen and it closes at 5120, he makes a profit of 40 points (£5/point x 40 = £200).

Traders trade Bungee bets on a range of assets from currency pairs, such as USD/EUR, GBP/USD, and USD/JPY, to crude oil and metals, such as gold and silver.

Use of the Elliot Wave Theory

Some traders seem to have a knack for making large profits by "catching the wave" in the financial markets. This is contrary to the belief held by most people that financial markets are completely random and there is no way of predicting the next move, either up or down.

The Elliot Wave theory offers a technique for forecasting the direction of the markets. It was developed by Ralph Elliot Nelson in the late 1920s after discovering that stock markets had distinctive patterns as opposed to the notion that they behave in a somewhat chaotic manner. He opined that they traded in repetitive cycles which he attributed to the main mindset of the populace at a given time. His claim was that the upward and downward swings of the common psychology always reflected in the same repetitive patterns, which were then divided into patterns now known as "Elliot Waves".

A relatively simple explanation of the Elliot Wave Principle is derived from the book, *The Elliott Wave Principle: Key to Market Behavior*, by Robert Prechter Jr. and A.J. Frost and is as follows:

Elliot pointed out that the stock market unfolded according to a basic rhythm or pattern of five waves up and three waves down to form a complete cycle of eight waves. The three waves down are referred to as a correction of the preceding five waves up. (See Figure 6.3.)

Figure 6.3 The Basic Structure of the Elliot Wave

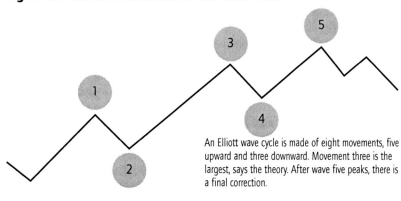

An Elliott wave cycle is made of eight movements, five upward and three downward. Movement three is the largest, says the theory. After wave five peaks, there is a final correction.

Source: City A.M.

The central theme is that as soon as the first move begins, the second wave (wave 2) subsequently takes the price down and then the third wave (wave 3) pushes it up again. From then on, a correction via the fourth wave (wave 4) leads to the fifth (wave 5) which is the final wave prior to the next correction.

Experts opine that Elliot Wave theory helps traders improve their trading in volatile market conditions in many ways including the following:

■ **Identification of trends** – The wave theory identifies the direction of the dominant trend, i.e. a five-wave advance identifies the overall trend as up while a five-wave decline shows that the predominant trend is down. This is crucial to trading activities, given that it is beneficial to trade in the direction of the dominant trend and offers the path of least resistance. It can be argued that there is greater probability that a commodity trade is successful if the trader takes a long position in wheat while there are sustained increases in the prices of other commodities.

■ **Identification of countertrends** – This is another way in which the theory helps traders. The three-way pattern serves as a corrective response to the previous impulse wave. Traders recognise that a recent price movement is only a correction within a broader trading market. They are aware that these corrections create opportunities for them to position themselves in the direction of the wider market trend.

Industry experts have concluded that the Elliot Wave theory is applicable to equities, foreign exchange and commodities markets. It is also applicable to different time frames from intra-day to daily, weekly, monthly and yearly charts.

The Volatility Index

Traders are increasingly using options prices offered up by the Chicago Board Options Exchange's Volatility Index, or VIX, to help determine market direction. This is because, in spite of their familiarity with trading options, most option traders are heavily dependent on volatility information to select their trades.

What is VIX?

VIX is an index that measures the implied volatility of a hypothetical 30-day option of S&P on the 500 index options. It is regarded as one of the financial markets' most acclaimed methods to assess stock market volatility.

The first version of the index was developed by the CBOE in 1993 and at the time was regarded as the benchmark for stock market volatility. It was calculated by using the weighted average of implied volatility for the Standard and Poor's 100 Index call and put options. In 2003, the index was updated to reflect the latest advances in financial theory. One of the key revisions was the use of the Standard and Poor's 500 Index in place of the Standard and Poor's 100 Index. This is because, in spite of the correlation of both indexes, the S&P 500 is the principal US stock market benchmark.

In some circles, VIX is referred to as the fear index and is regarded as a measure of investors' confidence, or lack of it, in market conditions.

In 2006, VIX options began trading on the Chicago Board Options Exchange. According to experts, these options allow traders to trade volatility without the need to factor in the price changes of the underlying instrument, dividend or interest rates. In essence, VIX options provide a way for traders to focus almost solely on trading volatility.

Figure 6.4 CBOE Volatility Index (VIX) in 2007

Sources: CBOE and Bloomberg

Benefits of VIX for Traders

▨ VIX creates opportunities for speculation and hedging.

▨ It allows investors to achieve effective portfolio diversification.

▨ VIX is negatively correlated with the S&P 500. According to the CBOE's website (www.cboe.com), since 1990 the VIX has moved in the opposite direction to the S&P 500 Index for 88% of the time. On average, VIX has risen 16.8% on days when the S&P 500 fell 3% or more. This offers diversification benefits and possibly an insurance cover against market disaster.

▨ VIX helps to determine market direction. An increase in its value indicates that the markets are going down while a decrease indicates that the markets are in an upward direction. Conventional wisdom would suggest that a rising stock market is less risky and a declining stock market more risky. The higher the observed risk in stocks, the higher the implied volatility and the more costly the associated put options. Therefore, implied volatility is about the implied risk related to the stock market as opposed to the size of the price swings. A market in decline triggers an increase in demand for put options. Increased demand indicates higher put prices and higher implied volatilities.

▨ VIX acts a contrarian indicator, measuring panic and complacency. Contrarians[70] often weigh VIX action against that of the market to unearth some

---

70 These are traders that adopt an investment style that goes against prevailing market trends by buying assets that are performing poorly and then selling when they perform well.

insightful clues on future direction or duration of a move. An increase in the value of VIX results in an increase in panic in the market. In contrast, a decrease in the value of VIX results in an increase in complacency in the market. Thus, as a contrarian indicator, VIX readings that are extremely low indicate a high degree of complacency and are generally considered to be bearish. Conversely, extremely high VIX readings indicate a high degree or anxiety or in some cases panic among options traders and are considered to be bullish.

Concept of Arbitrage

This chapter discusses the concept of arbitrage including the theoretical underpinnings and the different types of arbitrage.

Introduction

In the financial markets, arbitrage, also known as "riskless profit", is essentially buying in one market and simultaneously selling in another, profiting from a temporary price difference. In finance theory, arbitrage is described as a "free lunch", given that profits can be made without incurring risk.

An example of an arbitrage opportunity would be buying an iPod for £200 in, say, London when in Manchester the iPod is selling for £225. If Jane Abbi is able to buy the iPod in London and sell it in the Manchester market, she can profit from the difference without any risk because the higher price of the iPod in Manchester is guaranteed.

From a stock market perspective, there are arbitrage opportunities that traders can exploit. For instance, Vince Abby, a trader in New York, may buy a stock on the London Stock Exchange for 100p where the price is yet to adjust for the constantly fluctuating exchange rate. The spot exchange rate at the time of the transaction for GBP/USD is 1.8. The price of an equivalent stock on the New York Stock Exchange is 190p. Thus, the price of the stock on the London Stock Exchange is undervalued compared to the price on the New York Stock Exchange, and Vince makes a profit from this difference by buying in London and selling in New York.

Arbitrage opportunities in the stock market also include speculative deals such as the purchase of shares in a new issue in the hope that they can be sold after the issue and profits can be made.

In the FX market, a currency trader could buy a currency, say Japanese Yen, in one market and immediately sell it in another market at a better rate, making an arbitrage profit.

In the futures market, assume a cocoa futures contract trades on two different exchanges in New York and Chicago. If, at one point in time, the contract is bid at USD 27.05 on the Chicago exchange and offered at USD 27.00 on the New York exchange, a trader could purchase the contract at one price and sell it at the other to make a risk-free profit of USD 0.05.

If all markets were perfectly efficient, there would never be any arbitrage opportunities – but markets hardly ever remain perfect. It is vital to note that even when markets have a discrepancy in pricing between two equal goods, there is not always an arbitrage opportunity. If transaction costs are factored in, a possible arbitrage situation can turn into one that has no benefit to the potential arbitrageur. Considering the scenario with the iPods above, it would cost Jane Abbi a certain amount per iPod to get the iPods from London to Manchester. If it costs £25 per iPod, the arbitrage opportunity has been removed.

A market is said to have no arbitrage – or be arbitrage free – if prices in that market do not offer any arbitrage opportunities. This is a theoretical condition that is usually assumed for markets in economic and financial models. The assumption inspired the financial engineering theory of arbitrage-free pricing.

Definitions of Arbitrage

The simultaneous purchase and sale of an asset in order to profit from a difference in the price. This usually takes place on different exchanges or marketplaces. (Investopedia.com)

Attempting to profit by exploiting price differences of identical or similar financial instruments, on different markets or in different forms. (Investorwords.com)

A more theoretical definition of arbitrage is:

A trading strategy that does not involve the investment of capital, cannot lose money, and has a positive probability of making money.

Theoretical Underpinnings of Arbitrage

There are some economic theories that underpin the concept of arbitrage. These theories include the Efficient Market Hypothesis (EMH), the Law of One Price and the Purchasing Power Parity (PPP). These theories are discussed in brief in this section.

Efficient Market Hypothesis (EMH)

EMH is an investment theory that states it is impossible to "outperform the market" because stock market efficiency causes existing share prices to always incorporate and reflect all relevant information. According to the EMH, this implies that stocks always trade at their fair value on stock exchanges, making it impracticable for investors and traders to either buy undervalued stocks or sell stocks for inflated prices. As such, it should be impossible to outperform the overall market through expert stock selection or market timing, and the only way an investor or trader can possibly obtain higher returns is by buying riskier investments.

The efficient market hypothesis (EMH) was partly developed in the 1960s by Eugene Fama. A while back, the efficient market hypothesis was widely accepted by academic financial economists. It was generally believed that securities markets were extremely efficient in reflecting information about individual stocks and about the stock market as a whole. The established perception was that when information arises, the news spreads rapidly and is incorporated into the prices of securities without delay. Consequently, neither technical analysis, which is the study of past stock prices in an attempt to predict future prices, nor even fundamental analysis, which is the analysis of financial information such as company earnings, asset values, etc. to help investors select "undervalued" stocks, would enable an investor to achieve returns greater than those that could be obtained by holding a randomly selected portfolio of individual stocks with comparable risk.

115

The efficient market hypothesis is related to the idea of a "random walk," which is a term used loosely in finance literature to characterise a price series where all subsequent price changes represent random departures from previous prices. The logic of the random walk idea is that if the flow of information is unimpeded and information is immediately reflected in stock prices, then tomorrow's price change will reflect only tomorrow's news and will be independent of the price changes today. But news is by definition unpredictable and thus resulting price changes must be unpredictable and random. As a result, prices fully reflect all known information, and even uninformed investors buying a diversified portfolio at the tableau of prices given by the market will obtain a rate of return as generous as that achieved by the experts.[71]

Although it is a basis for modern financial theory, the EMH is highly contentious and often disputed. Supporters argue it is meaningless to search for undervalued stocks or to try to forecast trends in the market through either fundamental or technical analysis.

Law of One Price

The law of one price is a fundamental concept of finance theory. It states that in an efficient market, all identical goods must have only one price. The reasoning behind this law is that all sellers will gravitate to the highest prevailing price, and all buyers to the lowest current market price. In an efficient market, the convergence on one price is instant.

To illustrate the Law of One Price, it will be prudent to begin with the use of a real-world example. First, for the purpose of this illustration, it should be considered that:

- the law of one price says that identical goods should sell for the same price in two separate markets when there are no transportation costs and no differential taxes applied in the two markets.

Please note the additional consideration of transportation costs and differential taxes.

The goods to be considered in this illustration are iPods and the following is information about iPods sold in the UK and French markets:

Price of iPods in UK market, P_1 in GBP	£20
Price of iPods in French market, P_2 in Euro	€23
Spot exchange rate, S GBP/EUR	1.23

The sterling price of iPods sold in France can be calculated by dividing the iPod price in Euro by the spot exchange rate as shown:

71   Burton G. Malkiel, (2003), "The Efficient Market Hypothesis and Its Critics", *Princeton University CEPS Working Paper* No. 91, p3.

$P_2/S = 23/1.23 = £18.60/iPod$

The above shows that the law of one price does not hold in this circumstance since the sterling price of the iPod is less than the sterling price in the UK. If the law of one price held, then the sterling price in France should match the price in the UK.

The next issue to consider is what might happen as a result of the discrepancy in prices. Provided that there are no costs incurred to transport the goods, trading can provide a profit-making opportunity. For instance, UK travellers in France who recognise that identical versions of the iPod are selling there for a percentage less might buy iPods in France and bring them back to the UK to sell. This scenario is described as "goods arbitrage". It can be seen that an arbitrage opportunity arises whenever one can buy something at a low price in one location and resell at a higher price and therefore make a profit.

By applying basic supply and demand theory, the increase in demand for iPods in France would result in an increase their price. The increased supply of iPods on the UK market would drive the price down in the UK. Consequently, the price of iPods in France may rise to, say, €24 while the price of iPods in the UK may fall to £19.51. At these new prices, the law of one price holds because:

$P_2/S = 24/1.23 = £19.51 = P_1$

If there are no transportation costs or differential taxes or subsidies, identical goods should sell at identical prices in an integrated market and this should conform to the law of one price. If different prices existed then there would be profit-making opportunities by buying the goods in the low-price market and reselling them in the high-price market. If businessmen acted this way, then there would be convergence in price until equality was achieved.

Naturally, the law of one price does not hold even between markets within a country for many reasons. The prices of shirts, wine and CDs will possibly be different in Paris than in Marseille. The prices of these items will also differ in other countries when converted at current exchange rates. The basis for the discrepancies is that there are costs to transport goods between locations, there are different taxes applied in different regions and different countries, non-tradable input prices may vary, and people do not have access to perfect information about the prices of goods in all markets at all times. Therefore, as an economic "law", the law of one price is valid only to an extent.

In the financial markets, commodities, for example, can be traded where there will be a single offer price and bid price. Despite the small spread between these two values, the law of one price still applies (to each). In practice, traders will not sell the commodity at a lower price than the market maker's offer-level or buy at a higher price than the market maker's bid-level. If traders decide not to trade at the prevailing price then they won't have any counterparties to trade with or will be trading unprofitably.

Purchasing Power Parity (PPP)

This is an economic theory that uses the long-term equilibrium exchange rate of two currencies to equalise their purchasing power. It can also be described as the amount of adjustment required on the exchange rate between countries in order for the exchange to be equivalent to each currency's purchasing power.

PPP was developed by Gustav Cassel in 1920, and it is based on the law of one price.

This purchasing power exchange rate equalises the purchasing power of different currencies in their home countries for a given basket of goods. The best-known and most-used purchasing power parity exchange rate is the Geary-Khamis dollar (the "international dollar").

PPP exchange rate (the "real exchange rate") fluctuations are mostly as a result of market exchange rate movements. Apart from this volatility, there are consistent differences between the market and PPP exchange rates; for instance, (market exchange rate) prices of non-traded goods and services are usually lower where incomes are lower. (A US dollar exchanged and spent in the Seychelles will buy more yoga sessions than a dollar spent in the United States.) PPP factors in this lower cost of living and adjusts for it as though all income was spent locally. In other words, PPP is the amount of a certain basket of basic goods which can be bought in the given country with the money it produces.

PPP is:

$$£P (\$/£) = \$P$$

This means that the exchange rate that is equal to the value of a dollar of purchasing power (the PPP exchange rate) is:

$$(\$/£) = \$P/£P$$

If the actual spot rate is greater, it suggests that the £ is over-valued against the $. If the actual spot rate is less, it suggests that the $ is over-valued against the £.

For example, if a "model" consumption basket costs $3,000 in the USA and £2,000 in the UK, the PPP exchange rate would be $1.50/£. If the actual spot rate was $1.90/£, this would indicate that the pound was overvalued by 26%.

Purchasing power parity is often called absolute purchasing power parity to distinguish it from a related theory, relative purchasing power parity, which predicts the relationship between the two countries' relative inflation rates and the change in the exchange rate of their currencies.

Relative PPP relates the inflation rate (the change of price levels) in each country to the change in the market exchange rate.

The relative version of PPP is calculated as:

$$S = P_1/P_2$$

Where:

S is the exchange rate of currency 1 to currency 2

P_1 is the cost of item xyz in currency 1

P_2 is the cost of item xyz in currency 2

Big Mac PPP

This is an interesting measure of PPP made popular by *The Economist*, which looks at the prices of a Big Mac burger in McDonald's restaurants in different countries. With the Big Mac PPP, purchasing power is reflected by the price of a McDonald's Big Mac in a particular country. The measure gives an impression of how overvalued or undervalued a currency is.

The calculation of the Big Mac PPP-adjusted exchange rate looks at the price of a Big Mac in a given country and divides it by the price of a US Big Mac. To illustrate, the Big Mac in Singapore is considered. If a Singaporean Big Mac is 5.80 SGD and the US price is $2.90, then – according to PPP – the exchange rate should be 2 SGD for US$1. However, if the SGD was actually trading in the currency market at 4.12 SGD for US$1, the Big Mac PPP would suggest that the SGD is undervalued.

Types of Arbitrage

Forex Arbitrage

Forex arbitrage is a risk-free trading strategy that retail forex traders adopt to enable them to make a profit with no open currency exposure. In order to achieve this objective, traders have to act fast on opportunities presented by pricing inefficiencies, while they exist. This type of arbitrage trading entails the buying and selling of different currency pairs to exploit any inefficiency of pricing. The following example sheds light on how this strategy works.

Example – Arbitrage currency trading

The following are the current exchange rates of the relevant currency pairs in this illustration:

- EUR/USD: 1.2000
- EUR/GBP: 0.7400
- GBP/USD: 1.6400

The steps in the arbitrage transaction are:

1. Rex Abby, a forex trader, buys one mini-lot[72] of EUR (10,000 euros) for $12,000 USD. (10,000 x EUR/USD = 10,000 x 1.2000)

---

72 A Forex lot is used to measure the amount of a deal. Hence a mini-lot is similar to a regular lot, only it is smaller in size.

2. He then sells the 10,000 euros for 7,400 British pounds. (10,000 x EUR/GBP = 10,000 x 0.74000)
3. He sells the 7,400 GBP for $12,136 USD (7,400 x GBP/USD = 7,400 x 1.6400)
4. He makes a profit of $136 ($12,136 − $12,000) per trade with no open exposure because long positions cancel short positions in each currency.

The same trade using regular lots (rather than mini-lots) of 100,000 would yield a profit of $1,360. This can be sustained until the pricing error is traded away.

Rex Abby needed to act quickly to exploit the pricing inefficiencies. This is because, as with any arbitrage strategy, the act of exploiting the pricing ineffi- ciencies will correct the problem. Arbitrage opportunities are usually available for a very short time before being acted upon as a result of these corrections.

For arbitrage currency trading to be successful, real-time pricing quotes have be readily available and a trader needs the ability to act quickly on the oppor- tunities. Forex arbitrage calculators are available to help traders to seek out these opportunities.

Statistical Arbitrage

Statistical arbitrage, often referred to as "StatArb", is an arbitrage strategy that allows traders to make profits arising from pricing inefficiencies between secu- rities. These are usually identified through mathematical modelling techniques. Statistical arbitrage is not riskless as it is heavily dependent on the ability of market prices to return to a historical or predicted normal.

As a trading strategy, statistical arbitrage is a highly quantitative and com- putational approach to equity trading. Adopters of this strategy use data min- ing and statistical methods, as well as automated trading systems.

The evolution of StatArb can be traced to the less complex pairs trading strategy (see below), which entails pairing stocks according to fundamental or market-based similarities. In the event that one stock in a pair outperforms the other, the poorer performing stock is bought long in the hope that it will climb towards its outperforming partner; the other is sold short. This allows for hedg- ing of risk from whole-market movements.

Morgan Stanley, which was one of the biggest centres of statistical arbitrage in the early 1980s, defines statistical arbitrage as a model-based investment process, which aims to build long and short portfolios whose relative value is currently different from a theoretically or quantitatively predicted value. The constructed portfolios should represent industry, sector, market and dollar neu- trality. (Hedge Fund Research, Inc.)

The main motivation of statistical arbitrageurs is to attempt to profit from transitory deviations of equity prices from their original values. They use a mix of science (value theory, statistical decisions theory and time series among oth- ers), skills and experience to implement statistical arbitrage.

The efficient use of information gathered is one of the hallmarks of statisti- cal arbitrageurs. For instance, if an arbitrageur takes a long position in some stock in anticipation of an increase in its price but in reality it does not perform well, they can use that stock for short selling, which would lead to a reduced risk of the total portfolio holdings of the arbitrageur. The positive return of this strategy derives from two sources:

1. when the price of stock from the long side of the portfolio goes up;
2. from the short position;

but the strategy benefits should the price of the shorted equities drop, which implies that the arbitrageur can purchase the stocks they owe at a lower price.

Hedge funds and investment banks are the major adopters of statistical arbitrage. Many of the proprietary operations of these financial organisations are focused to a varying degree on statistical arbitrage trading. It is also widely used by sophisticated independent investors.

Hedge funds especially implement this strategy for the following reasons:

- Volatility is low.
- Returns of the strategy are independent and uncorrelated with the market.
- The strategy generates relatively high and constant return, irrespective of economic downturns.
- The strategy is complementary to others strategies used by hedge funds in their bid to increase portfolio diversification.

Experts identify a drawback in this strategy in the costs associated with short selling, as well as transaction costs. They are also concerned about the limited amount of stocks available for short selling and also the strict rules that prohibit short selling if the stock does not experience the previous uptick. Given that arbitrageurs are looking for highly liquid stocks to be short, it may happen that there is a limited availability of stocks to fulfil their objectives. This type of problem is known as capacity issue within the portfolio.

Risk Arbitrage

Risk arbitrage is a broad definition for three types of arbitrage that contain an element of risk:

1. **Merger arbitrage** – This is the concurrent purchase of stock in a company being acquired and the sale (or short sale) of stock in the acquiring company.
2. **Liquidation arbitrage** – This is a strategy adopted by arbitrageurs who seek to exploit the difference between a company's current value and its estimated liquidation value.
3. **Pairs trading** – This is the exploitation of a value difference between two very similar companies in the same industry that have historically been highly correlated. When the two companies' values diverge to a historically high level, arbitrageurs can take an offsetting position in each (e.g. go long in

one and short the other) because, as historical evidence shows, they will inevitably come to be similarly valued.

In this section, only merger arbitrage will be discussed.

Merger arbitrage

From a trading perspective, merger arbitrage is the business of trading stocks of companies that are the subject of mergers or acquisitions. This type of arbitrage takes advantage of the fact that takeovers involve a large price premium for the company. Provided that there is a price gap, ample rewards are potentially available even in spite of the risks inherent in betting on mergers.

What is merger arbitrage?

Merger arbitrage or "Merge-arb" is a strategy in which the stocks of companies engaged in mergers and acquisitions are simultaneously bought and sold for profit. Arbitrageurs look out for the public announcement of a potential merger and as soon as this happens, they buy the shares of the target company, which will most likely be selling below the acquisition price. Simultaneously, the arbitrageur will short-sell the acquiring company by borrowing shares, with the expectation that they will repay them at a later date with lower-cost shares.

If events occur as planned, the target company's share price should eventually rise to reflect the agreed acquisition price per share, and the acquiring company's price should fall to reflect what it is paying for the deal. The arbitrageur's potential returns are proportional to the spread or gap between the current trading prices valued by the acquisition terms.

The following is a typical example of a successful merger arbitrage deal.

BizCorp is a fictional oil service company that has invented a unique product which fills a gap in industry. At the moment, the share price for BizCorp is $30 per share. EssEnergy, a fictional integrated energy company, decided to bid $40 a share – a 33% premium – for BizCorp. The expectation is that the stock of BizCorp will rise sharply, but could eventually settle at some price higher that $30 and less that $40 until the takeover deal is approved and closed. However, if it happens to trade at a higher price, the sentiment in the market is that a higher bidder will come forward.

Assume that the deal is expected to close at $40 and BizCorp stock is trading at $37. Dave Madge, a risk arbitrageur, has been monitoring the events and grabs the price-gap opportunity by purchasing BizCorp stock at $38, pays a commission and holds on to the shares. Once the merger is closed, Mr Madge sells these shares for the agreed $40 acquisition price. From this aspect of the deal, Dave Madge makes a profit of $2 a share, or a 5% gain, less trading fees. The time frame between the announcement and the completion of the acquisition deal was four months. As this is a third of a year, the annualised return on the deal is 15% (5% x 3).

At the same time, Dave Madge short-sells EssEnergy's stock in the hope that its share price will drop in value. As it happens, EssEnergy's share price falls from $80 to $75, netting Dave Madge a profit of $5 per share or 6.25%. The annualised return on the deal is 18.25% (6.25% x 3).

A combination of the gains of the target's stock and the gains from the acquirer's stock translates into 33.25 % annualised return (less transaction costs) for Dave Madge.

Convertible Arbitrage

Convertible arbitrage is a strategy that involves the purchase of convertible securities and the subsequent shorting of the corresponding common stock. Conversion will offset the short position. This strategy allows the arbitrageur to attempt to exploit profits when there is a pricing error made in the conversion factor of the convertible security. This could be a market situation whereby there is a perception that the securities are priced lower than conditions merit.

The implementation of a convertible arbitrage commences with the purchase of convertible securities. These convertible securities may be in the form of a bond issue, but offer the chance to convert the bond into shares of common stock at some future date. The purchase of the convertible securities allows a trader to hold on to the security as it is, or exploit a conversion at a pre-determined price in the hope that the stock will rise in value in the short term.

At the same time, the process for a convertible arbitrage also involves the sale of any underlying equities associated with the company. This arrangement strengthens the position of the trader, given that the acquired securities were currently being undervalued. When the perception is corrected, the trader is left with security holdings that are considerably more valuable than they were at the time of purchase. Nevertheless, if it happens that the convertible securities were not undervalued after all, the loss will still be fairly minimal in most cases.

The following is an illustration of a convertible arbitrage trade using the cash-and-carry strategy.

Table 7.1 Example of US-style Cash-and-Carry Convertible Arbitrage Bond Trade

Trade Details: The initial price of the convertible bond is 108. The convertible arbitrage manager makes an initial cash investment of $202,500 (i.e. initial capital) plus $877,500 of borrowed funds for a total investment of $1,080,000 (i.e. the borrowed amount of $877,500 is just over 4 times the equity of $202,500). The bond's **conversion ratio**[73] is for 34.783 common shares. Note that 26,000 shares are initially sold short at a price of $26.625 (i.e. 26,000/34,783 shares = hedge ratio of 75%). We assume a 1-year holding period. (The example is gross of fees.)

---

73 The number of common shares received at the time of conversion for each convertible security. It is calculated by using this formula: Conversion Ratio = Par Value of Convertible bond/Conversion price of equity.

Determining Total Return

Return source	Return	Assumptions/Notes
Cash Flow		
Bond interest income (on long bond)	50,000	5% coupon on $1,000,000 face amount
Short interest rebate (on short stock)	8,653	1.25% interest on $692,250 short proceeds, based on initial hedge ratio[74] of approximately 75% (26,000 shares sold short at $26.625 = $692,250, relative to 34,783 shares of CB stock equivalency [i.e. 26,000/34,783 shares = **delta**[75] of 75%])
Less		
Cost of leverage	(17,550)	2% interest on $877,500 borrowed funds
Dividend payment (on short stock)	(6,922)	1% dividend yield on $692,250 (i.e. 26,000 shares sold short)
Total Cash Flow (1)	**34,181**	
Arbitrage Return		
Bond return	120,000	Bought at price of 108 and sold at a price of 120 per $1,000
Stock return	(113,750)	Sold stock short at $26.625 and stock rose to $31.00 (i.e. loss of $4.375 x 26,000 shares)
Total Arbitrage Return (2)	**6,250**	
Total Return (1) + (2)	**40,431**	**(Total dollar return of $40,431 is a 20% return on equity of $202,500)**
Analysing Return Sources		

Return Source	Contribution	Notes
Bond interest income (long bond)	4.6%	Interest of $50,000 earned/bond price of $1,080,000 x 100 = 4.6%

74 A ratio comparing the value of a position protected via a hedge with the size of the entire position itself.

75 The ratio comparing the change in the price of the underlying asset to the corresponding change in the price of a derivative. Sometimes referred to as the "hedge ratio".

Short (interest) rebate (short stock)	0.8%	Interest of $8,653 earned/bond price of $1,080,000 x 100 = 0.8%
Dividend payment (short stock)	-0.6%	Dividends $6,922 paid/bond price of $1,080,000 X 100 = -0.6%
Cost of leverage	-1.6%	Interest of $17,550 paid/bond price of $1,080,000 X 100 = -1.6%
Arbitrage return	0.6%	Return of $6,250 earned/bond price of $1,080,000 x 100 = 0.6%
Unleveraged Return	**3.8%**	**Total return of $40,431 earned/bond price of $1,080,000 = 3.8%**
Contribution from leverage	16.2%	The contribution from leverage is significant in this example
Total Return	**20.0%**	**Total return of $40,431 earned/capital of $202,500 = 20.0%**

Source: Arrow Hedge Partners Inc.

Index Arbitrage

Index arbitrage is the simultaneous buying of stock index futures and the selling (purchase) of some or all of the component stocks that make up the particular stock index to profit from sufficiently large inter-market spreads between the futures contract and the index itself.

By buying either the stocks or the futures contract and selling the other, a trader or investor can sometimes take advantage of market inefficiency for a profit. Like all arbitrage opportunities, index arbitrage opportunities vanish rapidly once information about the opportunity becomes widespread and many investors or traders act on it.

Index arbitrage can involve large transaction costs because of the requirement of simultaneous purchase and sale of many different stocks and futures, hence only large money managers are usually able to profit from index arbitrage. In addition, sophisticated computer programs are needed to keep track of the large number of stocks and futures involved, which makes this a very difficult trading strategy for individuals.

In order to provide an illustration of an index arbitrage, it would be prudent to briefly explain what an index futures contract is. Here is a simple definition:

A futures contract is a standardised contract, traded on a futures exchange, to buy or sell a certain underlying instrument at a certain date in the future, at a specified price.

The buyer of the contract agrees to deliver the product (or cash for financial futures) at the contract price on the expiry date. In the case of index futures, the contract is on a stock index such as the S&P 500. It is worth noting that the majority of futures contracts get "closed out" before the delivery date, thus no physical delivery actually takes place.

Whether an agreement is to buy or sell the S&P futures, it simply amounts to betting on how the index of stocks will behave over time. And because the terms of the futures contract are settled at a future date, the price of the contract generally leads to the price of the index in the hope that S&P 500 stocks will rise.

It is also necessary to define fair value, which is the equilibrium price for a futures contract. This is equal to the spot price after factoring in compounded interest and dividends lost because the investor or trader owns the futures contract as opposed to the physical stocks. This price is determined over the period of the futures contract. This rise or decline in the futures contract is usually calculated as a change from fair value.

Illustration of an index arbitrage trade

Stuart Indy notices that the S&P futures contract is trading above fair value (higher), before the market is about to open. He sells (short) the S&P futures contract and goes long (buy) on the underlying stocks within the S&P 500 index. He therefore profits from the increase in the stock prices until the S&P 500 index reaches fair value with the S&P futures contract.

Conclusion

The discussion on arbitrage in this chapter is not exhaustive, but underscores the importance of arbitrage in trading activities. Arbitrageurs' roles in the financial markets help to put into effect the law of one price, connect buyers and sellers and also repackage risks into forms that are beneficial to other traders.

Electronic and Algorithmic Trading

This chapter discusses the concepts of both electronic and algorithmic trading. Also included are discussions on concepts such as Implementation Shortfall, TWAP and VWAP.

Introduction

In the financial markets, the trading of financial instruments has traditionally needed face-to-face communication at physical locations. One of the first markets to use technology to replace physical interaction was the Nasdaq over-the-counter (OTC) stock market in the USA. Ever since then, the majority of stock exchanges in the world, including those in the major financial centres such as London, Tokyo and Frankfurt, switched to electronic trading. A number of major exchanges, such as the New York Stock Exchange, still combine the use of physical trading with the use of systems introduced to allow institutional and retail investors to engage in electronic trading.

Giant strides in computing and communications technology have brought about global electronic order routing[76] and the broad dissemination of quote and trade information, as well the implementation of new types of trading system. These innovative initiatives remove the requirement for direct person-to-person contact via trading floors or telephone networks. The impact of new technology has been to reduce the costs of building new trading systems, thereby lowering the barriers to entry for new competitors. In addition, advances in communications technology make faster order routing and market data transmission to a much larger group of participants possible.

Algorithmic trading was briefly discussed in Chapter 5, but to support the discussions in this chapter it will defined as follows:

In electronic financial markets, algorithmic trading, also known as algo, involves the use of computer programs for entering trading orders, with a computer algorithm making decisions on a number of aspects of the order, such as the timing, price or even the final quantity of the order.

Definition of Electronic Trading

[Source: The implications of electronic trading in financial markets.]

An electronic trading system is a facility that provides some or all of the following services: electronic order routing (the delivery of orders from users to the execution systems); automated trade execution (the transformation of orders into trades); and electronic dissemination of pre-trade (bid/offer quotes and depth) and post-trade information (transaction price and volume data). (Bank for International Settlements)

A narrower definition is: *Electronic trading systems are facilities that automate all aspects of the trading process, including trade execution.* (Bank for International Settlements)

---

76 This is the act of sending orders from their originators, mostly investors and broker-dealers, to the execution system.

Differences between Electronic Systems and Traditional Markets

There are a number of differences between electronic systems and traditional markets. Information technology facilitates the automation of parts of the trading processes and trading relationships both among dealers and between dealers and their customers. The effect is to potentially create a new way of trading that differs from both floor-based and telephone trading, as opposed to building a better telephone. Electronic trading (ET) offers cost savings, increased efficiency and improved risk management capabilities to users. According to the Bank of International Settlements, the identified differences between traditional systems and electronic systems are:

- **ET is location-neutral and also allows continuous multilateral interaction**. For trading purposes, a common physical location for users is unnecessary as long as they can connect to the system. However, unlike traditional location-neutral trading, such as telephone-based dealer markets, ET allows continuous multilateral interaction (telephone-based systems are bilateral almost by definition). Consequently, ET systems facilitate cross-border trading and cross-border alliances and mergers between trading systems to a greater extent than do traditional markets.
- **ET is scalable**. Electronic systems can be scaled up to handle more trades simply by increasing the capacity of the computer network. With traditional markets, the size of the floor has to be physically expanded, or the number and/or capacity of intermediaries active in a phone-based market has to be increased, which are much more costly processes. Thus, successful ET systems can potentially exploit economies of scale and reduce operational costs to a far greater extent than can traditional markets. Scalability also tends to widen the reach of dealers, who have access to a far wider customer base than formerly.
- **ET is integrated**. ET potentially allows straight-through processing (STP), i.e. the seamless integration of the different parts of the trading process, starting with displaying pre-trade information and ending with risk management. In traditional markets, different systems handle different parts of the trading process (for example, order placement and risk management). It is therefore worth noting that ET does not only affect front-office activities, but can also have implications for the setup and functioning of the back office.

Overview of Electronic Market Structures

[Source: Electronic Trading in Financial Markets]

The set of rules governing the trade execution mechanism and the amount of price and quote data released define a trading system's market structure. There are a number of diverse market structures identified in the financial markets. Three types of generic market structure are:

- a trading system with passive pricing;
- a continuous limit-order book;
- a single-price auction.

Passive pricing systems are electronic trading systems that determine trade prices by explicitly referring to other markets' pricing and sales activity. They have no independent price discovery mechanism and their prices are taken directly from a primary market.

In an electronic limit-order book, traders continuously post bids and offers on the system for other participants to view. In the order book, orders are displayed and usually ranked by price and then by time. An example of a limit-order book, that of Island (which is one of the largest electronic trading systems), is shown in Figure 8.1.

Buy orders are displayed on the left while sell orders are displayed on the right, with each order's price and quantity displayed. Buy orders are listed by descending price and sell orders by ascending price. As seen in the illustration, the highest bid price is $24.05 and the lowest price bid is $24.06, meaning that there is a spread between buy and sell prices of $0.01.

Here is the method by which orders are typically matched and executed on a limit-order book:

- A limit-order book does not normally display the user's identity, the order entry time, or the period for which the order is good.
- A market participant places a limit order in the book or instigates a trade with an order already on the order book.
- In the event that a bid or offer is in the book and a market participant enters an order on the other side of the market at the same price or better, the limit-order book automatically and immediately matches the orders, and a trade occurs.
- Matching of incoming orders can occur for more than one existing order.

Interaction between Various Market Participants in Electronic Trading

Regardless of the type of market, trading systems provide a link between market participants who can interrelate in a number of ways. This interaction can

Figure 8.1 A Sample Limit-Order Book

| refresh | island home | disclaimer | help |

GET STOCK

MSFT   go

SYMBOL SEARCH

LAST MATCH		TODAY'S ACTIVITY	
Price	24.0510	Orders	37,864
Time	13:15:23:745	Volume	6,972,147

BUY ORDERS		SELL ORDERS	
SHARES	PRICE	SHARES	PRICE
1,000	24.0500	5,000	24.0600
100	24.0500	2,000	24.0700
2,100	24.0320	4,000	24.0700
2,650	22.0240	500	24.0770
2,500	24.0240	300	24.0780
1,000	24.0220	700	24.0790
4,500	24.0210	1,000	24.0800
2,000	24.0200	2,600	24.0900
2,500	24.0200	3,000	24.0900
300	24.0100	2,000	24.0900
1,000	24.1000	1,000	24.0900
200	24.1000	750	24.0900
200	24.1000	1,200	24.0990
45	24.1000	5,400	24.0990
6,000	24.1000	100	24.1000
(498 more)		(587 more)	

Source: www.island.com

be used to describe the overall trading process. In order to properly assess the impact of electronic trading, it would be beneficial to have an understanding of the interaction between the various market participants in typical OTC markets such as foreign exchange and fixed income. A summarised diagrammatic representation of the interaction between market participants before the introduction of electronic trading is shown in Figure 8.2.

The assumption is that the diagram is straightforward. However, it would be prudent at this point to explain bilateral and multilateral interaction.

Historically, in traditional foreign exchange or fixed-income markets, when an end-user intended to execute a transaction, they incurred a search cost of

131

Figure 8.2 Interaction between Market Participants prior to Electronic Trading

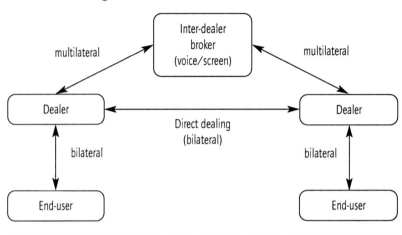

Source: Bank for International Settlements

contacting by telephone one or more of the dealers with whom they had a business relationship. Negotiation of a price would take place and a transaction executed at the best price available.

Should the dealer decide not to keep the acquired position, they would either seek out another customer with whom to conduct another transaction to offset this position or have recourse to the inter-dealer market. They could then directly contact another dealer to execute an offsetting transaction, or go through an inter-dealer broker, where dealers put up the bids and offers at which they are willing to trade. The former type of transaction is bilateral while the inter-dealer broker channel (bids/offers are transmitted either on screens or through voice contact) can be categorised as a multilateral interaction, given that quotes are pooled on a common platform and hence in direct competition with each other.

In recent times, electronic systems have been used to varying degrees for trading in the markets for foreign exchange and fixed income. The degree of adoption differs between markets, between market segments, between instruments, between types of trading and between the various stages of the trading process.

A summarised diagrammatic representation of the interaction between market participants after the introduction of electronic trading is shown in Figure 8.3. The dotted lines signify the lessened importance of the direct trading channels and the traditional inter-dealer broker channels.

Figure 8.3 Interaction between Market Participants after the Introduction of Electronic Trading

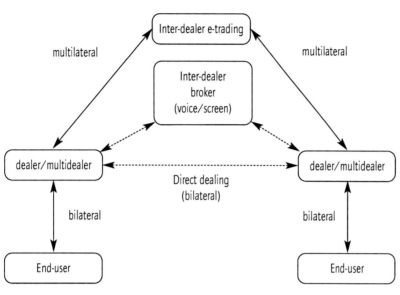

Source: Bank for International Settlements

Electronic Trading in Different Asset Classes

Observers of developments in the financial markets assert that the penetration of electronic trading in different sectors is uneven. The interaction between a number of factors, including the varied needs of traders, regulatory and competitive pressures, and existing market structure, is a contributor to the varied development patterns of electronic trading among asset classes (and market sectors within each of these).

A discussion of the penetration of electronic trading in the equity, fixed income and foreign exchange markets follows.

Equity Markets

Equity markets are the best known and most widely studied examples of electronic trading. The notion that electronic trading can penetrate different markets for the same assets in a different manner is evidenced by the contrasting patterns of development in Europe, Asia and the USA.

The US equity market has, in recent times, been characterised by an increase in the number of alternative electronic trading venues alongside relatively few traditional exchanges. Notable among these venues is BATS Trading, a platform established by trading organisations in the United States and backed by a host of financial institutions including Morgan Stanley, Merrill Lynch and Credit

133

Suisse. According to the *Financial Times*, as of January 2008, BATS had a market share of about 10% in US equities trading and, although only created in 2005, is the third largest share trading platform in the USA[77] behind the New York Stock Exchange and Nasdaq. This shows the level of penetration of electronic trading in the USA.

In contrast to the USA, most electronic trading facilities in Europe have developed within existing exchanges such as the London Stock Exchange (LSE) in the UK. Over a period of years, continuous electronic order books have been integrated into conventional exchanges, offering trading methods that were only available by "routing away" from the traditional venues.

However, the European Union's Markets in Financial Instruments Directive (MiFID), which came into force on 1 November 2007, allows the creation of a multi-trading facility across Europe, as domestic trades will no longer need to be reported on domestic exchanges. This has made room for the establishment of alternative trading venues in Europe, which will in effect end the domestic monopolies enjoyed by the likes of the London Stock Exchange (LSE). Notable among them is Project Turquoise, the pan-European equity trading operation, which was launched in 2008 by seven investment banks (Citigroup Inc., Credit Suisse Group, Deutsche Bank AG, Goldman Sachs Group Inc., Merrill Lynch & Co Inc., Morgan Stanley and UBS AG). While this represents a giant stride forward in Europe as far as electronic trading is concerned, the market penetration at the time of writing is still a long way off that of the USA.

In Asia, as at the time of writing, electronic trading has been slow to catch on. Nevertheless, with the build-up of infrastructure, the growing presence of bulge-bracket broker–dealers and technology offerings, this is set to change in the coming years. According to industry reports, the adoption of electronic trading in Asia is expected to increase appreciably by 2010. According to the Aite Group, an independent research and advisory firm, one of the key drivers for growth in electronic trading, and consequently algorithmic trading, in Asia will be the penetration of global broker–dealers in the local markets as US clients look to trade internationally more and more.

In addition, wider-spread Financial Information Exchange (FIX) adoption in Asia and increasing exchange cooperation in the markets will also help to drive electronic adoption.

Other industry experts assert that electronic trading growth in Asian markets is most likely to reflect the growth happening in Europe. While electronic trading quickly proliferated in the US markets, some experts point out that the Asian markets are more disparate, with different regulatory and trading requirements, similar to the pre-MiFID European climate.

Fixed Income

The adoption of electronic trading in fixed-income markets has been slower than for equities. Traditionally, bonds of all types were typically traded in tele-

77 Anuj Gangahar, 9 January 2008 "Banks throw weight behind BATS", *Financial Times*.

phone dealer markets.[78] But in recent times, the adoption of electronic execution by traders in the fixed-income markets has been accelerating.

According to data provided by operators of electronic trading systems for fixed-income securities, 74% witnessed an increase in trading volume during the first three quarters of 2006 compared to 2005. Nearly 68% saw an increase of over 5% in transaction volumes, 47% reported an increase of at least 10% and 28% said volumes increased 20% or more from 2005.[79]

According to the Securities Industry and Financial Markets Association, *"these data indicate the rapidly increasing adoption of electronic execution in the fixed-income markets globally. Since electronic trading in fixed-income securities first emerged in the late 1990s, trading platforms have become more sophisticated and have continued to offer services that reduce costs and risks and improve execution and trading efficiency. Increasing adoption of electronic execution enhances the liquidity of the trading platforms. In turn, enhanced liquidity, as well as efficiencies and cost reductions, continues to draw users to the electronic trading marketplace."*

There are reasons cited by experts for the later arrival of electronic trading in fixed-income markets in comparison with the equities markets. One notable reason is the distinct difference between the two. Fixed-income products are far less homogenous in the sense that there are more separate and individually less liquid issues than for equities, hence the more technical difficulty in introducing automated systems and the greater expense involved.

Foreign Exchange

Electronic trading has had a significant presence in the inter-dealer spot foreign exchange in recent years. According to the BIS triennial survey of December 2007, the spread of electronic trading platforms has also contributed to increased turnover in foreign exchange transactions between reporting dealers and other non-reporting financial institutions, such as non-reporting banks, hedge funds, pension funds and insurance companies, in part because it has enabled large financial institutions to set up algorithmic trading systems, and has provided trading facilities to retail investors.

For some years, there have been two major systems (Electronic Broking Services and Reuters) which have tended to specialise in particular major currency pairs. EBS dominates the EUR/USD and USD/JPY exchange. In 2006, the daily transacted volume in the EBS market exceeded 120 billion USD. As a

---

78 In a typical telephone dealer market (e.g. that for UK Gilts), traders receive telephone orders from customers and they are either obliged to quote prices or do so on a "best efforts" basis. The traders manage their inventories in an inter-dealer market, sometimes using an intermediary such as another dealer–broker or could deal directly with other traders.

79 Inderjit, C et al. (2006), "St. John's University Undergraduate Student Managed Investment Fund Presents Goldman Sachs Inc".

result, EUR/USD and USD/JPY rates posted on the EBS trading screens have become the reference prices quoted by dealers to their customers worldwide.[80]

Both systems have been designed as order books, in which traders are able to see the best bid and offer prices in the market, alongside the best bid and offer they could trade subject to their institutional credit limits structure.

According to BIS, these electronic systems are now used for the majority of spot inter-dealer trading in major currency pairs. As a result, the inter-dealer segment of the market has mostly, although not entirely, switched from voice brokering.

Algorithmic Trading

Algorithmic Trading Components

Some of the components of algorithmic trading as identified by the Tellefsen Consulting Group are:[81]

- real-time and historical market data;
- algorithms to:
  - perform correlation analysis;
  - identify trading opportunities;
  - determine optimal timing to launch;
  - measure trade execution against benchmarks (VWAP, TWAP etc.).
- order management/order processing;
- connectivity to liquidity pools:
  - exchanges, ECNs, inter-dealer brokers etc.
- integration with internal systems:
  - trading order management;
  - risk management;
  - compliance;
  - back office.

Algorithmic Strategies

Implementation Shortfall Measurement

In the quest for accurate measurement of the cost of trading, buy-side traders, such as traders in hedge funds, are increasingly concerning themselves with the

---

80 Chaboud, A. P., Chernenko, S. V., Howorka, E. R., Krishnasami, S., Liu, D. and Wright, J. H., "The High-Frequency Effects of US Macroeconomic Data Releases on Prices and Trading Activity in the Global Interdealer Foreign Exchange Market", *International Finance Discussion Papers*, 823 (2004).

81 Tellefsen Consulting Group, Inc. (January 2005), "Algorithmic Trading: Trends and Drivers". Available from www.tellefsen.com/Algorithmic_Trading_TCG.pdf.

Figure 8.4 Projected Algorithmic Trading Adoption in FX

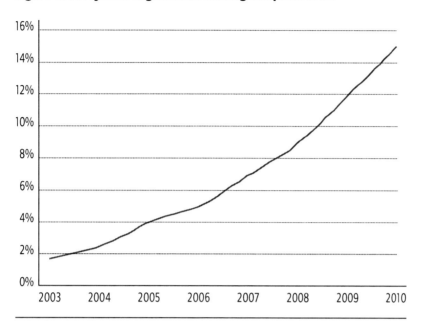

Source: Aite Group

comparison of execution prices against prices prevailing at the time they decide to trade. Any difference represents the cost to a specific fund of achieving its desired exposure, whether caused by delay in decision making, delay in trading or the impact of completing large orders in less liquid securities.

Implementation shortfall (IS) is one popular method that is used to measure ex-post execution costs when trading stocks. Implementation shortfall is a measurement of the difference between the value of the executed trade and the value of the same trade at the time the trading decision was made. It evaluates both the market impact of the trade and any intervening market events prior to trade execution. If the overall market had a significant move while the trade was pending execution, the opportunity cost of the trade can be isolated by subtracting the market return during the measurement period from the implementation shortfall.

The advantages of implementation shortfall as a measure of transaction costs include:

▨ direct linkage between trading and portfolio management, linking the cost of a trade to the value of the ideal;
▨ recognition of the trade-off between immediacy and price;
▨ allowance of attribution of implicit costs.

The disadvantages are that it needs extensive data collection and interpretation and that forces an unfamiliar evaluation framework on traders.

From a portfolio management standpoint, implementation shortfall can be measured as the difference between the dollar return of a paper portfolio (paper return), where all shares are assumed to transact at the prevailing market prices at the time of the investment decision, and the actual dollar return of the portfolio (real portfolio return). This is expressed mathematically as:

IS = Paper Return - Real Portfolio Return[82]

Before providing an illustration of implementation shortfall, it would be prudent to make a distinction between some categories of portfolios. According to Barclays Global Investors,[83] implementation shortfall can be distinguished by three categories: the paper portfolio, the actual portfolio, and the "rabbit portfolio:

1. **Paper portfolio** – This is a representation of the model situation in the sense that all securities transactions take place at benchmark prices. Transaction costs, bid-ask spread, liquidity impact, opportunity costs, market trends and slippage do not occur.

Figure 8.5 Diagrammatic Representation of Implementation Shortfall

Paper Returns	Implementation Shortfall	Real Returns
Returns if all trades were executed simultaneously with zero cost at decision price	Direct costs: Commission, settlement, taxes Indirect costs: Delay costs, Timing Gain/Lost Market Impact Opportunity Costs	Trades partially executed at prices achieveable in the market or not executed at all

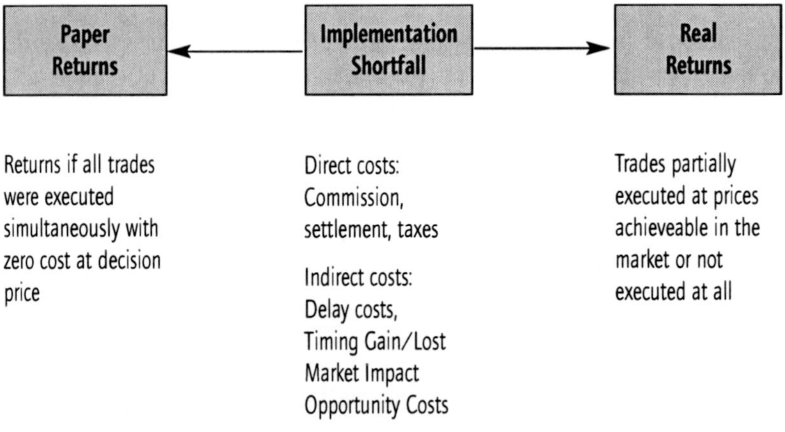

Source: George Midgley, A Guide to Transaction Cost Analysis

82 Robert Kissell, (2006), "The Expanded Implementation Shortfall; Understanding Transaction Cost Components", *Journal of Trading*, pp 3–5.

83 Minder Cheng, "Pre-trade Cost Analysis and Management of Implementation Shortfall," AIMR Conference Proceedings July 2003, no. 7 (DOI 10.2469/CP.V2003.n7.3349).

2. **Actual portfolio** – This portfolio is a reflection of reality in the sense that all transactions take place in real markets. Market impact, commissions, bid-ask spread, liquidity, opportunity costs and slippage are incorporated.

3. **Rabbit portfolio** – This portfolio represents expected trading costs in that all securities are transacted in expected markets. While the paper portfolio has no trading costs and the actual portfolio has high trading costs, the rabbit portfolio is the benchmark by which traders measure performance.

Illustration of IS

A case of implementation shortfall that involves complete execution of all shares transacted can help in gaining a thorough understanding of how transaction costs affect portfolio returns. An illustration of this case is as follows.

Big Fund, a hedge fund, intends to buy X shares of BizEnergy stock that is currently trading at $\$P_s$ per share. Supposing at some future date (e.g. the end of trading) the stock price is $\$P_t$, the total dollar paper return is computed as:

Paper return = $X.P_t - X.P_s$

Where: $X.P_s$ represents the starting value of the portfolio (e.g. the amount of money to invest) and $X.P_t$ represents the ending value of the portfolio (e.g. the portfolio value at the end of trading)[84]

If all the X shares were transacted, $\Sigma X_j = X$, the actual portfolio return is calculated as:

Portfolio Return = $X.P_t - \Sigma x_j p_j - fixed$

Where: x_j is the number of shares executed in the jth transaction, Σx_j is the total number of shares executed, p_j is the price of the jth transaction, and $\Sigma x_j p_j$ is the total transaction value, that is the cash invested. The fixed fees signify the commission, taxes, clearing and settlement charges, ticket charges, etc. and result in a reduction in portfolio return. In addition, $X, x_j > 0$ is an indication of a buy order (cash investment) and $X, x_j < 0$ indicates a sell order (cash redemption).

Thus, implementation shortfall is then calculated as shown below:

$IS = (X.P_t - X.P_s) - (X.P_t - \Sigma x_j p_j) - fixed$

$\quad = \quad \Sigma x_j p_j - X.P_s - fixed$

It should be noted that in this case, implementation shortfall measure is simply the total transaction value minus the value at the time of the investment decision fixed cost and does not depend on the future stock price P_t at all.

---

84 Almgren, R. and Chriss, N., (2000), "Optimal execution of portfolio transactions", Journal of Risk (3) 2, pp. 5-39.

Volume-Weighted Average Price (VWAP)

Volume-weighted average price (VWAP) is the ratio of the value traded to the total volume traded over a particular time horizon (typically one day). It is used to measure the average price a stock traded at over the trading horizon.

VWAP is often used as a trading benchmark by traders and investors who aim to be as passive as possible in their execution. In practice, traders' performance is evaluated by their ability to execute orders at prices better than the VWAP over the trading horizon.

VWAP is also used as the published closing price of a security.

The obvious closing price is the last price at which a security traded before trading stopped for the day. The problem with this is that a small transaction at the end of the day can change the closing price. This means that the closing price can reflect capricious trades (e.g. one resulting from the accidental entry of a buy at a very high price or a sell at a very low price). Even worse, it can open the way to deliberate distortion of the price through the placing of orders at very high or low prices just before trading closes.

The use of VWAP helps to solve this problem. It is the average price at which a security traded over a period prior to the close of trading. The period runs for a fixed time, ending with either the close of trading or at the time of the last trade in the security. The exact method used to calculate a VWAP will depend on the trading rules of the market in question.

Nevertheless, VWAP is calculated by adding up the dollars traded for every transaction (price multiplied by number of shares traded) and then dividing by the total shares traded for the day.

The formula for calculating VWAP is as follows:

$$\text{VWAP} = \Sigma \text{ Number of shares bought x Share price/Total shares bought}$$

Figure 8.6 shows some definitions of VWAP.

Impact of Benchmark Choice on Trading Strategy

The questions that need to be answered at this juncture are: What is the impact of the choice of performance benchmark on traders' decisions? And, what is the impact on trading strategy?

The choice of performance benchmark will impact on a trader's decisions with regard to factors including:

- order placement strategy (limit versus market orders);
- trading horizon;
- choice of venue (primary market, upstairs market or crossing systems).

These decisions in turn have a significant impact on realised trading costs and hence measurement of net performance on a risk-adjusted basis (i.e. net alpha).

As for VWAP benchmarks, the main impact on strategy is related to trading horizons. Daily VWAP benchmarks encourage traders to spread their trades out

Figure 8.6 VWAP Definitions

Measure	Definition	Remarks
Full VWAP	Ratio of the dollar volume traded to the corresponding share volume over the trading horizon, including all transactions	Standard definition, usually computed the day of the trade. Some traders use multiday VWAP (in the case of orders broken up for execution over several days) or intraday VWAP for orders executed strictly within the trading day. Unambiguously defined.
VWAP excluding own transactions	Ratio of dollar volume traded (excluding own volume) to share volume (excluding own volume) over the trading horizon	When the trader's order is a large fraction of volume, excluding the trader's *own* transaction volume corrects for bias. Excluding own trades, however, may produce a misrepresentative benchmark since VWAP is an average of prices before and after the bulk of the trading has occurred.
Non-block VWAP	VWAP computed excluding upstairs or block trades	Excluding large-block trades is reasonable for small traders who cannot access upstairs liquidity (Keim and Madhavan, 1996; Madhaven and Cheng, 1997). While some markets flag upstairs trades, others, including those in the US, do not. It is common to exclude trades of 10,000 or more shares as a proxy for upstairs trades.
VWAP proxies	Proxies for VWAP, including simple average of open, low, high and close	In emerging markets where tick-level data are unavailable, proxies are readily computed.
Value-weighted average price	Prices weighted by dollar value of trade, not share volume	Value-weighting is reasonable for volatile securities because the weights are determined by the economic value of the transaction. Other weighting schemes also exist.

Source: Ananath Madhavan, VWAP Strategies

over time to avoid the risk of trading at prices that are at the extreme for the day. There are considerable risks associated with this practice, given that delay and opportunity costs arising from passive participation trading can significantly erode alpha.

Trading Strategies Adopted to Attain VWAP

VWAP strategies typically fall into one of three categories: **sell** the order to a broker–dealer who guarantees VWAP; **cross** the order at a future date at VWAP; or **trade** the order with the goal of achieving a price of VWAP or better:

1. **Guaranteed principal VWAP bid** – This entails giving a trade list to a broker–dealer which charges a fixed per share commission and guarantees the day's VWAP for each stock.
2. **Forward VWAP cross** – This entails electronic matching of buyers and sellers and execution at the end of the day at a price equal to full-day VWAP.
3. **VWAP Trading**:
   - **Direct access** – where the order is traded by the investor, either through a participation strategy or with a view to timing the market to beat VWAP.
   - **Agency trading** – where the order is given to a broker–dealer to trade on an agency basis with a view to obtaining VWAP or better.
   - **Automated participation strategies** – which entail breaking up orders over the day to participate proportionately in the day's volume, trading as intelligently as possible and with the minimal market impact.

VWAP trading alternatives and their advantages and disadvantages are summarised in Table 8.1.

Table 8.1 VWAP Trading Alternatives

Strategy	Advantages	Disadvantages
Guaranteed principal VWAP bid	Low commission, guaranteed execution.	Exposure to significant adverse price movements. Leakage of information, especially in thinly traded stocks.
Forward VWAP cross	Low commission, no market impact.	Non-execution risk; residual must be traded. Exposure to significant adverse price movements.
Agency trading or direct access	Control over trading process, including the ability to cancel during day.	VWAP is not guaranteed. Commission costs; ticket charges add up. Significant time commitment.
Automated participation strategy	Ability to cancel during day; low cost. Can be somewhat customised.	VWAP is not guaranteed. Possibility of significant shortfalls on days with unusual price or volume patterns.

Time-Weighted Average Price (TWAP)

Time-weighted average price (TWAP) allows traders to "time slice" a trade and impose parameters (volume, limit) to achieve transaction goals. In contrast to

VWAP, this usually trades fewer stocks when the market volume drops. TWAP will trade an equal amount of stock spread out throughout the time period specified in the order.

TWAP is most advantageous for orders that must be completed by a specific time or for trades in illiquid stocks where the trader doesn't want their execution schedule to depend on volumes.

Figure 8.6 Diagrammatic Representation of TWAP

TWAP trades an equal number of shares each interval

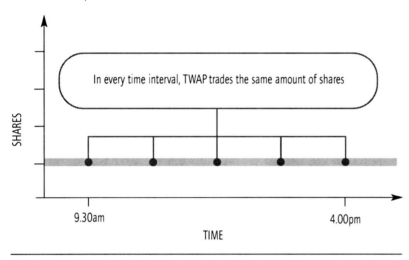

Source: Instinet Algorithms

Sample TWAP Trading Scenario

This scenario deals with an unpredictable volume pattern.

Peter T. Wopp, a trader, decides at 14:00 EST that he needs to exit a position in an illiquid stock (BizDry Chemicals – Symbol BZDY) by the 16:00 EST close. He would like his execution rate not to depend on market volumes. By placing the order in the TWAP rule, it will be executed according to a predictable time schedule between 14:00 EST and 16:00 EST.

The following is the specification of the deal ticket to reflect this order:

Sell 100,000 BZDY
Start time – 14:00
End time – 16:00
Volume constraint – 25%

Transaction Cost Analysis

No discussion of electronic and algo trading is complete without a mention of transaction cost analysis (TCA).

Transaction cost analysis (TCA), or the ability to measure effectiveness, is essential to the value proposition and the basic principle of algorithmic strategies. An algorithm's performance is defined in terms of market impact or deviation from a benchmark. The appropriate selection of a model, the parameters and constraints applied, the timing, the market venue and many other implicit and externally derived factors contribute to an algorithm's performance and results. The provision of a snapshot of trade-specific and market condition details and execution performance results are usually complete by the end-of-trade date or T+1.

Traders typically source TCA reports from both the algo providers and independent third-party services. The information provided by brokers will show results at the trader and algo level; while independent services, in addition to being unbiased, provide the added advantage of comparing execution quality across brokers. Services exist that permit interactive analysis across multiple brokers, or are able to segment trades by broker, market sector, venue, trader or portfolio manager. The use of specific trade-level details and related market data at the time of the trade (e.g. size, volume and volatility) for analysis allows users to improve their selection of dealers and the use of specific algorithms for future trades based on past results.

Common Systems Used in Trading and Exchanges

9

This chapter discusses systems commonly used in trading and in exchanges. A comparison of open outcry and automated trading is also included.

Introduction

Information Technology has been a major contributor to the development of trading and the exchange industry. Not so long ago, growth in the volume of securities transactions was constrained by the physical burden of paper-based transactions and the capacity to communicate information. However, once information could be reduced to electronic form, large amounts of financial information as well as value could be processed and transferred across markets.

As seen from previous chapters, the business processes in trading as well as exchanges are complex. This complexity, coupled with explosive growth in the number of securities traded, brings about the need to speed up the processing of trades in the face of increasing volumes of data. To this end, market participants, including brokers, traders and exchanges, require IT systems that can deliver the required operational efficiencies.

There is a plethora of IT systems available in the market place, from order management systems, trading systems, and risk management systems to software components for the dealing room, which ensure that trading will become an instantaneous electronic exchange of information between buyers and sellers, anywhere in the world, at any time.

Comparison of Open Outcry and Automated Trading Systems

Historically, open outcry was the unique method of communication between professionals on a stock exchange or futures exchange. It involves shouting and the use of hand signals to convey information primarily about buy and sell orders. The section of the trading floor where this takes place is known as a pit.

Hand signals are the preferred method of floor communication, especially in the financial futures pits, for three key reasons:

1. **Speed and efficiency** – They are a major benefit in terms of speed and efficiency as hand signals allow for fast communication over relatively long distances (as far as 30 or 40 yards) between the pits and order desks and within the pits themselves.
2. **Practicality** – In terms of practicality, hand signals are more convenient for communication than voice, given the number of people on the floor and the general noise level.
3. **Confidentiality** – Hand signals offer confidentiality, making it easier for customers to maintain anonymity, since large orders do not sit on a desk, subject to accidental disclosure.

Common Hand Signals
The most common hand signals used on the floor of most exchanges are:

146

- Buy/Sell
- Price
- Quantity
- Expiration months (for futures contracts)
- Expiration cycles
- Market signals such as those to indicate, for instance, if an order is completely filled or if an order is a working order that a broker has not filled but is still attempting to do so.

An Example of a Hand Signal

The following is an example of a hand signal used to indicate a buy or sell order.

When a broker intends to indicate that they want to buy (indicating a bid), the palm of the hand always faces towards them (see Figure 9.1). When making an offer to sell (indicating a bid), the palm always faces away from them.

Figure 9.1 Buy and Sell Hand Signals

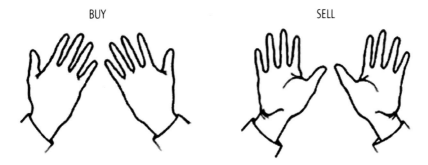

As seen in Chapter 8, there is an ongoing proliferation of electronic trading. This has prompted speculation that the open outcry system is quickly becoming obsolete. New advances in screen-based trading have forced both traders and exchanges to keep up with rapidly evolving technological developments.

Table 9.1 shows a comparison between open outcry and automated systems.

The Procedure of Online Order Execution

One of the greatest impacts of IT on trading has been the ability for traders and investors to trade online. The internet has caused major shifts in both trader and investor behaviour as well their expectations. No other sector of the world's economy has been affected by the rapid development of e-commerce as much as the securities industry. Accordingly, investors want the instantaneous trading and access-to-information capabilities that only online technologies can provide. Worldwide, markets and regulators have responded quickly to fulfil their needs.

Investors and traders alike often do not have a full understanding of what happens when they click the "enter" button on their online trading account. The

Table 9.1 Comparison of Open Outcry and Automated Trading Systems

	Open outcry trading	Electronic trading
Liquidity	Perceived to be inherently more liquid by some of the world's largest exchanges (CBOT, CME, NYSE)	Recent empirical studies have found evidence that ET may be better.
Immediacy	Orders are changed/cancelled faster, and price discovery maintained in markets under stress.	Especially during market stress, order cancellation procedure may cause delays and discourage limit orders; system may slow down or fail.
Efficiency	Different prices may exist, orders may not be fairly matched (front-running and curb-trading), with scope for human errors.	Transparent price discovery, reduced frauds and human errors.
Cost	High fixed and operating costs.	High development costs, low operating costs.
Anonymity	Provide more information about counter-party.	Adverse selection in block trades, limiting the growth of order size.
Global link	Segregated exchanges	24-hour, globally linked trading possible.

Source: Adapted from Tsang, 1999.

misconception is that their order is always filled immediately after they click the button in their account.

Investors are generally of the opinion that an online account connects them directly to the securities markets. This is not the case. When an investor places a trade, whether online or over the phone, the order goes to a broker. Upon receipt of the order, the broker then looks at the size and availability of the order to make a decision on the best way for it to be executed.

A broker can attempt to fill the trader's or investor's order in a number of ways:

- ■ **Order to the floor** – In the case of stocks trading on exchanges such as the New York Stock Exchange (NYSE), the broker can route the investor's or trader's order to the floor of the stock exchange, or to a regional exchange. In some cases, regional exchanges will pay a fee for the benefit of executing a broker's order, referred to as payment for order flow. Given that there is a human element to the order flow, it can take some time for the floor broker to get to the order and fill it.
- ■ **Order to third market maker** – For stocks trading on an exchange like the NYSE, the brokerage can direct the order to what is known as a third mar-

ket maker. A third market maker is a firm that stands ready to buy or sell a stock listed on an exchange at publicly quoted prices. This type of firm is likely to receive the order if: a) they entice the broker with an inducement to direct the order to them, or b) the broker is not a member firm of the exchange to which the order would otherwise be directed.

- **Internalisation** – Internalisation happens when the broker decides to fill the order from the inventory of stocks their brokerage firm owns. This allows for quick execution. This type of execution allows the broker's firm to make additional money on the difference between the purchase price and the sale price, i.e. the spread.
- **Electronic communications network (ECN)** – As seen in Chapter 5, ECNs automatically match buy and sell orders. These systems are used mostly for limit orders because the ECN can match by price very quickly.
- **Order to market maker** – For over-the-counter markets such as the Nasdaq, the broker can direct the trade to the market maker in charge of the stock the investor or trader wishes to purchase or sell. This is usually timely, and some brokers make additional money by sending orders to certain market makers (payment for order flow).

Figure 9.2 Brokers' Choices for Fulfilling Orders

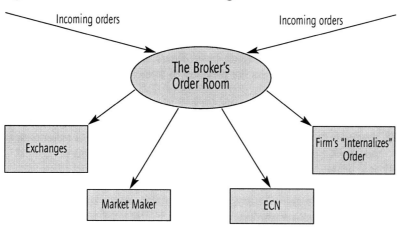

Profiles of Systems

Vendor: Progress Software
System: Apama
Proven in the most demanding of markets, Apama offers a broad, deep and flexible platform for building event-driven applications. Apama allows both business users and IT to exploit the power of complex event processing.

Progress Apama is a platform for algorithmic trading, enabling both sell-side and buy-side traders to leverage proprietary trading strategies, rather than rely-

149

on packaged "black box" algorithms. Apama's "white box" platform puts control in the hands of traders, who can create, test, deploy and manage their own algorithmic trading strategies.

In the fast-moving, increasingly fragmented FX world, traders also need speedy access to multiple liquidity venues to find the right price and depth. Traders need to get them from a trading platform that offers a sustainable, competitive advantage.

Apama's Market Aggregation Accelerator combines FX integration adapters with an integrated and pre-built (but modifiable) Apama trading dashboard that gives traders a bird's-eye market view. The FX Accelerator supports FX data streams from dealing banks, FX aggregators, and electronic crossing networks (ECNs).

Obviously in today's market, surveillance is key, but all too often market surveillance and control systems fail to deliver. Built on top of Progress Apama's Complex Event Processing (CEP) technology, the Market Surveillance Accelerator monitors, analyses and acts on fast-moving market conditions, generating alerts to analysts who can then respond while there is time.

Vendor: Horizon Software
System: Market Maker

Horizon Market Maker is a multi-purpose trading application designed for sales people and traders of investment banks to animate derivative products in real time on listed or internal markets and official platforms or via a website.

Horizon Market Maker is able to handle thousands of products via a global architecture and a global trading team. Direct exchange links to European, Asian and American markets are provided so trades can be performed worldwide.

Thousands of products are supported:

- Any type of securitised product – leverage, participation, yield enhancement and capital protection – ranging from vanilla to exotic products.
- Any underlying asset classes – equity, rates and FX products, commodities, and hybrids. There is absolutely no limitation regarding the asset class.
- All products types – futures, options, warrants, notes, certificates, spread warrants, knock-out warrants, mini-futures, barrier discount certificates, reverse convertibles, barrier reverse convertibles, capital protected products, etc.

Within the organisation, the solution is used by different areas:

- Traders, to execute orders;
- Sales, to request information;
- Administration/Compliance to control and monitor traders and sales business.

Horizon Market Maker is designed in a modular way in order to adapt to the investment bank environment, which requires high flexibility. Horizon Market Maker enables a global trading team to manage a high volume of instruments and trades thanks to shared use of a global deployment. To match trading activ-

150

ities' real-time needs, Horizon Market Maker was designed to react with delays of a few milliseconds.

The Horizon Market Maker application has different purposes, all with the same aim – to contribute continuously to the different markets:

▦ Animate investment products and leveraged products on different markets by continuously contributing bid and ask prices via pricing modules and automatons. The scope of animated products is broad, from options and warrants to structured products.
▦ Manage pricing context so that data (volatility, dividends) used for volatility calibration/price validation, for quoting and for position keeping intraday valuation, can be different. It allows the user to configure different environments on the same instrument in order to use different parameters according to the trading functions.
▦ Broadcast prices on several exchanges/platforms.
▦ Automatically generate hedging orders based on a set of user-definable rules.
▦ Allow traders to define and trade baskets.
▦ Manage risks in real time.

Horizon Market Maker is a client-server architecture composed of four main groups of functional components:

1. **Horizon Trader** – Horizon Trader is an EMS with enhanced features (mouse trading, complex order management, risk management).
2. **IMS** – The IMS provides the connectivity to markets and market feed providers.
3. **Animation Unit** – The animation unit does the market making. It is composed of three components:
   ▪ The Spotter, which produces a reliable spot for each underlying.
   ▪ The Price Streamer, which requests as few exact prices to the pricing infrastructure as possible, and performs interpolation to provide real-time prices.
   ▪ The Automaton Manager, which converts the real-time spreads provided by the Price Streamer into orders maintained on the market. It takes care of all the market events, such as executions, market status changes, etc.
4. **Pricing Unit** – The pricing unit performs the calculation of prices and provides them to the Price Streamer upon request.

At a security level, Horizon Market Maker provides users' rights management, encryption and specific protocol, audit trail and monitoring functionalities.

Key benefits
Thanks to technological interconnectedness between trading desks around the globe, Horizon Market Maker is a useful tool for implementing "follow the sun" market making. This architecture is a real asset for investment banks that are permanently present on the market.

Ease of use is highly important for traders' activities. They need to work in a friendly environment, similar to their habits, in order to bring an efficient and quick contribution to the market. Designed to facilitate traders' work, Horizon Market Maker provides a flexible and customisable GUI, allowing users to create their own workspaces handled with different sets of associated views.

Technology

Horizon Market Maker has a distributed architecture, written in Java and based on a proprietary middleware bus. This makes the system very scalable for handling increasing product and trade volumes and for implementing a fault-tolerant architecture. Horizon Market Maker industrialises the animation of a large number of products (retrieval of market data stream, pricing, animation).

The graphical interface is written in Java (Swing) and is modular thanks to its framework. Horizon provides a plug-in development kit, allowing any developer to customise or extend the software.

Vendor: Sungard
System: Front Arena

SunGard's Front Arena is a cross-asset trading infrastructure serving a range of financial institutions. Front Arena provides straight-through processing, integrating sales and distribution functions with trading capabilities, risk management and operations support. Front Arena's components can be configured to meet trading needs in both local and global installations.

As a trading solution, Front Arena supports all the market segments shown in Table 9.2 in a single solution:

Table 9.2 Market Segments supported by Front Arena

Asset Classes	Workflows
Equities	**Sales and Distribution**
It offers an order management system, while providing a trading and risk management platform across multiple markets. It also delivers straight-through processing from investors to execution venues and from original orders to confirmations.	Across asset classes, the system allows electronic connection to customers. Via a browser-based or Java client, customers are offered order management and position-keeping tools that allow them direct or internal market access.
Fixed Income and Repo	**Market Making and Proprietary Trading**
High-volume government bonds, illiquid corporates, funding instruments – the system enables all of this through pricing and credit risk management in a single view, as well as electronic distribution to multiple liquidity channels.	Front Arena offers traders ideal functionality from pre-deal pricing and direct quoting into markets to opportunity watch lists, whilst also offering deal capture, position keeping and desk-level risk management. Everything is integrated to present a unified view of risk across all asset classes.

Credit Derivatives

Front Arena offers packaged functionality for this asset class, including support to price, risk manage and process a wide range of credit derivatives, including synthetic CDOs, using semi-analytical model and base correlation. In addition, the modelling capability is extendable for proprietary valuation.

Risk Management

Front Arena allows risk management in the same system using the same analytics as Front Office. It allows for risk management of portfolios using simple greeks, applying scenario analysis and even computation of value at risk (VAR).

Interest Rate Derivatives

Front Arena allows real-time pricing and risk management of plain vanilla as well as complex instruments. Many pricing models are available including a Libor market model. An API allows for easy use of external valuation libraries. Cross-asset class trading and risk management are integrated.

Middle Office, Operations and Back Office

Front Arena supports settlement, confirmation, accounting and middle-office functions in a unified environment and helps to eliminate data integrity issues and reduce complexity.

Foreign Exchange, Money Markets, FX Options and Treasury Sales

Front Arena's financial product coverage and scalability are designed to meet all trading and treasury needs and the expanding business demand of the future.

Market and Price Connectivity

Offers connection to markets directly whilst also providing connections to real-time data vendors.

Vendor: ULLINK
System: UL TRADER

ULLINK provides connectivity and trading software solutions for the international financial community. It helps its customers build modular, scalable, vendor-neutral trading environments that custom-fit their business needs.

UL TRADER, ULLINK's order management system and trading front end, is an application which empowers front-office desks with trading capabilities.

How it is used in the trading industry

The broker's sales staff are responsible for managing client orders, i.e. orders given by the broker's buy-side clients by phone, fax, email, or electronically in an EMS. The latter buy-side electronic orders are integrated, without manual intervention. Other orders are created "electronically" in the system by the sales staff, using a dedicated interface, and according to the client's instructions.

Once the order is created, the salesperson forwards it to a trader. It is possible for them to select a specific trader (one who knows the stock well, for example) or to let automatic, broker-defined routing rules decide (such routing rules enable faster treatment).

UL TRADER is designed for both traders and sales-traders. It integrates into the broker's trading environment without impacting the underlying infrastructure.

UL TRADER is natively connected to UL ODISYS, ULLINK's order management system, and thus to the multiple execution venues available in the UL BRIDGE connectivity platform.

A number of natively integrated modules complement the UL TRADER solution:

- Basket trading (sending a number of orders simultaneously);
- Waving (slicing a large order into several smaller orders to ensure discreet execution);
- Scheduling (sending orders at specific hours or at specific time intervals during the day);
- Algorithmic trading (sending orders at prices and quantities calculated automatically);
- All four modules can be combined with Excel to leverage trading strategies;
- Real-time Excel link (using Microsoft RTD technology).

Benefits of using the system

Dealers are responsible for the execution of client orders in the best possible conditions. UL TRADER provides them with trading tools which help them achieve this objective. The UL TRADER's dedicated Dealer interface enables the trader to:

- display market data from any vendor (real time and history);
- manage client orders (manual creation, order monitoring, re-assignment);
- manage market orders (creation, executions, multi-asset class trading);
- handle post-trade (allocation, commissioning, archiving);
- support multiple execution channels (DMA, brokers, routing networks, algorithmic engines);
- aggregate multiple exchanges (MiFID & RegNMS);
- customise their interface according to their needs and preferences.

UL TRADER is readily available for any institution looking for a comprehensive order management and trading system.

Three major global brokers are already in production with UL TRADER, using the system to trade across global markets and across asset classes.

List of Other Systems

Table 9.3 shows a list of some of the other systems used in the trading and exchanges industry, the vendors and the uses of these systems.

Table 9.3 Systems, Vendors and Uses

System	Vendor / Provider	Uses
Baxter Trading Platform	Baxter Solutions	Used for pricing, order matching, trade execution and validation as well as distribution of liquidity
dConfirm	Digiterre	Used for automation and consolidation of post-trade confirmations
Endur	Openlink Financial	An integrated front-through-back solution used for trading and risk management in energy markets such as crude oil and natural gas
EZE OMS	BNY ConvergEX Group	This is a multi-class order management system used to monitor real-time performance, perform and track program trading and capture data for best-execution analytics
Fidessa Trading Platform	Fidessa	A multi-asset class trading system used for trading a wide range of securities and routing orders to the appropriate execution venues
I-Trader	Swissrisk Financial Systems	This is a platform used by issuers, traders and market makers to trade and quote instruments on multiple exchanges and ECNs concurrently
kACE^2 The Analytics Platform	Kalahari	Used by traders for complex financial modelling
Longview Trading	Linedata Services	A trade order management solution used by the buy side for order generation and trade execution
Microgen Cortex+	Microgen Plus	This is a web-enabled trading solution used for trading derivatives including e-minis
MX.3	Murex	Used for trading and risk management across asset classes such as equities and commodities
ORS Order Management	Acquin Components GmbH	Used for automation of the order process
Pyramid	Ferential Systems Inc.	Used for supporting front-to-back derivatives processing including initial deal entry and valuation

Reuters Trading for Exchanges	Thomson Reuters	Used by traders who use Reuters 3000 Xtra to create and route orders to a choice of executing/clearing brokers, using the prices they see on the desktop, for any exchange-traded instruments including equities and energy derivatives
SLIB OMS	SLIB	An instrument trade book used by broker-dealers to automate order flows according to predefined routing rules
Tradis Workstation	3i Infotech	This is a trade order management system used by traders and brokers that has multi-instrument coverage including commodities, equities, futures and options

Factors Driving Users' Choice of Electronic Trading Platforms

Electronic trading involves a change in trading technology that potentially allows new market structures to appear. The possibility of this happening and the degree to which users adopt the new structures are dependent to a large extent on the explicit and implicit costs of trading in these systems. Nevertheless, historical factors as well as potential entry barriers due to first-mover advantages also affect the choices of users and so the system with the least cost for a particular user may not actually be chosen.

Explicit Trading Costs
In most wholesale markets, the explicit costs of trading are made up of market access fees, commissions, tax, clearing and settlement costs, and staff and IT overheads. While fixed IT costs may at the moment be higher in electronic trading than in traditional markets, electronic trading has the potential to significantly reduce many of the variable cost components of processing orders. Therefore, provided that the trading volume is of sufficient scale, the average cost of trading will be lower in electronic markets than in traditional trading.

Furthermore, the scalability of electronic trading allows market participants to take advantage of economies of scale to a far greater extent than was possible in traditional markets.

Implicit Trading Costs
The implicit costs of trading include the bid-ask spread paid to a liquidity provider and the price impact of the trade (i.e. the degree to which the trade price moves away from the current market price as a result of the trade). In dealer markets, investors pay the trader a bid-ask spread as compensation for sup-

plying liquidity, i.e. immediacy of trade execution. The trader's bid-ask spread must cover their explicit trading costs, their profit margin and a liquidity risk premium (i.e. the risk of being unable to unwind the transaction at a predictable cost). ET systems potentially reduce all components of the dealer's bid-ask spread, and thus the implicit costs.

First Mover Advantages

Users' choice of trading system may be limited by various external factors arising from the nature of the IT industry. Advantages for so-called "first movers" include being able to set the standard for a particular type of trading system, after which users can be "locked in" because the cost of changing over to another system with a different standard is considered be on the very high side.

Historical and Institutional Factors

Users' choice of trading system may also depend on the historical evolution of that market and its existing structure (usually referred to as "path dependency"), vested interests and the relative market power of the various institutions that may limit the scope for market evolution.

Electronic Trading Platform Characteristics and Services

Electronic trading platforms may have characteristics and offer services according to the requirements of market participants. Table 9.4 shows the characteristics and services of some notable electronic bond trading platforms.

Table 9.4 Characteristics and Services of Electronic Bond Trading Platforms

Platform Name	Type of System	Trading Method	Trading Platform Participants	Pre-trade Prices Available	Information Available to Participants
Autobahn	Single dealer-to-(buy-side) customer.	Order driven. Market-making or cross-matching. Request for quote.	Institutional investors.	Executable.	Spread.

Automated Bond System (ABS)	Inter-dealer.	Order driven.	Dealers as providers of liquidity. Dealers as consumers of liquidity. Institutional investors.	Executable. Last traded price.	Price, Yield, Size.
BondWeb	Inter-dealer.	Multiple dealer-to-(buy-side) customer.	Market-making or cross-matching. Request for quote. Dealers as providers of liquidity. Dealers as consumers of liquidity. Institutional investors.	Executable. Indicative.	Price, Yield, Spread, Size.
CreditTrade	Inter-dealer.	Order driven.	Dealers as providers of liquidity. Dealers as consumers of liquidity.	Executable. Indicative. Last traded price.	Price, Bid/Ask, Size.
eSpeed, Inc.	Inter-dealer.	Order driven.	Dealers as providers of liquidity. Dealers as consumers of liquidity.	Executable. Indicative. Last traded price.	Price, Yield, Bid/Ask, Size.
Eurex	Multiple dealer-to-(buy-side) customer.	Order driven. Market-making or cross-matching. Request for quote. Auction.	Dealers as providers of liquidity. Dealers as consumers of liquidity. Institutional investors.	Executable. Last traded price.	

MarketAxess	Multiple dealer-to-(buy-side) customer.	Request for quote.	Dealers as providers of liquidity. Institutional investors.	Indicative. Last traded price.	Price, Yield, Spread, Size.
SWX Eurobonds	Multiple dealer-to-(buy-side) customer.	Order driven.	Dealers as providers of liquidity. Dealers as consumers of liquidity. Institutional investors.	Executable.	Price, Size.
TradeWeb LLC	Multiple dealer-to-(buy-side) customer.	Request for quote.	Dealers as providers of liquidity. Dealers as consumers of liquidity. Institutional investors.	Indicative.	Price, Size.
ValuBond, Inc.	Inter-dealer	Market-making or cross-matching. Request for quote.	Dealers as providers of liquidity. Dealers as consumers of liquidity.	Executable. Indicative. Last traded price.	Price, Yield, Size.

Source: eCommerce in the Fixed-Income Markets, SIFMA

IT Projects

This chapter discusses IT projects that can be undertaken in organisations that engage in trading as well as in traditional exchanges.

Introduction

IT projects are the lifeblood of the support role that IT plays in the trading and exchange industries. As seen in previous chapters, competition is rife in the exchange industry with the proliferation of alternative execution venues.

As for trading, there is increasing activity from the retail investor community looking to trade anything from shares and currencies to contracts for difference (CFDs), with technology being the main enabler for the increase in this type of trading activity.

To keep abreast of competition, exchanges need to plan and execute IT projects that enhance their IT infrastructure as well as deliver sustainable competitive advantage. In addition, with the introduction of new financial instruments, the popularity of multi-asset and cross-asset trading and the attendant increase in data volumes, exchanges have to upgrade their existing systems and implement new systems to ensure that they offer their customers the desired level of service.

CFD providers and non-bank foreign exchange trading platforms also have to plan for an increase in trading activity and execute IT projects accordingly. Additionally, they need to continually improve their level of service to maintain their competitive position. Planning and execution of the appropriate IT projects play an important role in the achievement of this objective.

Implementation of Electronic Trading Systems

IT projects involving the implementation of trading systems are some of the most strategic undertakings at exchanges, brokerages, investment banks and other market participants. Front-office trading systems are essentially the backbone of the IT infrastructure and support traders by processing their transactions. The implementation of electronic trading systems has been instrumental to the transformation of the landscape of trading venues, thereby enforcing changes in market architecture and trading possibilities. The advent of cutting-edge technology has allowed for the design of trading systems to feature linkages to electronic order routing and dissemination of trade information, and also linkages to clearing and settlement systems.

In most exchanges, brokerages and investment backs, a trading system is typically linked to a number of internal and external applications. In order to achieve seamless integration front-to-back through straight-through processing, systems architects usually design appropriate trade workflows.

What is the Basic Role of a Trading System?

As seen in Chapter 2, the trading life cycle involves a sequence of events from deal capture through to accounting. Regardless of the type of trade, the various trade events can be categorised into front-office, middle-office and back-office activities. The workflow of trading systems is designed to mirror these sequences of events. Thus, the basic role of trading is to:

- capture trades of a trading desk;
- enable traders to track their positions and both realised and unrealised profit and loss (P&L);
- allow risk managers to have access to trade data that can be used to monitor risk across portfolios, strategies and trading desks;
- allow for checks on the compliance of the trading operation with regulatory or internal rules and conformity to market procedures;
- establish a connection to back-office, accounting and other downstream systems.

An implementation project for a new trading system can either be a greenfield project, i.e. a project that is starting completely from scratch and thus having no existing code base, or an upgrade project that involves the replacement of an existing system. One of the greatest challenges faced by IT functions in recent times has been the implementation of true electronic multi-asset trading systems. Not only are there many technology integration issues, there is also a broad range of cultural sensitivities that IT staff need to navigate when bringing various business lines closer together on one trading platform.

Project Phases
The following are the six project phases of a typical trading system implementation project; some are generic to any type of systems implementation and others specific to the implementation of this type of system.

Figure 10.1 Project Phases of Trading Systems Implementation

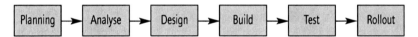

Planning
This is generic to the implementation of any type of system. At this stage, the objective of the implementation project is outlined.

Analyse
This entails the following:

- identification of financial instruments, workflows, and trade life cycle of the system;
- organisation of a high-level system architecture that takes account of all the interfaces to the system that need to be built during the project;
- development of the relevant project plans for the design and build phases as well as the data migration and testing.

Design
This involves the following:

- organisation of user access rights;
- specification of portfolio/book structure;
- determination of static data requirements;
- how instruments to be traded will be captured;
- specification of workflow and trade cycle events;
- modelling of interest rate curves and spread curves;
- specification of P&L and risk measures.

Build

In this phase some of the activities involved include:

- coding;
- customisation, if required;
- technical architecture implementation, which encompasses the set-up of the production and test environment;
- test phase preparation;
- unit testing.

Test

Activities in this phase include the necessary testing activities:[85]

- **System test** – Depending on the development methodology employed, once all modules have been developed and unit-tested, system testing should be executed. This involves validation and verification of the workflows as well the report generation to ensure that they are functioning as designed. In addition, it is essential to verify that the user access rights structure supports the workflow design.
- **Integration test** – The objective of this test is the verification of the proper functioning of cross-system workflows and data flows as well the interfaces to these other systems, both individually and collectively.
- **Data migration test** – This is a dress rehearsal for data migration, i.e. migration of both static and transactional data.
- **User acceptance test (UAT)** – This is the stage at which the users of the trading system will test it to ensure it meets the requirements specified in the analysis and design phases.

Rollout

This is the final phase of the implementation where the trading system is productionised. Activities in this phase include:

- data migration/loading;
- deployment of the system into the production environment;

85 The activities in the test phase vary as there are different methodologies used in modern software development. Therefore, it will be beneficial to regard this discussion as a guide.

■ user training.

Data Considerations
Market data

Market data refers to quote and trade-related data associated with financial instruments such as equity, fixed income and derivatives. The term market data traditionally refers to numerical price data originating from trading venues, such as stock exchanges. The price data is attached to a ticker symbol and additional data about the trade.

Market data is vitally essential to trading, given that this information is increasingly indispensable for the timely and accurate execution of every individual step of the trade process and all derived processes.

Trading systems require a market data feed so that they can receive the current pricing information, and place and manage orders. Thus, implementation of a trading system is not complete without ensuring connectivity to a market data provider such as Bloomberg.

In most cases, the data feed is received via trading software and an API (programming interface). APIs are usually in several different programming languages such as C/C++ and Java, and enable market data to be used by independent order entry systems.

Potential static data issues

When implementing trading systems, there are potential static data issues which should be considered as they could cascade through the front-to-back trade flow resulting in settlement failure. Regardless of whether the implementation is a greenfield project or an upgrade, the data migration strategy has to be well thought out.

Data analysis should be a prerequisite to data migration and should involve a two-step process: data profiling and mapping. Data profiling entails performing a detailed study of the source data in order to gain an understanding of its content, structure, quality and integrity. As soon as the data has been profiled, an accurate set of mapping specifications should be developed based on this profile in the next process, data mapping. The combination of data profiling and mapping comprises the crucial first step in any successful data migration project and should ideally be completed prior to attempting to extract, scrub, transform and load the data into the target database.

Implementation of Cloud Computing in Exchanges

Implementation of cloud computing brings the electronic stock market to desktop computers. Some industry observers define cloud computing narrowly as an updated version of utility computing: basically, virtual servers available over the internet. Others go very broad, arguing that anything consumed outside the firewall is "in the cloud", including conventional outsourcing.

Cloud computing fulfils an increasingly important role in IT, i.e. increasing capacity or adding capabilities rapidly without any new investment in infrastructure, training of new personnel, or licensing of new software. In essence, cloud computing includes any subscription-based or pay-per-use service that, in real time over the internet, extends IT's existing capabilities.

What is Cloud Computing?

The term "cloud computing" probably derives from (at least partly) the use of a cloud image to represent the internet or some large networked environment. Some industry experts assert that it is essentially a black box that can be depended upon for reliably sending and receiving data. Others maintain that cloud computing is now associated with a higher-level abstraction of the cloud. In place of data pipes, the routers and servers are now services. The underlying hardware and software of networking is, of course, still in existence but there are now higher-level service capabilities available that are used to develop applications. Behind the services are data and computer resources. A user of the service doesn't necessarily care about how it is implemented, what technologies are used or how it's managed, only that there is access to it and it has a level of reliability essential to the fulfilment of the application requirements.

It is, in essence, distributed computing. An application is built using the resources from multiple services, potentially from multiple locations. At this point, users still typically need to know the endpoint to access the services rather than having the cloud provide them with available resources. This is also referred to as "software as a service". Behind the service interface is usually a grid of computers to provide the resources. The grid is usually hosted by one company and consists of a harmonised environment of hardware and software, making it easier to support and maintain. The minute that users start paying for the service, and the resources utilised, it could be classed as utility computing.

The following is a breakdown of what cloud computing is all about:

- **SaaS** – This is a type of cloud computing that delivers a single application through the browser to customers using a multi-tenanted architecture.
- **Utility computing** – This form of cloud computing has been around for a while and is getting a new life from a number of providers who offer storage and virtual servers that the IT function can access on demand. Organisations that were early adopters typically use utility computing for supplemental, non-mission-critical requirements.
- **Platform as a service** – This is a variation of SaaS and is a form of cloud computing that delivers development environments as a service. Applications can be built that will run on the provider's infrastructure and can be delivered to users via the internet from the provider's servers.
- **Service commerce platforms** – This is another variation of SaaS and is a form of cloud computing that offers a service hub which users interact with, and is common in trading environments.

Case Study on the Implementation of Cloud Computing

A case study on the implementation of Nasdaq Market Replay will be used in this section to illustrate cloud computing.

Nasdaq Market Replay[86]

A universal experience in the stock market is wondering "what happened?" A trader sees a situation flash by on their trading screen and wonders whether a similar opportunity may arise again. An investor receives a trade confirmation and wonders why the trade occurred at a price they weren't expecting. What these people need is a way to rewind and replay the market, slow it down and zoom in to the second and even the millisecond level to see exactly what happened.

Since its inception, the NASDAQ stock market has continuously invested to increase market transparency by rolling out new and improved data products. As trading accelerated over the years, NASDAQ OMX realised that even their most sophisticated market participants were losing the ability to understand what was happening. Market events happen too fast and the datasets are too large and expensive to store and retrieve. Even participants with large budgets have to take older data offline to prevent their databases from becoming too slow and expensive. NASDAQ saw the problem and began looking for a way to provide low-cost, permanent instant replay for the market.

Unfortunately, they met the same hurdle faced by their customers. The NASDAQ stock market trades all NASDAQ-, NYSE-, and AMEX-listed stocks, some 6,000 companies in all. Even limiting their product to the most fundamental information produced 50 GB of data each day. The cost of keeping years of data in a database ready for immediate retrieval looked set to put their product at a price point that would have been prohibitive to most investors.

During the summer of 2007, they learned about two new technologies, Adobe AIR and Amazon S3, and realised that they could combine them to solve their data challenges. Adobe AIR enabled them to build a powerful client-side application that would do most of the data manipulation and rendering on their client's computer. That enabled them to build a very simple data service, storing the market data in text files that they could make available on Amazon's inexpensive, scalable and reliable Simple Storage Service (S3).

Data model

NASDAQ OMX could avoid using a database on the server side because the data required for replay and analysis is very well organised. It's entirely sequential by date, stock symbol and time. There is a very clean and simple way to break the data into individual files. One file covers a single stock symbol on a single day for a single 10-minute time period (all time periods are standardised

---

86 By Claude Courbois, Associate Vice President, Global Data Products, NASDAQ OMX Group.

9:25–9:35, 9:35–9:45, etc.). The filename identifies the stock, date and time period of the data in the file. They run a process that transforms real-time market data into the required files and sends them to Amazon S3.

A user begins a replay by entering a stock symbol, date and time. The client application translates that symbol, date and time information into a filename. The client then reaches out to S3 and asks for the file that it needs. S3 is very, very fast at finding files and sending back the contents.

There are many advantages to building their data product on a commodity service like Amazon S3. The most important is that they have a huge ability to scale their product in terms of the amount of data they store and the number of customers they serve. Amazon S3 already contains billions of files and has no problem handling millions of requests incredibly quickly. Even their most ambitious growth expectations will not tax the infrastructure.

Amazon provides them with a level of reliability that would have been very expensive to build in on their own. All of the data is stored on servers in three different data centres. If one copy is overloaded or corrupted, another copy immediately takes its place.

On the cost side, there are two main advantages to building the product in the cloud. The first is that they get this enormous scalability in very small increments. They pay only for what they use, but always have more capacity available. Buying the same level of scalability on their own would require large incremental costs, part of which would be for servers that would be sitting idle.

Second, their costs are entirely predictable. Amazon has a published price list of each increment of service that they use. They know exactly how much it costs to store their data and they know exactly how much it costs for each customer query. This facilitates planning and enables them to price the service as competitively as possible without any "padding" for unexpected costs.

User interface

Because of the size and complexity of stock market data, NASDAQ OMX could not have stored the data in text files on Amazon S3 without a powerful client application. They needed the capacity to prepare the data for the visualisations and calculations required by users. The combination of Adobe Flex and AIR enabled them to create the client application they needed.

AIR supports more robust data processing on the client side than they could have achieved in a browser. This made it possible for them to push most of the workload of creating a replay and other analysis to the user's desktop. For example, the client application calculates the consolidated best bid and offer for every millisecond in a replay without any help from their servers.

NASDAQ OMX also had the benefit of beginning their application user interface with standard Adobe Flex 3 components. They made modifications to those components for their particular application, but it saved development costs to start with tools that were already available and tested. As an additional benefit, the components they built can now be shared across web properties, enabling them to share the maintenance cost of the application components across multiple products.

These advantages helped NASDAQ OMX create a user interface with the latest Web 2.0 features that were not offered by other historical market data clients. Market Replay enables users to view the quotes and trades at any point in time, replay the market in simulated real time and zoom to view events at the millisecond level. Investors can validate the quality of their trades. Brokers and traders can review events at the time when their trades occurred to determine whether there was a problem or a missed opportunity. Brokers can send clients a NASDAQ-validated screenshot of the moment a trade occurred to validate their performance.

Conclusion

Web 2.0 and cloud computing enabled NASDAQ OMX to launch a revolutionary stock market tool by dramatically reducing the cost of storing, distributing, and manipulating that data. They can provide every quote and trade update for every US-listed security to an unlimited number of end-users without delays and without ever needing to take data offline. And they do it in a user interface that brings the latest Web 2.0 features to financial data for the first time.

For professional market participants, Market Replay has greatly reduced the cost of analysing market data. For example, brokers can reduce the time and costs associated with fielding calls from customers or regulators about the quality of their trades. Analysts can quickly revisit the market impact of news and other events to find opportunities they can use in the future.

For individual investors, Market Replay increases confidence in the market by enabling them to see exactly what happened at the time of their trades. This is a level of accessibility to market information that has traditionally only been available to the most sophisticated professional traders. NASDAQ OMX now makes this level of access available at a price point that makes it possible for individual investors to get access through online brokers and financial portals.

Infrastructure Optimisation – Front to Back Office – Trade to Settlement

The information technology (IT) infrastructure is regarded as a strategic asset and the fundamental base upon which software can provide the services and user applications that a business requires in order to achieve both success and operational efficiency.

Industry observers acknowledge that infrastructure optimisation facilitates the realisation of the value of investments in IT infrastructure. In the case of financial services, where the business is totally dependent on technology, this applies across the trade life cycle – buy side, sell side, exchange, settlement and payments, to name but a few components. It also allows the IT infrastructure to be viewed as a strategic asset that allows for varying degrees of agility, and ultimately helps such organisations create an infrastructure for a business that is "people and business-enabling". In today's climate, adaptability at speed and cost is crucial. For example, trading organisations need to view their stance on

169

low latency and the ROI in staying in the race, and exchanges or brokerages need to look at the implications of MiFID from a compliance and competitive standpoint. That the infrastructure is people- and business-ready means they are able to adapt to trading environments and capable of bringing new products and services to market in a timely and cost-effective fashion through a linkage of people, information and business processes that can help eradicate inefficiencies as well as enhance market responsiveness.

In this section, fasterLAB will be showcased as a model product that can be used for optimising infrastructures in exchanges and other firms such as brokerages across the financial life cycles. Use of the fasterLAB can be an ideal IT project for infrastructure testing, evolution and optimisation.

fasterLAB[87]
Tuning front-office infrastructures for Formula 1 trading performance

RegNMS in the USA, MiFID in Europe, decimalisation and the natural competitive challenges of the marketplace, combined with leaps in technological capability, have all conspired to make the trading arena of financial services a cauldron of focus for speed and performance in the execution of trades across global markets. While today's challenges raise uncertainty, trading volumes have increased and with them market data volumes continue to multiply. Whatever the economic prognosis, the technology infrastructure challenge does not go away.

Technology is both an enabler and disruptive force as the market evolves – enabling higher performance and lowering the barriers to entry to new players who can respond to the markets changing, competitive and regulatory dynamics.

Massive technology investments have and are being made in the trading arena – making it critical to make the correct choices, mixes and matches with the component parts which make up the enabling infrastructure on which to build new trading business practices.

Traditionally, the focus of technology has been on the writing or buying of software functionality to support business applications – concentration on infrastructure stopped at the consideration of operating system and hardware vendor. In recent times, investigation into the performance edge that technology can give is diving deep into the elements within the hardware and inner workings of the total computer environment. Chip processors, data and computer grids, standards-based messaging, virtualised architectures, high-speed interconnects, "wire speeds", real-time middleware and acceleration tools are now becoming important parts of the mix and adding to the headache of setting technology strategies.

Optimised (trading) infrastructures are on the edge of performance, innovation and stability. The drive for low latency has to take each element into consideration, but how can the risk-return of deploying technologies be seen, measured and taken forward into production?

87   By Nigel Woodward, European Head of Financial Services at Intel.

The elements have to be tested in combination for the optimum mix – combining Formula 1 performance with operational sustainability to stay on the track for the course of the race.

How to do this – where can test beds be found with enough access to the technology mix to show the effects of different combinations? How are systems tested and battle-hardened before entering the trading fray – and managing the operational risk of change and enhancement?

No one place currently exists – until, that is, the creation of Intel's fasterLAB facility.

Taking the technology solution stack, we can see the many-layered components, from the very base with Intel's processors to application software and user interfaces. Vendors at every level provide their own testing facilities and, of course, the now infamous "Proof of Concept" as lures into the sirens' den of a visible way forward to solution glory!

So, the challenge is how to achieve a critical mass of variety, mix and match technologies, add new components and test the different combinations in a cost-effective manner with a level of independence which protects the objectivity of the activity.

The market favours and drives open standards – across messaging and underlying technologies – from the success of Unix and Java through SOA, AMPQ plus open source, the Linux explosion and X86 as the homogenising standard in the processor infrastructure.

To achieve a trading edge, capital cost has not been the priority, and hence many Tier 1 firms in the market can simulate environments in-house, albeit stretching resources to the limit. The best brains in the market can be hired, but access to technology firms' resources and motivation is not a core skill set. For Tier 2 and beyond, the optimisation task is to all intents impossible.

Intel has been the major driving force behind the establishment of X86 and its effect on lower hardware prices and higher processor performance across the industry. Intel Architecture (IA) has become the market share leader in the infrastructure layer and as such is an accepted common denominator for technology.

Building on this de facto industry position, Intel uses its architectural and market influence to draw together, through the fasterLAB, the additional components which together make up the (trading) solution stack. Intel's strong market presence and reputation for consistent innovation means that for many firms across the market, working in IA (Intel Architecture) is an acceptable default strategic position. Building on this base, the fasterLAB can facilitate the juxtaposition of layers higher up the infrastructural stack – and draw together best-practice combinations which are most likely to deliver at the leading edge.

Moving from "now" to the "future" and evolving the current infrastructure is a complex task of handling fast-moving parts, with severe consequences if the order of engineering destabilises the whole environment.

During the last 24 months,[88] the market has become obsessed with low

---

88 24 months from the time of writing.

latency – and a technology-enabled edge is an arms race that has ensued. Whether this will continue in the same away is a moot point (October 2008) as the future is rewritten – but what is consistent is that the skills to win with optimised technology will apply to any ongoing scenario.

Through the fasterLAB, Intel is using its de facto open standards market position to draw in the components of contributing partnering companies. Allying this to deep software and hardware engineering, plus consulting, data centre and project management skills in their Software Services Group, and the quest for the trading low latency combination comes into focus.

So how does the Intel fasterLAB achieve this? Starting with the base layer – from interdependent relationships with all the major hardware vendors, the fasterLAB is equipped with the most recent products and hardware combinations. Layered on top of the hardware foundation, the fasterLAB adds a range across the choices of high-performance and acceleration technologies, all measured by sophisticated monitoring tools. Additionally, deep in the silicon, IA's own unique acceleration tools and specialist processor cards, e.g. IO acceleration, have enhanced FIX message throughput by up to 30% and FAST market data compression is enabling the handling of data volumes in line with the projection of the graphs from the markets' major venues.

Engagements with the fasterLAB deliver tangible, rapid benefits. Intel's Core 2 and Nehalem micro architectures with dual, quad and multi processors are being implanted in existing X86 architectures with immediate performance uplift. This provides business execution speed and, of course, the reciprocal benefit of reduced energy consumption for the same workloads – assisting the eco elements of the agenda. Whether it be front-office trading speeds or middle- and back-office settlement volumes – optimisation is always relevant.

Benchmarks go only so far, and provide only indicative statements of performance – albeit exciting tools for the salesperson and marketer. The fasterLAB goes a step further. Testing out best-known combinations of technology is a new dimension, as is the ability to work on clients' own code.

Low latency – as with other performance-related measurements – is not achieved at a single end point. We must follow the trade on its round-trip life history – from the execution venues' export of market data, to its arrival into the front office and marriage with the trading engine, which itself has to be synchronised with the client orders and compliance before routing for execution – while ensuring that "best" is achieved and auditable as such.

Which element, therefore, contributes most to lower latency, what are the operational risks in exposing a currently stable infrastructure to technical open-heart surgery in the quest for higher trading stamina?

The fasterLAB deploys project management disciplines

To unlock the lab's potential, first discovery and understanding of the target technology organs for surgery or treatment have to be achieved. Normally undertaken by workshop under strict NDA conditions by the Intel team and potentially selected pre-qualified partnering technologists, the discovery session feeds the construction of proposals to identify the best bets for lab activity leading to latency gains. Deliverables in this phase are detailed architectural analyses, and the early pointers and roadmap towards repairing, improving or replacing current speed bumps in the infrastructure.

Time, resources and physical assets cost money and in this respect the fasterLAB has a cost to all participating parties – contributors and client beneficiaries. Leveraging the principle that technology companies' core business is "product" not services, the fasterLAB delivers on a cost recovery basis. Designed to keep parties motivated, it encourage sights to be ranged on the end goal of successfully deployed technologies which can be tuned on an ongoing basis rather than a short termism of focus and experience.

Ongoing – the Formula 1 analogy continues. Between races in the season, the optimisation continues and the same can be true in today's world of trading and operation in financial markets. New technologies and interpretations of their optimum combination are streaming into the market with relentless velocity. The fasterLAB is both the fully equipped pit stop and factory outlet – an innovative meeting point that can facilitate the leading teams' successes.

Commonly Used Terminology

This chapter contains a list of terminology commonly used in the trading and exchanges industry.

Introduction

Trading is perhaps the most prominent and complex aspect of the financial services industry, more so than lending, deposits and advisory services. It is also safe to assume that readers agree that the terminology used in trading is outside the diction that they are familiar with. Thus, it is essential to have an appreciation of the jargon used in trading and exchanges.

Movies such as *Wall Street* and *Trading Places* starring Michael Douglas and Eddie Murphy contain scenes of trading in stocks and commodities respectively, and in these scenes a lot of the terminology that is still relevant to exchange trading in more recent times was used. It is advisable for readers to pick up copies of these movies and pay attention to the scenes specific to trading.

Below is a list of some of the terms used in trading and exchanges.

List of Terms

Above Par This term is used to refer to the situation where the market value of a security, especially a bond, is above its face value.

Around Quoting jargon used by dealers in FX when the forward premium/discount is near parity. For example, "two-two around" means 2 points to either side of the present spot rate.

Auctioning system A trading platform in which a trader requests a price from a pricing source, and then makes a buy or sell decision based on the quote offered.

Automated trading This is the type of trading whereby prices can be published and executed by IT systems.

Backtesting A computer-aided process employed by traders when trying to estimate how financial instruments would have performed in the past had a particular mechanical trading system been employed to trade them.

Basis point One one-hundredth of a per cent or 0.01%.

Bear market A market where prices are declining.

Bear raid This is a situation where a trader attempts to drive down the price of a particular security by heavy selling or short selling.

Bearer securities Securities that are not registered.

Best execution This is the term used to describe the responsibility of brokers to provide the best price and order execution for their clients.

Beta A measure of a security's sensitivity to changes in the overall market.

Big figure Dealer expression used in the forex market for the first few digits of an exchange rate. These digits are omitted in dealer quotes, as they rarely change in normal market fluctuations. For example, a USD/YEN rate would be quoted verbally without the first three digits, i.e. "31/36" – instead of 102.31/102.36.

Bilateral netting An agreement between two parties under which they exchange only the net difference between what each owes the other. The main aim is to reduce exposure to credit and settlement risk.

Black box trading This terminology is used to describe the use of automated trading programs which seek to profit from market price swings, as well as arbitrage, between trading exchanges. Black box trading systems, i.e. those running these types of program, are often used to determine optimal trading practices. These systems construct many different types of data including buy and sell signals.

Blind broker A broker who acts as principal and does not give up names to either side of a brokered trade.

Bond Debt security that requires the issuer to pay the holder interest during the term of the bond, with some exceptions, and the principal at or before maturity.

Book The summary of a desk's or trader's total positions.

Book-entry system[†] An accounting system that permits the electronic transfer of securities without the physical movement of certificates.

Book value Value computed from historical costs and expenses using accounting rules rather than current market value.

Break a trade This is the practice whereby a long or short position is prematurely unwound in a security with respect to the intended trading strategy.

Bull market A market where prices are rising.

Buy-in A purchase of securities in the open market by a lender (or its agent) in order to replace loaned securities that a borrower has not been able to return.

Cable The GBP/USD exchange rate, which derives its name by virtue of being transmitted via a transatlantic cable, beginning in the mid 1800s.

Carry The interest cost of financing a securities inventory; may be either positive or negative.

Cash and carry An arbitrage strategy that generally consists of the purchase of a particular security and the sale of a similar security (often the purchase of a security and the sale of a corresponding futures contract).

Cash flow Net cash produced by an asset, as opposed to earnings calculated by accounting rules.

Cash trade A non-financing transition sale or purchase of securities.

Central securities depository (CSD) An institution for holding securities, which enables securities transactions to be processed by means of book entries.

Physical securities may be immobilised by the depository or securities may be dematerialised (so that they exist only as electronic documents).

Cheapest to deliver The bond from among the deliverable bonds most likely to be selected for delivery into the futures contract.

Churning A period of intense trading with few sustained price trends and small movements in stock market indexes.

Circuit breaker A number of measures used by stock exchanges during large sell-offs to avert panic selling.

Circular trading A fraudulent trading scheme whereby sell orders are entered by a broker who knows that offsetting buy orders, the same number of shares at the same time and at the same price, either have been or will be entered.

Close-out (and) netting An arrangement to settle all existing obligations to and claims on a counterparty by one single net payment, immediately upon the occurrence of a defined event of default.

Closing (or back) leg[†] Second leg of a pair of transactions in the same securities, i.e. a securities lending transaction – one for a near value date, the other for a value date further into the future.

Cocktail swap A complex transaction based on several different types of swaps and involving more than two counterparties.

Collateral pool A portfolio of securities, each with a specified yield (or yield formula) and expected term to maturity, that is purchased by a lender with cash collateral received in connection with a securities loan.

Collateral yield The annual rate of return on a collateral portfolio, expressed as a percentage. Also referred to as reinvestment yield.

Commission A transaction fee charged by a broker.

Composite A group of individual portfolios, retaining their original attributes, that are treated as a single portfolio for analysis.

Conduit borrower An intermediary in the securities lending chain, acting as principal, that borrows securities in order to lend them at a higher spread to another borrower whose credit may not be acceptable to the original lender or whose credit facility is filled with the original lender.

Corporate action This is a corporate event, initiated by a company, which brings about material changes that impact on its shareholders. In some cases, shareholders may or must respond to the corporate action or select from a list of possible actions. Typical events include spin-offs, mergers and stock splits.

Country code The code that identifies the country from which a security was issued.

Coupon The periodic interest payment on a security paid by the issuer to the holder, usually quoted as an annual percentage of the face amount.

Coupon frequency The number of interest payments made on an annual basis.

Crack spread The spread created as a result of a purchase of oil futures and the offsetting of the position by selling gasoline and heating oil futures.

Cross border trading Trading that occurs between counterparties from different countries.

Cross hedge This is the practice of hedging a risk in a cash market security by buying or selling a futures contract for a similar, but not identical, instrument.

Cross trade An illegal practice outlawed on most major stock exchanges in which buy and sell orders for the same stock are offset without recording the trade on the exchange.

Custody risk This is the risk that occurs from the inability to hold secure custody of assets or from incurring loss by failing to obtain or release the correct secure custody when conducting purchase and sale transactions.

Dark liquidity pools These are private intra-bank or inter-bank platforms used for trading in stock away from traditional exchanges.

Daycount method The method used to count the days in a month and the days in a year, denoted as follows: (days in a month)/(days in a year).

Daylight exposure The risk that a market participant faces when related transactions are not settled simultaneously but at different times during the trading day, especially relevant when dealing in different time zones.

Decision price This is the price of a stock that informs the decision to buy or sell.

Defensive stock This is a type of stock such as oil, tobacco and utilities that is illiquid and tends to remain stable under difficult economic conditions.

Delist The removal of a stock from an exchange due to a violation or a failure to meet certain requirements.

Dematerialisation[†] The elimination of physical certificates or documents of title which represent ownership of securities so that securities exist only as accounting records.

Depth of market This is the ability of the market to maintain relatively large market orders without affecting the price of the security.

Direct market access (DMA) This is a service offered by broker–dealers that enables clients to place buy and sell orders directly on electronic exchanges.

DK A questioned trade; a trade that is rejected because of some type of problem or operational error.

Dragon bond A bond that is issued in Asia but denominated in US dollars because the currency is more stable and might entice foreign investors.

179

DV01 ("Dollar value of .01") The approximate change in price (for $100 face value) for a one basis-point change in yield (0.01%).

Economic indicator A government-generated statistic that reflects current economic growth and stability. Such indicators include employment rates, gross domestic product (GDP), inflation etc.

Efficient portfolio A portfolio that provides the greatest expected return for a given level of risk.

Equity price risk The risk of loss incurred as a result of movements in equity prices.

Escrow (securities lending) A service that involves collateral management services, including marking to market, repricing and delivery, by a third party.

Exchange seat The membership on an exchange that is a requirement for transacting business on that exchange.

Execution risk This is the risk associated with trade execution that is the possibility that an order may be slipped in price or lost entirely, resulting in loss or reduced profit.

Exhaustion This is a situation whereby the majority of participants that trade in the same asset are either long or short and leave few investors to take the other side of the transaction when participants wish to close their positions.

Failed transaction A securities transaction that does not settle on the contractual settlement date.

Fill or kill An order given to a broker that must immediately be filled in its entirety or, if this is not possible, totally cancelled. Fill or kill orders require the transaction be filled completely and immediately, or not at all.

Financial information exchange (FIX) protocol This is a series of messaging specifications for the electronic communication of trade-related messages, developed for securities transactions and markets.

Fourth market This refers to the direct trading of large blocks of securities between institutional investors through a computer network, rather than on an exchange.

Front running The unethical or illegal practice of a broker trading an equity based on information from the analyst department before their clients have been presented with the information.

Global custodian[†] A custodian that provides its customers with custody services in respect of securities traded and settled not only in the country in which the custodian is located but also in numerous other countries throughout the world.

Goldbrick shares A stock that bears the surface appearance of quality and worth, which could in reality be worth very little.

Gross-paying securities[*] Securities on which interest or distributions are paid without any taxes being withheld.

Hedge The method for making offsetting commitments to reduce the impact of adverse movements in the price of a security.

Highs This term is used to refer to stocks that have reached new 52-week high prices in the current or most recent trading session.

High-touch trading This is a trading method whereby prices are quoted over the phone.

Historical data This is past information about a company, such as historical price, price/earnings ratio, revenues and revenue growth, that is used in the process of forecasting the company's future.

Hit the bid This is a situation where a dealer agrees to sell at the highest price offered ("bid") by another dealer for a given stock.

Income attribution This is the breakdown of total income by its sources.

Indemnification An agreement to compensate for damage or loss.

Index A statistical composite that measures changes in the economy or financial markets.

Indicative price (quote) Bid or offer price provided by way of information rather than as the level at which a trader is willing to trade. Indicative prices (quotes) enable a customer to plan a transaction but the transaction does not proceed until firm prices are provided.

Integrated portfolio A portfolio whereby a funding and collateral portfolio are combined.

Interest rate risk This is the risk that the value of a security might be reduced as a result of a change in interest rate levels.

Jitney This is a situation in which a broker who has direct access to a stock exchange performs trades for another broker who does not have access.

Leading indicators These are statistics that are used to anticipate future economic activity.

Legal risk[†] The risk of loss because of the unexpected application of a law or regulation, or because a contract cannot be enforced.

Liquidity The ease with which a security can be traded on the market.

Listing The acceptance of a security, such as a company's stock, for trading on a registered exchange.

Lot Multiple shares held or traded together, usually in units of 100.

Lows Stocks that have reached new 52-week low prices in the current or most recent trading session.

Margin Margin is a good faith deposit that a trader puts up as collateral to hold a position.

Margin buying A technique that entails the purchasing of securities with borrowed money.

Margin call A call from a broker to a client or from a clearing house to a clearing member. Also referred to as a maintenance margin call.

Market price This is the last reported sale price of a security that is traded on an exchange, or, if traded over the counter, its ask and bid prices in the open market.

Marking-to-market Revaluation of a security in a trade to current market values.

Matched book A portfolio of assets and portfolio of liabilities that have equal maturities.

Matching (or comparison)[†] The process for comparing the trade or settlement details provided by counterparties to ensure that they agree with respect to the terms of the transaction.

Matrix trading The swapping of bonds, designed to profit from unusual yield curve differentials between bonds of different ratings or classes.

Mechanical investing This is the practice of buying and selling stocks according to a screen based on predetermined criteria, usually ranking stocks using relative strength or momentum as the central indicator, but other indicators can also be used.

Migration risk This is the risk that is associated with the possibility that a change in the credit quality of a security issuer will either increase or decrease the value of the security that it has issued.

Municipal bond A bond issued by a state, city, or local government, where the revenue is used to raise capital for the government's day-to-day activities.

Net paying securities[*] Securities on which interest or other distributions are paid net of withholding taxes.

New money The amount by which a replacement issue of securities exceeds the original issue (more money is raised for the borrower).

Off-floor order This is an order placed with a broker that does not occur on the floor of an exchange.

Offsetting transaction This is a trade that cancels or offsets some or all of the market risk of an open position.

Open transactions Transactions that have no fixed maturity date and there is a chance that the transactions may be terminated or the rebate rate renegotiated on a daily basis.

Orphan stock A stock that has been largely disregarded by research analysts, but may be an undiscovered bargain.

OTC bulletin board This refers to an electronic quotation system, used for unlisted, over-the-counter securities.

Overnight A trade that is open until the next business day.

Pair off[*] The netting of cash and securities in the settlement of two trades in the same security for the same value date. Pairing off allows for settlement of net differences.

Par Face value of a bond. Its value as it appears on the certificate or instrument.

Payup Cash required of the buyer to settle a trade. In a securities swap, payup is required when the securities bought are more expensive than the securities sold.

Price transparency Describes quotes to which every market participant has equal access.

Principal A party to a transaction that acts on its own behalf. In acting as a principal, a firm is buying/selling from its own account for position and risk, expecting to make a profit.

Proprietary trading[*] Trading activity conducted by an investment bank for its own account rather than that of its client.

Quote An indicative market price normally used for information purposes only.

Quote size This refers to the number of shares that is being offered for purchase at the bid price, often expressed in terms of hundreds of shares.

Real-time gross settlement (RTGS) The continuous (real-time) settlement of funds or securities transfers individually on an order-by-order basis (without netting).

Repricing The process of marking to market.

Resistance level This is the price at which a stock or market can trade, but not exceed, for a certain period of time.

Risk-adjusted return The return on a lender's lending activity based on the risks it took to generate the revenue.

Roll Renewal of a trade at its maturity.

Rolling settlement[†] A situation in which settlement of securities transactions takes place each day, the settlement of an individual transaction taking place a given number of days after the deal has been struck. This is in contrast to a situation in which settlement takes place only on certain days – for example, once a week or once a month – and the settlement of an individual transaction takes place on the next settlement day (or sometimes the next but one settlement day) following the day the deal is struck.

Samurai bond A yen-denominated bond issued in Tokyo by a non-Japanese company that allows the company to access investment capital available in Japan.

Screen-based trading Trading executed through a network of electronic terminals.

Secured bond This is a type of bond, such as a mortgage bond, which is backed by an asset from the issuer, which serves as collateral for the bond.

Securities settlement system (SSS) A system in which the settlement of securities takes place.

Settlement interval The amount of time that elapses between the trade date (T) and the settlement date, typically measured relative to the trade date, e.g. if three days elapse, the settlement interval is T+3.

Shaping* A practice whereby delivery of a large amount of a security may be made in several smaller blocks so as to reduce the potential consequences of a fail.

Short and distort This is an illegal practice used by unethical internet investors who engage in short-selling a stock and then spread uncorroborated rumours and other kinds of unconfirmed negative news in an attempt to drive down the equity's price and realise a profit.

Solvency risk The risk of loss owing to the failure (bankruptcy) of an issuer of a financial asset or to the insolvency of the counterparty.

Squawk box A speaker and intercom system used on trading desks that allows a firm's analysts and traders to communicate with the firm's brokers through speakers on the brokers' desks.

Straight-through processing The automated end-to-end processing of trades, which entails the automated completion of trading life-cycle activities such as confirmation, generation, clearing and settlement of instructions.

Subcustodian A custodian bank that is responsible for the safekeeping of securities within a single country and in only one currency. In contrast, a global custodian manages a network of subcustodians in order to perform custody operations for its clients worldwide.

Sushi bond This is a Eurobond issued by a Japanese company.

Takeout The cash balance on hand as of the final settlement date.

Take the offer Expression for a stock buyer's willingness to accept a floor broker's (listed) or dealer's (OTC) offer price at an agreed-upon volume. Opposite of hit the bid.

Technical analysis This is a technique that is used to forecast the future direction of security prices through the study of past market data, primarily price and volume in a financial market.

Term transactions[†] Transactions with a fixed end or maturity date.

Thin market[*] A market in which trading volume and issue liquidity are low and in which bid and ask quote spreads are wide.

Tick The standard minimum pricing unit in a particular market.

Ticker symbol This is a combination of letters used to uniquely identify a stock or mutual fund listed and traded on an exchange.

Tomorrow next (tom/next) The simultaneous purchase and sale of a currency for delivery the following day.

Trade blotter A log of trades and the details of the trades made over a period of time (usually one trading day). The details of a trade will include such items as the trade date, price, order size and a specification of whether it was a buy or sell order. Trade blotters are used to carefully document the trades so that they can be reviewed and confirmed by the trader or the prime broker.

Trading desk A dedicated desk in an investment bank or brokerage firm where transactions for buying and selling securities occur.

Trading halt This occurs when the trading of a particular security on one or more exchanges is paused, typically in anticipation of a news announcement or to correct an order imbalance.

Trading range The spread between the high and low prices traded during a period of time.

Tranche A portion of a share issue.

Unit This is a specific quantity accepted as a standard for exchange.

Unit of trading This is used to denote each single, indivisible amount in a transaction. An example is the unit of trade for stocks which is a share.

Unmatched book (open book, short book)[*] When the average maturity of a bank's or a portfolio's assets exceed the average maturity of its liabilities.

Variation margin This is an additional margin payment that is made by clearing members to their respective clearing houses in the event of market fluctuations of the futures contracts that these members hold.

Wash trading This is a stock trading practice that is illegal and entails an investor simultaneously buying and selling shares in a company through two different brokers.

Whipsaw This is a sharp price movement that is quickly followed by a sharp reversal in a highly volatile market.

Yield curve The yield curve describes the relation between the interest rates and the maturity dates of bonds for a given currency.

Zero coupon bond This is a type of bond that does not offer any interest (a coupon), but trades at a deep discount of face value, offering the potential for return when the instrument matures at full face value.

Zero-sum game This is used to describe a situation where one market participant's gains are only the result of another participant's losses. For instance, futures trading is a zero-sum game because for every holder of a profitable contract, there is another investor or series of investors holding the losses reflected in the other side of that contract.

*   Source: "An Introduction to Securities Lending", © Mark C. Faulkner

†   Source: "Securities lending transactions: market development and implications", © International Organisation of Securities Commissions and Bank for International Settlements 1999. All rights reserved.

The Future

*This chapter discusses the future
of trading and exchanges from both
an IT and business perspective.*

The Future: What does it hold for IT and Business in Trading and Exchanges?

The future of IT and business in trading and exchanges will be shaped by the turmoil that has beset the financial markets since the turn of the century. First, it was the dot-com bubble that burst in the early 2000s, caused by investors' disenchantment with technology stocks. This occurred because of the unknown and innovative nature of online business that led to the abandonment of many standard business models in the early 1990s in favour of radical new models which focused on brand building and networking before giving any consideration to profits. The idea placed emphasis on increasing market share whilst operating at a loss. The novelty value of these companies, and the difficulty in valuing them properly, led to an incredible excitement with which stocks in the new dot-com companies were purchased. This in turn led to them being increasingly over-valued, perpetuating the enthusiasm for buying stocks. This enthusiasm cooled when there was a market correction to the value of these technology-based stocks. Between 2000 and 2002, $5 trillion in the market value of technology companies was wiped out on Nasdaq, the exchange on which most of these stocks were traded.

Secondly, there was the terrorist attack on the United States on 11 September 2001. Financial markets remained closed for the next four trading sessions. When stocks began trading again on 17 September, the Dow Jones industrial average (a stock market index) fell 684.71 points, its biggest one-day point loss in history.[89]

In more recent times there has been the credit crunch, which has been thrust upon the financial markets since 2007. At the time of writing, the full effects of the credit crunch are unknown. Judging from the way in which major stock market indexes around the world, from the USA to Russia, have been fluctuating in the wake of such events as the collapse of Bear Stearns and Lehman Brothers, and the bail-out of AIG, Freddie Mac and Fannie Mae by the US government, it is difficult to predict investor sentiments towards financial stocks in the future.

Nevertheless, the following is an attempt to predict the future of trading and exchanges from both a business and IT perspective.

Consolidation in the Exchange Sector

If past events are to be used to predict the future, then there will be continued consolidation, especially cross-border mergers, of the global stock exchange sector. The benefits offered by cross-border mergers to the larger stock markets include access to higher liquidity, new markets and an increased number of list-

89 Alexander Winn, "Stocks: 5 Years after 9/11", 11 September 2006. Available from http://money.cnn.com/2006/09/08/markets/markets_fiveyearslater/index.htm.

ings. Despite the difficulties inherent in these cross-border deals such as legal requirements, differences in management styles, and disagreements over where (and under what laws and regulations) a combined company should be based, they are still set to continue in the future.

Sharing of IT assets between stock exchanges as well as collaboration of development projects will also proliferate to enable round-the-clock trading. A typical example was witnessed in 2007 when the London Stock Exchange (LSE) and the Tokyo Stock Exchange (TSE) formed a business alliance.

Increased Competition from Alternative Execution Venues

In recent times, a number of alternative execution venues have been created to compete with the traditional exchanges. They range from dark liquidity pools to trading venues such as Chi-X. However, a notable execution venue provides a glimpse into the future of the competitive environment of exchange trading, and that is a multi-lateral trading platform known as Project Turquoise.

Project Turquoise has been designed as a low-cost trading platform to compete with Europe's stock exchanges, as well as to access hidden pools of liquidity that are often off-exchange. Advances in technology and the European regulation, MiFID, have been instrumental in the successful creation of this platform. Under MiFID, a market participant has an obligation of best execution from traders, so they have to check against all execution venues including alternatives like Turquoise. The key to gaining increasing market share will be to offer lower costs, to be faster and to be more reliable than traditional exchanges. In addition, they will have to overcome connectivity issues given that MiFID allows for market participants to connect to more than one execution venue in the quest for best execution.

Increasing Role of Technology in Trading

Technology will play an increasing role in trading in the future, especially in the area of risk management. There will be increasing demand for risk management systems that can prevent trading losses such as the incident of January 2008 at Société Générale Bank, when the bank lost approximately €4.9 billion closing out trading positions over three days of trading starting from 21 January 2008. These losses were allegedly as a result of fraudulent transactions created by Jérôme Kerviel, a trader with the firm. The trader was alleged to have admitted to exceeding his credit limits.

Whilst it could be argued that inadequate risk management practices might have been responsible for the actions of the trader in exceeding his credit limit unnoticed, the implementation of appropriate risk management systems could have prevented this from happening. Appropriately designed risk management

189

systems can generate reports that fully capture the entire population of trades within each category of trading activity and aggregate total credit exposures across all product lines on a system-wide basis. These systems could help generate reports that identify violations of credit guidelines resulting from an inability to recognise collateral or the failure to adjust credit lines.

Risk management systems will help in the monitoring of the consistency of information contained in a firm's trade processing and financial reporting and prevent the omission of certain accounts and activities from the risk monitoring function. They will help to ensure that the appropriate risk measures are utilised and are commensurate with the complexity of products traded.

The increasing complexity of derivative instruments traded nowadays is partly to blame for the recent credit crisis in the financial markets. It could be argued that had the appropriate risk management systems been in place, the losses at some of the world's largest investment banks could have been minimised.

Exchanges, investment banks and brokerages will continue to use algorithmic trading systems to trade more profitably. However, we contest the prediction by IBM that by 2015 there will be 90% fewer traders employed by the top investment banks as they lose their jobs to computer systems.[90] Whilst algorithmic trading may offer speed as well as the ability to operate around the clock without wages, it is still bereft of the ability that human traders possess to take strategic risk positions that computer systems are less able to determine.

Exchanges will continue to update their IT systems, given the evidence that technology platforms help to increase trade volumes on exchanges. According to industry reports, a total of 212 million electronic equity trades took place at the London Stock Exchange and its subsidiary Borsa Italiana in 2007, for instance, as a result of the adoption of a new technology platform, TradElect. Average daily numbers of trades were reported to be up 55% over the year to 839,244, while the average daily value traded grew 41% to £12.8 billion.[91]

Emergence of New Trading Hotspots

The future will witness the emergence of new trading hotspots looking to rival exchanges in the more developed financial institutions such as New York, London, Hong Kong and Tokyo. Notable among them is the Dubai International Financial Exchange (DIFX). Once regarded as a trading hub, it is set to rank among the top exchange groups in the world in the international capital markets.

The exchange, according to its website, www.difx.ae, lists shares, structured products and conventional bonds as well as Islamic bonds (Sukuk). It is part-

90 Tim Ferguson, "Computers to replace city traders by 2015?", 3 October 2006. Available from www.silicon.com/financialservices/0,3800010322,39162911,00.htm.
91 Tom Young, "Stock Exchange IT improves Trade Volume", 9 January 2008. Available from http://www.computing.co.uk/computing/news/2206850/lse-improves-trading-volume.

owned by the Nasdaq OMX and Borse Dubai, which is the majority stakeholder with two-thirds of the shares. The other third of the shares is owned by Nasdaq OMX.

Analysis of its DIFX market model document shows that its trading platform, the DIFX trading platform, is *"an anonymous, order-driven market but allows for market makers to make markets in the products listed"*. Also, all the types of orders discussed in Chapter 3 are available on this platform.

DIFX also has a clearing function as well as a central counterparty (CCP) facility.

Exchanges in Africa will also become trading hotspots in the long term. Prior to 1989, there were just five stock markets in sub-Saharan Africa and three in North Africa. As of August 2007, there were 19 stock exchanges ranging from starts-ups like the Uganda and Mozambique stock exchanges to the Nigeria and Johannesburg stock exchanges.[92] Experts assert that despite the rapid development of stock markets on this continent, even the most advanced African stock markets are relatively immature. They also state that in the majority of these stock markets, trading occurs in only a few stocks, which account for a considerable part of the total market capitalisation. Additionally, these markets suffer from the problem of low liquidity. The implication of this low liquidity is that it will be harder to support a local market with its own trading system, market analysis, brokers and the like because the business volume will simply be too low.

Despite these shortcomings, industry observers believe that the African stock markets are set for a period of rapid growth as long as they can overcome a number of challenges including:[93]

- regionalisation of stock markets in Africa as a panacea to the problem of low liquidity;
- demutualisation to help solve the governance and profitability problems;
- how to achieve a wider dissemination of information on these markets, the implementation of robust electronic trading systems, and the adoption of central depository systems.

Changes in the Nature of Trading

Short-selling of stocks has been a profitable way for traders at hedge funds especially to generate huge fortunes for their firms. Short-sellers are often looked upon with suspicion because, in the view of many, they profit from the misfortune of others. The practice is not illegal but it is unpopular with company directors. Short-selling has been blamed for being a contributing factor in crashes as far back as the Dutch tulip market in the 17th century. It was banned

---

92 Charles Amo Yartey and Charles Komla Adjasi, (August 2007), Stock Market Development in Sub-Saharan Africa: Critical Issues and Challenges. IMF Working Paper WP/07/209.

93 Ibid.

in England in the 18th century and regulations were imposed on it in the USA after some believed it was responsible for the Wall Street Crash of 1929.[94]

However, in the wake of the recent credit crises, short selling has been under the spotlight in a number of countries as it is perceived as one of causes of the decline of financial stocks. In the UK, for instance, short sellers targeted the shares of HBOS, selling them short and at the same time driving the price of the shares down. This led to the eventual takeover of the bank by a high-street rival, LloydsTSB.

Industry observers advocate a return to the "buy and hold" model in the wake of the subprime crises. Some, however, are of the opinion that the "originate and sell" model, the antithesis of the "buy and hold", will not see a elemental reversal, but rather will undergo a more narrow set of changes, addressing specific failings that were exposed mainly on the business execution side.

Generally, the following are some of the characteristics common to the organisations that were impacted:

- **failure to create transparency** with regard to aggregate risk exposures and sensitivities in stress scenarios;
- **poor risk control, underwriting and pricing discipline**, including the acceptance of maturity mismatches;
- **over-reliance on rating agencies**, sometimes ignoring the fact that ratings for CDO tranches are far from equivalent to bond rating standards.

Without a doubt it will take a while to work through these issues; but fundamental economic considerations around arbitrage and performance leverage, which resulted in the emergence of securitisation, will not become unpopular. Experts opine that the industry and external parties will use the lessons learnt from recent failures to ensure future successes by making necessary adjustments, especially:

- **improved governance and market discipline, as well as stricter standards** (lending and pricing), both at the front end of origination and on the side of the regulators;
- **increased transparency** regarding packaged risks, implying simpler structures (most likely with less leverage), and active preparation for life beyond rating agencies;
- **independent, "educated" investors** with a clear appetite for, and understanding of, underlying risks.[95]

In the future, the volume of derivatives traded either on exchanges or over the counter will be reduced, given the role of credit derivatives in the credit crises in recent times.

94 Daily Telegraph, "What is Short Selling", 22 March 2008. Available from www.telegraph.co.uk/money/main.jhtml?xml=/money/2008/03/21/nhedgie321.xml.
95 Oliver Wyman, "State of the Financial Services Industry", 2008 Annual Report.

How did Credit Derivatives contribute to the Credit Crunch?

The following will be used to illustrate the contribution of credit derivatives to the credit crises:

1. Suppose a US citizen, Stephanie Derry, was given a sub-prime home loan of 250,000 USD in 2003 by a lender, despite her ineligibility for a loan of this magnitude.
2. At the time, the lender had no problem in raising the funds. It bundled up Stephanie's loan with tens of thousands of others in a collateralised debt obligation (CDO), a credit derivative.
3. The lender then sold the CDO to another bank and received cash in exchange for the right to receive regular mortgage payments from Stephanie and other borrowers in the bundle.
4. This practice now continued, with banks trading CDOs with one another – either by using CDOs as collateral to borrow funds or selling them outright.
5. By the middle of 2007, Stephanie and a vast number of other American mortgagees were unable to meet their mortgage repayments, and the value of real estate in the USA began to tumble. This marked the beginning of the end of the US housing bubble. There were a lot of home repossessions and the number of mortgagees that would default was uncertain.
6. Holders of CDOs ran into problems as they were not sure of the quality of the mortgagees in their bundle, i.e. whether they were good or "toxic". As a result, the market values of these CDOs began to plummet to almost zero as the market for them dried up. Unfortunately, banks still had loans to repay.
7. The fallout from this was the reluctance of banks to lend to each other. They increased the interest rate they charged each other for loans. In essence, it was the inability to borrow money that caused the demise of the likes of Lehman Brothers.

On the evidence above, it would be logical to conclude that the trading of credit derivatives will be on the decline in future.

Conclusion

Trading will continue to be the lifeblood of the financial markets, and exchanges around the world will continue to facilitate the trading activities of traders and investors alike. The future is bright for IT professionals who are willing to increase their knowledge of trading as well as the workings of the numerous types of exchanges.

Figure 12.1 Chronology of the 2007 Mortgage Crisis and Subsequent Crises

Fear	Panic	Fallout recognition
Rising defaults and risk	Spreads, equity, markets	Sizing and fire-fighting
January–June	**July–September**	**October–December**
January HSBC issues first profit warning because of US$10.5bn bad debt charges over US mortage book. **February** Fremont General sells subprime business. New Century stops issuing loans. **April** New Century files for bankruptcy. NAR: 5.4% slump in existing home sales in Feb, largest monthly fall in 18 years. **June** Bear Stearns' hedge funds near collapse; Merrill Lynch accepts US$850m for collateral assets.	**July** Credit agencies downgrade subprime bonds. IKB bailed out. **August** Bear Stearns' hedge funds bankrupt. Central Banks (FED, ECB BoJ) pump funds of ~US$280bn into repo markets. FED cuts discount rate by 50bp to 5.7%. **September** Countrywide plans 12,000 job cuts. Bank of England bails out Northern Rock. FED lowers funds and discount rates by 50bp.	**October** Citigroup declares write-downs of US$5.9bn. Group of banks discloses plan of launching superfund M-LEC. Merrill Lynch revises total write-downs to US$8.4bn; CEO O'Neal steps down. UBS confirms write-downs of US$3.4bn. FED lowers funds and discount rates by 25bp. **November** Citigroup declares further write-downs of US$8.11bn; CEO Prince resigns. Swiss Re writes down US$1.07bn. Citigroup to sell stake to Abu Dhabi Investment Authority for US$7.5bn. E-trade receives US$2.6bn from Citadel; CEO Caplan steps down. **December** UBS writes down further US$10bn, sale of stakes to GIC and Middle East investor. FED lowers funds and discount rates by 25bp. Five big Central Banks team up for cash loans of >US$100bn; ECB to flood market with record two-week tender of US$500bn. Largest decline ever recorded for Case-Shiller US home price index; new US home sales at 12-year low in November.

Source: Oliver Wyman press research

Appendix

Bibliography

Adjasi, C. K. and Yartey, C. A. (2007). "Stock Market Development in Sub-Saharan Africa: Critical Issues and Challenges". *International Monetary Fund Working Paper WP/07/209*, pp6–8.

Aima. "Convertible Arbitrage Strategy", *AIMA Canada Strategy Paper Series*, Number 6, September 2006.

Allen, H., Hawkins, J. and Sato, S. (2001). "Electronic Trading and its Implication for Financial Market Systems", *BIS Papers No. 7*. pp34–36.

Amenc, N. and Martellini, L. (2002). "Portfolio Optimization and Hedge Fund Style Allocation Decisions".

Amos, G. and Nolan, D. (2001). *Mastering Treasury Office Operations*, Financial Times, Prentice Hall.

Baltazar, M. (2004). *The Beginner's Guide to Financial Spread Betting*, Harriman House Publishing.

Bank for International Settlement (January 2001). "The implications of Electronic Trading in Financial Markets", *Report by Committee on Global Financial System*, pp3–8.

Bauch, M. "The Global Electronic Stock Market". Available from http://investopedia.com/printable.asp?a=/articles/06/globalelectronic market.asp.

Berstein, P. "A Primer on Exchange-Traded Funds", *Journal of Accountancy*, January 2002.

Borio, C. "Market Liquidity and Stress: Selected Issues and Policy Implications", *BIS Quarterly Review*, November 2000.

Brady, N. (January 1989). *Report of the Presidential Task Force on Market Mechanism*, Washington, D.C. Government Printing Office.

Brokers Advisory Committee, "The Role of Interdealer Brokers in the Fixed Income Markets", Securities Industry and Financial Markets Association.

Carsey, T. W. "The Electronic Investor", *Barron's*, 07 July 2008.

Chisholm, A. (2002). *An Introduction to Capital Markets*, John Wiley and Sons.

Choi, J. Y., Salandro, D. and Shastri, K. (1998). "On the Estimation of Bid-Ask Spreads: Theory and Evidence". *Journal of Financial and Quantitative Analysis*, 23(2):245–69.

City AM. "Cashing in on Assets You'll Never Even Buy", *City AM Contracts For Difference Supplement*, 13 May 2008.

Collins, C., Frost, A. and Pretcher, R. (2000). *The Elliott Wave Principle: Key to Market Behavior*, John Wiley & Sons.

Cripps, E. "Demand for DMA", *FT Mandate*. November 2007.

Davies, R. "Former Casenove Partner Faces Insider Dealing Case", *City AM*, 25 July 2008.

Dealing with Technology, "Dipping into Cross Assets", *Cross Asset Trading Special Report*, 12 May 2008.

Dealing with Technology, "Exploiting New Reality Trading Technology", *DWT 2008 Special Report*, 26 May 2008.

Degryse, H. and Van Achter, M. "Alternative Trading Systems and Liquidity", *Centre for Economic Studies Discussion Paper Series*, p2. Available from www.econ.kuleuven.be/ces/discussionpapers/default.htm.

Depository Trust & Clearing Corporation, "Following a Trade", *A Guide to DTCC's Pivotal Roles in How Securities Change Hands*, p5.

Dubai International Financial Exchange, "DIFX Market Model", 23 June 2006. Available from http://www.difx.ae/Files/downloads/DIFX_Market_Model.pdf.

Elder, A. (2002). *Come into my Trading Room*, John Wiley & Sons.

Elder, A. (2008). *Sell and Sell Short*, John Wiley & Sons.

Elliott Wave International, "How the Wave Principle Can Improve Your Trading". Available from www.elliottwave.com.

Fackler, M. "In Japan, Day-Trading like It's 1999", *The New York Times*, 19 February 2006.

Faithorn, J. "Turn the Trading Floor into a Casino", *City AM*, 11 June 2008.

Falush, S. "Banks Compete for Growing Retail FX Business", *Reuters*, 30 November 2007.

Galper, J. (August 1999). "Three Business Models for the Stock Exchange Industry", *MIT Sloane School of Management*, pp4–10.

Gangahar, A. and Grant, J. "Responding to Liquidity Pools", *Financial Times*, 23 June 2008.

Gatheral, J. *The Volatility Surface: A Practitioner's Guide*, John Wiley & Sons.

Goya, P. and Lawande, S. (2006). *Grid Revolution: An Introduction to Enterprise Grid Computing*, McGraw-Hill Osborne.

Harris, L. (2002). *Trading and Exchanges: Market Microstructure for Practitioners*, OUP USA.

Hawkins, K. "Exchange-Traded Funds (ETFs)".
Available from www.investopedia.com/university/exchange-traded-fund/.

Hendershott, T. "Electronic Trading in Financial Markets", *IT Pro*, July/August 2003.

Hope, K. "The Secret to Doing Deals Without Tears", *City AM*, 17 June 2008.

Hope, K. "Why Japanese Housewives Go Crazy for Forex", *City AM*, 25 June 2008.

Hope, K. "Use Spreadbets to Protect You When Markets are Stormy", *City AM*, 23 July 2008.

Inderjit, C. et al. (2006). "St. John's University Undergraduate Student Managed Investment Fund Presents Goldman Sachs Inc."

Instinet, "TWAP", *Instinet Algorithms*. Available from www.instinet.com.

Investopedia Staff, "Gauging Sentiments with the Volatility Index". Available from http://investopedia.com/printable.asp?a=/articles/technical/02/081202.asp.

Iran Daily, "The Ultimate Money Machine", *Economic Focus*, 7 May 2007.

Jadega, S. "How Wave Power can Help You to Read the Markets", *City A.M.*, 26 August 2008.

Johnson, J. and Tabb, L. (January 2007). "Groping in the Dark: Navigating Crossing Networks and Other Dark Pools of Liquidity". Available from www.tabbgroup.com/research.

Jones, D. "Use Binaries, Bungees and Other Tricks to Make a Killing", *City A.M.*, 30 June 2008.

Joys, J. "Electronic Trading Systems and Fixed Income Markets: 2001", *Tuck School of Business at Dartmouth*, Case No. 6-0006.

Kaljuvee, A. (2008). *Straight Through Processing for Financial Services*, Academic Press.

Katz, A. "Leverage Your Returns with a Convertible Arbitrage". Available from www.investopedia.com/articles/bonds/08/leverage-convertible-hedge.asp.

Keeper, J. "Traders' and Investors' Role in the Marketplace". Available from http://www.investopedia.com/articles/basics/07/trading_investing.asp.

Keeper, J. "Using Options Instead of Equity". Available from www.investopedia.com/articles/optioninvestor/07/options_instead_equity.asp.

Kendall, K. (2007). *Electronic and Algorithmic Trading Technology*, Academic Press.

Kissell, R. "The Expanded Implementation Shortfall: Understanding Transaction Cost Components", *Journal of Trading*, Summer 2006.

Knorr, E. and Gruman, G. "What Cloud Computing Really Means", *The New York Times*, 7 April 2008.

Kolb, R. (2007). *Futures, Options and Swaps*, Blackwell Publishers.

Lamb, K. "Understanding Structured Products". Available from www.investopedia.com/articles/optioninvestor/07/structured_products.asp.

Lerman, J. (2001). *Exchange Traded Funds and E-mini Stock Index Futures*, John Wiley & Sons.

Lhabitant, F. S. (2006). *Handbook of Hedge Funds*, John Wiley & Sons, Ltd.

Lhabitant, F. S. (2002). *Hedge Funds – Myths and Limits*, John Wiley & Sons, Ltd.

Lien, K. (2006). *Day-Trading the Currency Market: Technical and Fundamental Strategies to Profit from Market Swings*, John Wiley & Sons.

Madhavan, M. "VWAP Strategies", *Transaction Performance*, Spring 2002.

Malkiel, B. G. (April 2003). "The Efficient Market Hypothesis and Its Critics", *Princeton University CEPS Working Paper No. 91*, p3.

McClean, H. "Retail FX Providers", *e-Forex*, October 2006. pp118–122.

McClure, B. "Trade Takeover Stocks with Merger Arbitrage". http://investopedia.com/printable.asp?a=/articles/stocks/06/merger arbitrage.asp.

McKhann, C. "Introducing the VIX Options". Available from http://investopedia.com/printable.asp?a=/articles/optioninvestor/06/NewVIX.asp.

Mehrling, P. "Monetary Policy Implementation: A Microstructure Approach", Department of Economics, Barnard College, Columbia University. (March 2006).

Miller, M. (2008). *Cloud Computing: Web-Based Applications That Change the Way You Work and Collaborate Online*, QUE.

198

Moore, E. "Stock: Going Short as Markets Falter", *Financial Times*, 13 March 2008.

Norman, J. "A Good Trading Plan is the First Step if You Want To Make Money with CFDs", *City AM.*, 23 July 2008.

Norman, J. (2008). *CFDs: The Definitive Guide to Trading Contracts for Difference*, Harriman House Publishing.

Picarda, D. "Fixed-Odds: A Bet for Every Moment", *Investor Chronicle*, 4 July 2008.

Plummer, T. and Poser, S. (2003). *Applying Elliott Wave Theory Profitably*, John Wiley & Sons.

Poole, A. (2007). *Statistical Arbitrage: Algorithmic Trading Insights and Techniques*, John Wiley & Sons.

Pryor, M. (2007). *The Financial Spread Betting Handbook: A Guide to Making Money Trading Spread Bets*, Harriman House Publishing.

Richards, A. (2007). *Understanding Exchange-Traded Funds*, McGraw-Hill Professional.

Rime, D. (2003). *New Economy Handbook*, Elsevier Science (USA).

Robinson, S. "Citi and Goldman Break into Retail FX", *FX Week*, 26 November 2007.

Rosenberg, L. (2008). *ETF Strategies and Tactics*, McGraw-Hill Professional.

Sarr, A. and Lybek, T. (2002). "Measuring Liquidity in Financial Markets", *IMF Working Paper WP/02/232*, p4.

Schmerken, I. "Direct Market Access Trading", *Wall Street and Technology*, 4 February 2005.

Sclossberg, B. "Trend Trading or Range?". Available from http://investopedia.com/printable.asp?a=/articles/forex/05/050505.asp.

Shamah, S. (2003). *A Foreign Exchange Primer*, John Wiley & Sons Ltd.

Shaw, E. "In Volatile Market Times There are Still Investments That Offer a Safe Haven", *City A.M.*, 1 August 2008.

Tellefsen Consulting Group, Inc. "Algorithmic Trading Trends and Drivers", January 2005 presentation.

Temperton, P. "Trading with the Help of 'Guerrillas' and 'Snipers'", *Financial Times*, 19 March 2007.

The Definitive Guide to Swing Trading. Available from www.SwingTrader Guide.com.

The Economist. (April 2007). "It's all Derivative", *Market View*. Available from www.economist.com/finance/displaystory.cfm?story_id=E1_JDNPSDQ.

The Economist. (June 2007). "The Best Newsreaders May Soon be Computers". Available from http://www.economist.com/finance/displaystory.cfm?story_id=9370718.

Timmons, H. "A London Hedge Fund That Opts for Engineers, Not MBAs", *New York Times*, 18 August 2006.

Upper, C. (February 2000). "How Safe Was the 'Safe Haven'? Financial Market Liquidity During the 1998 Turbulence", *Discussion Paper 1/100 Economic Research Group of the Deutsche Bundesbank*, pp6–8.

Van Bergen, J. "Investor Intelligence Sentiment Index". Available from http://investopedia.com/printable.asp?a=/articles/trading/03/100103.asp.

Wachman, R. "Hi-Tech Newcomers Challenge Mighty LSE for Trading Crown", *The Sunday Times*, 11 September 2008.

Woods, R. "Seven Days That Shook the World", *The Sunday Times*, 11 September 2008.

World Federation of Exchanges. "The Significance of the Exchange Industry", July 2004, 5th Edition, pp2–7.

World Federation of Exchanges. "2007 Market Highlights", 25 January 2008, pp1–3.

Young, T. "Stock Exchange IT improves Trade Volume", *Computing*, 6 December 2007.

Young, T. "Turquoise Takes on The City", *Computing*, 6 December 2007.

Index

List of Useful Websites

American Stock Exchange	www.amex.com
Athens Stock Exchange	www.ase.gr
Australian Stock Exchanges	www.asx.com.au
Bank for International Settlements	www.bis.org
Bolsa de Madrid (The Madrid Stock Exchange	www.bolsamadrid.es
Bolsa Mexicana de Valores (The Mexican Stock Exchange)	www.bmv.com.mx
Bloomberg	www.bloomberg.com
Bombay Stock Exchange	www.bseindia.com
Borsa Italiana (The Italian Stock Exchanges)	borsaitaliana.it
Business Week	www.businessweek.com
Caracas Stock Exchange	www.caracasstock.com
Chicago Mercantile Exchange	www.cme.com
Chicago Board of Trade	www.cbot.com
Chicago Stock Exchange	www.chx.com
Committee of European Securities Regulators	www.cesr-eu.org
CNBC TV	www.cnbc.com
CNN	www.cnn.com
Deutsche Borse Group (The Frankfurt Stock Exchange)	http://deutsche-boerse.com
Dow Jones	www.dowjones.com
Dubai International Exchange	www.DIFX.com
Euronext Amsterdam	www.aex.nl
European Central Bank	www.ecb.int
Financial Services Authority	www.fsa.gov.uk
Financial Times	www.ft.com
Fitch	www.fitchibca.com
Hong Kong Stock Exchange	www.hkex.com.hk
Karachi Stock Exchange	www.kse.com.pk
Johannesburg Stock Exchange	www.jse.co.za
Korea Stock Exchange	www.kse.or.kr
Bursa Malaysia (Kuala Lumpur Stock Exchange)	www.klse.com.my
Indonesia Stock Exchange	www.idx.co.id
Institutional Investor	www.institutionalinvestor.com
International Monetary Fund	www.isda.org
Instinet	www.instinet.com
Istanbul Stock Exchange	www.ise.org
London Stock Exchange	www.londonstockexchange.com
LCH Clearnet	www.lchclearnet.com
MEFF:(Spanish Financial Futures & Options Exchange)	www.meff.com
Moody's Investor Services	www.moodys.com

NASDAQ	www.nasdaq.com
New York Stock Exchange	www.nyse.com
New Zealand Stock Exchange	www.nzx.com
NYSE Euronext	www.euronext.com
OMX Nordic Exchange	www.omxnordicexchange.com
Russia Trading Systems Stock Exchange	www.rts.ru
Securitization News	www.securitizationnews.com
Security and Exchange Commission	www.sec.gov
Shenzhen Stock Exchange	www.szse.cn
SIX Swiss Exchange Ltd.	www.swx.com
Standard and Poor's	www.standardandpoors.com
Stock Exchange of Singapore	www.ses.com.sg
Tel Aviv Stock Exchange	www.tase.co.il
The New York Times	www.nytimes.com
The Depository Trust and Clearing Association	www.dtcc.com
The Economist	www.economist.com
The South African Futures Exchange (Safex)	www.safex.co.za
Santiago Stock Exchange (La Bolsa de Comercio de Santiago)	www.bolsadesantiago.com
Sao Paulo Stock Exchange	www.bovespa.com.br
Taiwan Stock Exchange	www.twse.com.tw
The Stock Exchange of Thailand	www.set.or.th
Tokyo Stock Exchange	www.tse.or.jp
Toronto Stock Exchange	www.tsx.com
Turquoise	www.tradeturquoise.com/
Wall Street Journal	www.wsj.com
Wiener Börse AG (The Vienna Stock Exchange)	http://en.wienerborse.at/
World Federation of Exchanges	www.world-exchanges.org
World Trade Organisation	www.wto.org

Introducing Bizle.biz

Bizle.biz is the first online portal dedicated to the alignment of IT and business. When fully operational, Bizle will be the reference point for IT students and professionals that want to keep abreast of issues concerning IT and the alignment with the business community. It will also provide answers to "on-the-job" queries that professionals might have during the course of their everyday tasks.

Bizle.biz will have the following features:

- IT jobs adverts partitioned into the industry sectors to allow both candidates and advertisers to tailor their job requirements
- Recommended Books
- Industry News
- 'Ask' support service
- Glossary of Terms
- Forum
- Content in different languages

Other Titles in the Bizle Professional Series

Business Knowledge for IT
in Global Investment Banking

Business Knowledge for IT
in Pharmaceuticals

Business Knowledge for IT
in Private Equity

Business Knowledge for IT
in Insurance

Business Knowledge for IT
in Islamic Finance

Business Knowledge for IT
in Mobile Telecoms

**These and other exciting titles can be pre-ordered
on Amazon sites worldwide or on www.essvale.com**

Lightning Source UK Ltd.
Milton Keynes UK

175930UK00001B/20/P